San Francisco 49ers

Great Teams' Great Years

San Francisco 49ers

by Creative Services, NFL Properties, Inc.

A National Football League Book

Macmillan Publishing Co., Inc.

New York

Collier Macmillan Publishers

London

Other Books in This Series
Cleveland Browns
Dallas Cowboys
Detroit Lions
Kansas City Chiefs
Los Angeles Rams
New York Giants
Pittsburgh Steelers
Washington Redskins

A National Football League Book
Prepared by Creative Services Division, National
Football League Properties, Inc.
Publisher: *David Boss*
Editor: *John Wiebusch*
Managing Editor: *Tom Bennett*
Associate Editors: *Patricia Cross, Doug Kelly*
Project Coordinator: *Bill Von Torne*
Production Manager: *Patrick McKee*
Production Staff: *Amy Yutani, Rob Meneilly, Jere Wright*
Executive Director: *Jack Wrobbel*

Macmillan Publishing Co., Inc., 866 Third Avenue, New
York, N.Y. 10022. Collier-Macmillan Canada Ltd.

Library of Congress Catalog Card Number: 73-21301
First Printing 1974
Printed in the United States of America

Contents

Introduction

July. A place called Goleta, site of the Santa Barbara campus of the University of California.

When the Green Bay Packers worked out here in 1967, their coach, Vince Lombardi, spent $3,000 to erect a "spy screen" around the practice field so nobody could watch. In contrast now, there are sets of wooden bleachers, behind the endzone at the practice field; you can even step over a low fence and wander onto the field itself. No one will stop you. Some professional football training camps are the best-kept secrets since the Manhattan Project. This isn't one of them.

In the summer haze, the not-so-distant Santa Ynez mountains seem reduced to indistinct purple. All the scenery — the nearby dormitory buildings, the bay trees clustered in tired groups at the other end of the field, and even the parched yellow of the grass itself — has the feel of America's medieval past, of the time when Father Junipero Serra stood barely a mile away and watched the waves of the Pacific glide almost like surreptitious suitors to kiss the shoreline of the New World.

Another part of the Goleta scenery is the splendor and finery of the National Football League team working out here now — the whiter-than-white shirts and bold red numbers of their offensive unit; the sealing-wax red jerseys and blinding white numbers of their defensive unit; the sparkling gold of their helmets.

An old man, long since retired, sits in the bleachers. He played for Amherst, he tells you, when William Howard Taft was President. But as he watches the practice, his face is younger by far than the seamed, intense faces of the rookie receiver and free safety who now tumble, each cursing in self-criticism.

The old man says he moved here from Massachusetts in 1949. The campus occupied its present site in 1954. But the football team — the San Francisco 49ers — has been around forever.

Forever? Wait a minute. The 49ers didn't even field a team until 1946, and that was in the old All-America Football Conference.

From the date of their origin, the 49ers have played all their home games in the same city under the same management. True, they have played in two different leagues, but that was because two different leagues wanted them. Unlike the Steelers, they never combined forces with another team in another city just to keep the franchise going. Unlike the Bears, they did not begin in some whistle-stop town. Unlike the Rams, they never took a title team and left town. Unlike the Giants, they never thought of moving someplace else.

The institutional quality of this team derives not only from its own longevity — but also from the fact the city of San Francisco guarantees instant antiquity. In San Francisco, today's immigrant is tomorrow's native, and today's new skyscraper is tomorrow's landmark.

This institutional quality even applies to the team's name. No Jets, Expos, Astros, Rockets or SuperSonics are they, but 49ers, a rollback to the Old West and a century of gold prospectors. By the calendar the 49ers are less than 30 years old, and it should be simple for the average fan to rattle off the names of the six men who have occupied the post of head coach within that postwar time. But the calendar lies, and the task is not simple; even an ardent fan may blow it. Maybe he'll forget that Jack Christiansen came between Red Hickey and the present incumbent, Dick Nolan. Even more likely, he'll forget that Red Strader came between Buck Shaw and Frankie Albert.

Lapses of this sort are not evidence of the fan's inattention. To the contrary, the sin of the 49ers' fan is that, like Othello, he loves not wisely but too well. The team's move from Kezar Stadium, an ancient intimate structure, to spacious, impersonal Candlestick Park was accelerated one afternoon when the faithful pelted their heroes, not only with beer cans, but also with can-openers — not to mention a few entire picnic baskets. Next day the 49ers' management, perhaps the most thoughtful in the industry, went to see the chief of police about constructing a moat.

The point is that the same San Franciscans who can't name the six 49ers' coaches can identify whole herds of interior linemen from two decades and more into the past. It is no special task to identify the three quarterbacks — Frankie Albert, Y. A. Tittle, and John Brodie — who animated the team's first three decades. The memories are no less distinct of Howard Mudd, John Thomas, Bruno Banducci, Bob Toneff, Marv Matuszak, or Hardy Brown, of whom one opposing ball carrier likened contact with him on a third-down play to stepping on a mine.

Sit down with a 49ers' fan and be prepared to be regaled with high tales of John (Strike) Strzykalski, Joe Arenas, Len Eshmont, and Norm Standlee; of Bob St. Clair, Leo Nomellini, Charlie Krueger, Bruce Bosley, Cedrick Hardman, and Tommy Hart; of Matt Hazeltine and Dave Parks and Frank Nunley. Live again the exploits of Gene Washington, Gordy Soltau, or R. C. Owens, and of Hall of Famers like the piston-driven fullback Joe Perry. Perry did not need to run to daylight: On one occasion he was obliterated by a pile of nine enemy tacklers, but before the play was blown dead, the whole pile started to move in the same direction Perry was going to begin with, for six more yards and a first down.

Work your way through Billy Wilson, Dave Wilcox and J. D. Smith; Jimmy Johnson and Ted Kwalick; Clifton McNeil and Forrest Blue. Be prepared, if you can, to sense that one function of this guided tour through a 49ers fan's memory, so enriched by the formidable achievement of so many skilled professionals, is to perform the public service of identifying number thirty-nine. As halfbacks go, the exploits of a Gale Sayers or O. J. Simpson are established fact. For nine seasons in the NFL, by contrast, number thirty-nine was mostly rumor, and the day after a game against San Francisco, it was a religious exercise for opposing defenders to consult their morning newspapers in an effort to discover who the hell that was. He not only carried the ball from scrimmage, but he also caught passes and punts. Sometimes he returned punts in unconventional ways. One time, on a field left slick by an overnight frost, he covered an incredible number of yards on a weaving touchdown runback. Every enemy tackler had a shot at him; most of them had more than one. One huge defender took a dive at him, missed, and wound up sliding on his stomach to the feet of his head coach on the sideline. "Get up, you s.o.b.," the coach said, not unkindly. "He'll be back in a minute."

Even the newspapers were not always helpful in identifying number thirty-nine. From one coast to the other, they tended to call him what he was: the King. Others referred to him, with equal accuracy, as the greatest "thrill runner" in the history of the sport. For the record, his name was Hugh McElhenny.

From Shaw through Nolan, 49ers coaches have tended to symbolize the low profile, the quiet demeanor, and the direct answer to a direct question. Nolan was asked about the 100-degree heat which sidelined his quarterback and four other starters in the 49ers' opening loss at Miami in 1973. "It was just as hot for the Dolphins," he snapped. At least equally to the point, a generation earlier, was the verdict of Norman Strader, Buck Shaw's successor as 49ers coach. When asked whether it was his or his players' fault when the team was doing badly, his reply was brief, quick, and philosophical. "Theirs," he said.

The 49ers' owners are light-years removed from the domineering, flamboyant owner types like George Preston Marshall, Ted Collins, Carroll Rosenbloom, or Dan Reeves. Control of the San Francisco 49ers rests in the hands of two gentle widows and a mild-mannered man who moved up from office helper to president of the club.

This strange troika consists of Josephine Morabito, whose late husband Tony founded the team; Elizabeth Jane Morabito, widow of Tony's half-brother Vic, who took over as club president upon his older brother's death in 1957; and Lou Spadia, who began as the guy who went for coffee and whose chief connection was with a friendly laundry that let him have free shirt cardboards on which to check off seat locations. It is Spadia who runs the show.

In one incredible season — 1957 — the 49ers helped set the all-time pro football attendance mark as 102,368 fans watched them at Los Angeles. That year in the divisional playoff game against the Lions, the 49ers set the all-time television audience record of its era for an event telecast live from the Pacific Coast.

But it was in the first half of the 1957 season, before a crowd of 56,693 at Kezar Stadium, that the football club really let loose. The 49ers were trailing the Chicago Bears 17–7 at halftime. Privately, the news was brought to the dressing room: Tony Morabito, the owner of the team, had suffered a heart attack in the stands. He had been taken to St. Mary's Hospital, four blocks away. Frankie Albert, the 49ers' coach, told his players. Then he went back to a clipboard and continued to read off his notions of how to play the second half.

Midway in the third quarter, a piece of paper was slipped into Albert's hand on the sideline. It said two words: "Tony's gone."

To this day, neither the Bears nor the game officials, let alone the world at large, have any true appreciation of what happened then. All the officials knew was that they were calling one penalty after another against the 49ers — and not for any of the polite reasons, like too much time, offside, or backfield in motion. They were calling them instead for running into the kicker, personal foul, roughing the passer, pass interference, and clipping. The 49ers seldom had the ball. But when the Bears did, they would see a giant like Leo Nomellini pouring in on them with tears streaming down his face. They saw Joe Perry, hobbled by a severe knee injury, coming into the game without even being sent in, demanding the ball, and hitting for eight yards up the middle. They saw Ed Henke smack them three times hand-running and then drop from exhaustion. Unbelievably, the Bears found themselves behind 21–17 with 12 minutes still to go. In those final 12 minutes, the Bears had the ball for 25 plays against 9 for the 49ers. But the Bears haven't scored yet.

After the game, a functionary from the Bears came to the 49ers' dressing room and sought out coach Albert. "We didn't hear about it 'til now," he said.

Albert took his face from his hands and looked at him. "If he was going to die," said the man from the Bears, trying to say the right thing, "it would have made him happy that you beat us by four points."

Frankie Albert's face crumpled. "If he was going to live," he responded, "it would have made me happy to lose by a hundred points." He looked up, and there were newspapermen standing there. "Write that down," Albert said, and then the coach of the most exciting crowd-drawing team in professional football history began to sob. The words came out slowly, as he held a hand before his eyes and his shoulders heaved from crying. "I wish we'd lost by a hundred points . . ."

It is Christmas day, 1971, at Candlestick Park in San Francisco. Their faces lined with anxiety, coach Dick Nolan and members of the 49ers' defense watch the offense line up for a fourth-down play at the goal line of the Washington Redskins. Number 52 is linebacker Skip Vanderbundt, and at the far right is trainer Linc Kimura. San Francisco scored on the play and went on to defeat the Redskins 24-20 in a playoff game and qualify for the NFC championship game against Dallas a week later.

The Great Years

Young Tony Morabito (left), a partner in a San Francisco lumber firm, organized the 49ers in 1946. One of his first steps was to sign well-known players from Bay area college teams. Four of the best were Frankie Albert and Norm Standlee of Stanford, and Alyn Beals (second from right) and Visco Grgich of Santa Clara.

On the desk of Franklin Mieuli, owner of the Golden State Warriors franchise in the National Basketball Association, sits a photograph of the darkly handsome Anthony J. Morabito, founding father of the San Francisco 49ers. The inscription reads: "I don't agree with you but that is why you're my partner."

One may speculate how much this says about Mieuli, who had — and has — at best only a minor financial interest in the 49ers and a commensurately minor influence on the team's policy. But it says a great deal about Tony Morabito: his occasional flair for old-world aphorism; his undoubted capacity to occasional hyperbole, and his fierce degree of loyalty (Mieuli started as an advertising salesman, pushing a beer account for the 49ers' radio broadcasts, and became, by his own recollection, the first "outsider" privileged to buy 49ers stock).

If you belonged to the 49ers — as official, player, coach, or investor — there was nothing Tony wouldn't do for you. By the same token, if there was something he didn't like, he threw it out the window, at times literally. More than one passerby, walking on the sidewalk beneath his office window, found himself dodging flying objects from above. On one occasion it might be a felt hat, on another a fluttering deck of cards.

But if Morabito disliked the hat one of his players wore during a visit to his office and threw it out the window, he would also give the player a $5 bill to buy a new hat. And if the way the gin rummy game was turning out upset him, out the window would go the cards. But the next day he'd be playing the same opponent with a fresh deck.

In his lifetime and even after, Morabito was described both as "controversial" and "colorful." He disliked the second adjective even more than the first, because he was an intensely private individual, the success of whose private dream — to bring big league sports to San Francisco — threw

him into a public world he never wanted.

That Morabito would become a public figure was logical and inevitable, but for years he fought it. The 49ers' press brochure from the team's initial season in 1946 lists him as owner of the team at one point, and merely as its secretary-treasurer at another. The latter struck some outsiders as an overly modest designation, and they were right.

What they failed to take wholly into consideration was the degree to which privacy warred with fame in Tony Morabito. Perhaps more important, they failed to seek out the reasons why.

Rebuffed by the established National Football League, Morabito formed his team as a charter member of the old All-America Football Conference instead. He already sensed this meant war with the NFL, but there are wars and wars. Tony was willing to fight this one.

Holder of a postwar trump — the best team in the new sports territory, the Pacific Coast to which area he divined all major sports would come — he found himself something of an outsider even among his fellow AAFC clubowners. The key segment of that last word is "club." To a degree Morabito had not foreseen, other AAFC executives played a kind of gentlemanly footsie with their NFL counterparts, even while headlines called it all-out war.

To Morabito it was all-out war. What other kind of war was there? He raided the other league for talent, because that was what you did. The result was that no fewer than 12 of the first 49ers had already played for National Football League teams: Giants, Eagles, Rams, Lions, Bears, Steelers, and Redskins. Morabito went for a nucleus of established talent. He could see no other way.

There was another way. AAFC club officials seemed almost at times to interlock with NFL club officials. They shared ball parks, catering services and the same table at Toots Shor's. They

had baseball, boxing, even horse racing interests in common. Even Arch Ward, sports editor of the *Chicago Tribune,* whose brainchild the AAFC was, found no reason not to preserve meticulously the greatest single promotional event the rival NFL had: another one of his brainchildren, the annual preseason game between the NFL champion and the College All-Stars.

Today, 49ers president Lou Spadia says that one of the team's earliest mistakes was to align itself with one San Francisco newspaper, the *Examiner,* in a five-year preseason charity-game deal between the 49ers and the Washington Redskins.

By San Francisco standards, Spadia is undoubtedly right. But Tony failed to see it. If AAFC founder Ward could retain the All-Star game and if New York City's *Herald Tribune* could sponsor an annual game of its own between the All-Stars and the local football Giants . . . then what was wrong with playing a game for a worthy cause?

Morabito found out what was wrong — from both ends: when he refused to renew the deal with the *Examiner,* the other three San Francisco papers, led by the *Examiner's* morning rival, the *Chronicle,* refused the deal because the *Examiner* had had it previously.

The result, known locally as the Eighteen-Year War, pitted Morabito against the San Francisco press. It was not one-sided; blows were delivered from both encampments. It certainly was not famous: A generation of fans outside the immediate Bay area may be bemused to discover that it existed at all. And its aftereffects were hardly noticeable: Today's relationship between the 49ers and San Francisco's football writers is standard up-beat fare. The team makes all provision for the press, and the press in turn responds gratefully, generating powerful publicity for the 49ers and only periodically suggesting that parking fees at the stadium be lowered, the coach be fired, the quarterback be replaced and the scouting and player-draft machinery be revised.

The matter is introduced at the outset here because if Tony Morabito or his younger brother Vic, who survived him by barely six years, were still alive, the war might still be on. It's simplistic to say that cooler heads have since prevailed; of course they have. But the creed was that a Morabito would go to hell to defend a matter of principle, which in a business sense, Tony damn near did. Those first years were lean years.

"I told him he had to be prepared to lose a lot of money," said the late *Chronicle* sports editor Bill Leiser. And if Tony Morabito wasn't prepared to do just that, he soon took the gamble.

At the outset, Morabito established a partnership with his coexecutives in Lumber Terminals of San Francisco (Allen E. Sorrell and E. J. Turre). It is emblematic of the mists of time that today some people give credit to Sorrell, others to Turre, for having come up with the name of the team.

In those days the name was spelled out — *"Forty-Niners"* not *"49ers"* — but by all odds it was an extraordinarily fitting name for a San Francisco sporting enterprise. The original visual symbol of the club yielded the full flavor of San Francisco's past — a booted prospector with lumberjack shirt, checkered pants, hat blown off, mustache and hair askew, splayed feet and a pair of six-shooters in full fire (one aimed narrowly to miss his foot, the other even more narrowly to miss his brain).

In a word, the guy had to be drunk. "He *was* drunk," Lou Spadia has recalled. "In the original picture, which was featured on the side of railway freight cars, there was a saloon in the background." The 49ers had wiped out the saloon and left the patron.

The symbol remained persuasive nonetheless: The 49ers would shoot at anything. While Morabito was raiding National Football League teams for talent, other All-America Football Conference clubs were treating the problem of how to stock their rosters with big-name help in a far more civilized and infinitely more hypocritical fashion.

With a backlog of four war years, the talent was coming out of the colleges, not just the pre-war pro ranks. So the prevailing approach among the other AAFC teams was to outbid the NFL for collegians, and not for established professionals.

This made good sense to Tony Morabito, up to a point. He not only went to the colleges, he also stressed colleges from the San Francisco vicinity, with the result, *inter alia,* that he picked up an additional 11 players for his first squad from colleges within the North Pacific Coast area. One of these was a little 5-foot 8-inch quarterback, Frankie Albert. He couldn't see over the big guys, and (even worse) he was left-handed in a right-handed world. He'd attended Stanford, with Norm Standlee, another 49ers acquisition, a fullback who'd been the rookie sensation of the Chicago Bears in 1941.

Five players came from Santa Clara: Ken Casanega, Eddie Forrest, Rupert Thornton, Alyn Beals, and Visco Grgich. Beals and Grgich were among the most brilliant pass receivers and middle guards, respectively, of their time. The coach also came from Santa Clara: the lean, handsome, prematurely gray Lawrence T. (Buck) Shaw, who had turned down one professional offer after another, subliminally awaiting the day when the call would come from a nearby place. Meanwhile he had gently built his reputation as one of the half-dozen finest coaches in the nation.

In all this, there was a plane of ethics involved. If you had graduated from college, were on somebody's draft list, or had played pro ball before, you were fair game. To Morabito's astonishment, other AAFC teams seemed to prefer at times to go after other kinds of game. They were signing stars whose credentials had been proved with wartime service teams, but who had not yet graduated from college. With each announcement of such a signing came the pious disclaimer that the boy had pronounced himself willing and anxious to return to college to complete his degree at the first opportunity. "I won't sign a youngster unless he tells me he'll go back to college," one AAFC coach said, to great applause. To Tony Morabito, things appeared less complex: If the boy had finished college, or had quit his studies, you went after him. You didn't talk him into quitting, and you didn't rob cradles. Most important of all, you didn't extract a promise from the boy that some day he'd go back to school, then relay that churchly news to the headline writers.

Call it what Tony called it — a defense of principle — or call it anything you like, but this approach took its place in the survival of the San Francisco 49ers. Comprised largely of former NFL players and local names, the 49ers may have been designed to withstand the college-robbing of other teams, but the 49ers' survival certainly was in doubt for some time. Morabito's first approach to the established NFL — "this is a big country," meaning the Pacific Coast would take its rightful place in the scheme of big league sport after World War II — came back now to haunt him. For maybe it was too big a country. Other teams had their own stars — never mind how they got some of them — and Tony, losing money, took the gamble of his life. He borrowed $100,000, bought out his original partners, and split the ownership of the 49ers on a 75-25 basis between himself and his brother Vic.

Said Harry Wismer, famed sportscaster and

The 49ers and teams in seven other cities formed the All-America Football Conference, postwar rival of the established National Football League. Admiral Jonas H. Ingram (left, standing between the co-owners of the Los Angeles Dons, actor Don Ameche and businessman Ben Lindheimer) was the commissioner of the AAFC in 1947. Jim Crowley, once a member of the Four Horsemen at Notre Dame, had been the first AAFC commissioner; he resigned to coach the Chicago Rockets (right, an advertisement that appeared in the 1947 issue of Pro Football Illustrated).

Washington Redskins patron, "There's this nut with a hearing aid in San Francisco who is putting his own money into his damn team."

But Tony had his reasons, and if anything they hardened from 1946 through 1949, four seasons during which the struggling AAFC went through a cornucopia of trauma. The league's first commissioner was Jim Crowley, one of the Four Horsemen of Notre Dame. But Crowley resigned to accept an offer to coach the Chicago Rockets, an AAFC entry which may have been the worst and funniest football team in professional football history, and he was succeeded as commissioner by a procession of retired World War II admirals. The postwar job market for admirals being bearish, one of the admirals-turned-commissioner said his main ambition was to retire permanently to La Jolla and "rose raises."

To know that old All-America Football Conference is to have known Arch Ward, the Chicago sports editor who thought the whole thing up. Ward had conceived not only the College All-Star game, but also major league baseball's All-Star game. His attention to detail did not always match his soundness of overall approach. To express it in short form, he felt that no new football league could succeed without a Chicago franchise. In and of itself, that was a brand of thinking beyond reproach. Then things started to go wrong.

One of the first problems was the appearance of evidence suggesting that there was a contract out for one of the owners of the Chicago Rockets. Upon this and other depressing findings, Ward had to agree that the team's ownership ought to change hands. It did. Four times in four years.

Another problem was that the Rockets were the third team in a city already inhabited by two others – both of whom won. The Chicago Bears, who played at Wrigley Field, were established beyond question. The Chicago Cardinals (the team that later moved to St. Louis) occupied Comiskey Park and were making their own move. Under the spiritual guidance of piano-playing coach Jim Conzelman, who confessed early and often that he did not have the slightest idea what his players had in mind, the Cardinals put together the most inventive, most talented backfield in the history of professional football: Paul Christman at quarterback, Pat Harder at fullback, Elmer Angsman and Charley Trippi at halfbacks. They were not just a quartet: they were a quintet, for the greatest all-around back they had — Marshall Goldberg of Pitt — had to play safety on defense. They invented plays on the spot and sent incoming substitutes back to the bench with instructions not to bother them — not even when the substitute was no substitute at all, but an eleventh man, representing Conzelman's desperate attempt to inform them they'd been playing with 10 men for the last six plays.

In those immediate postwar years, the Cardinals slammed to prominence and championship, and their classic games always were against the crosstown Bears. That left the Rockets looking for a few things, including a place to play. The only place empty at the time was wind-frozen Soldier Field on the waterfront of Lake Michigan. The Bears play there nowadays, but under more amenable conditions. Automobiles, freeways and modern mass transit were not available in the immediate postwar years. The stadium was only slightly easier to reach than the south col of Mt. Everest, and almost as cold. Unwilling to be confronted with direct competition from the Bears and Cardinals, one or the other of which was always at home on a Sunday, the Rockets took to scheduling their games at night, when it was colder. One rookie who never got into a game used to sit on the bench, frozen beyond caring and completely enveloped

in a hooded parka. In the last game of the season, Dick Hanley, the Rockets' first coach, finally noticed him. "You!" he cried. "Get in there!"

"He'll be with you in a minute, coach," one of the other players said. "He's developing a picture."

In desperation the Rockets sent a delegation to the University of Chicago, which had given up football and turned its renowned old stadium, Stagg Field, into a research center for the atom bomb. The elders of the university were astounded to learn that somebody wanted to lease the place for football. One by one, they ticked off the drawbacks: The streetcar line that used to run there had been torn up; the south grandstand had been torn down; they had no lights; and somebody would have to pay the financial penalty if, upon this incursion of private enterprise, their tax-free status as a site of the Manhattan Project was threatened.

"One other thing," a man from the university said as the Rockets' people edged toward the door. "You'd better check the showers. They may be radioactive."

So the Rockets stayed at Soldier Field where, in due course, their fortunes were guided by three player-coaches: Bob Dove, Ned Mathews, and Wee Willie Wilkin. On one memorable occasion all three were in the game at the same time when the Rockets drew a penalty. That put them in an excellent position to argue with the officials. The argument failed. "By the Rockets' red ink," as one writer described the incident, "the flag was still there."

In final desperation, the Rockets even changed their name. For the 1949 season they were known as the Chicago Hornets, choosing yellow shirts with black stripes as their color motif. The football they used for home games, under the dim and uncertain lights of Soldier Field, also was yellow with black stripes.

Y. A. Tittle would quarterback the 49ers in the 1950s, but in 1946 he was at Louisiana State University (left). The lineup for San Francisco in its opening game, a preseason match September 1, 1946, against the Chicago Rockets, is shown at right. Along the front line were, left to right, Bob Titchenal, John Woudenberg, Bruno Banducci, Art Elston, Dick Bassi, John Mellus, and Bill Fisk, and in the backfield, John Strzykalski, Frankie Albert, Norm Standlee, and Len Eshmont. Substitute Parker Hall passed 16 yards to Alyn Beals for the 49ers' first touchdown in history (pages 20-21). One of the Rockets' players who turned away disconsolately after Beals' second-quarter touchdown was Elroy (Crazylegs) Hirsch, number 40. The 49ers won 34-14.

"How can we tell which one of them has the ball?" one rival player asked his coach.

"Tackle the first two guys you see," the coach replied. "The rest of them will fall down by themselves."

It would be inviting to say that this situation was not typical of the All-America Football Conference — inviting, but not correct. Commissioners came and went. Franchises shifted and merged. More than a few bills remained unpaid. At one point, in 1947 and 1948, there were not only three professional teams in Chicago, but there were also three in New York — two in the AAFC: the New York Yanks and Brooklyn Dodgers. The latter's 1948 season resulted in a 3–10–1 won-lost-tied record. That should have been bad enough for last place in the league's Eastern Division, but it wasn't: Baltimore was 2–11–1 that same year.

Records indicate that somebody else had to be doing some winning. True. In fact, there were two somebodies, both in the Western Division: the Cleveland Browns and the San Francisco 49ers. The 49ers were 9–5–0 their first year, 8–4–2 their second, 12–2–0 their third and 9–3–0 their fourth. Yet they did not win an All-America Football Conference division title. For those same four seasons, Cleveland was 12–2–0, 12–1–1, 14–0–0 and 9–1–2.

This was not without its frustrations for the San Francisco team. Indeed, Morabito is known to have confided to a few friends that his team was never supposed to have been in the All-America Football Conference. Morabito claimed that George Halas of the Bears — a powerful influence in the established National Football League — had promised San Francisco an NFL franchise. But if such a promise was made, it was poorly timed. Before sounder actuaries could prevail, the AAFC was a reality. Many of the AAFC's eager participants believed the postwar sports dollar was there for anyone

who cared to put a team on the field.

It could be supposed that Tony Morabito, pioneering the least-explored territory on the big league map, was taking the biggest chance of all. Certainly his enthusiasm (he had played football himself until a shoulder injury ended his career shortly after his enrollment at Santa Clara) was outmatched by none, and if anyone stood to be blinded to the truth of things, it was Morabito.

Actually, Tony's plan was the most realistic of anybody's. Although San Francisco was geographically remote from other places, that splendid isolation meant no direct competition from rival organizations. And Tony foresaw an extraordinary bonus pool in attendance: San Francisco had served as the chief port of embarkation for the war in the Pacific and the postwar tourist boom would cause hundreds of thousands of servicemen who had passed through San Francisco to return.

The son of an immigrant father whose own business had faded during the depression, Morabito had risen, in only a few years in the thirties, from an $80-per-month truck driver to a thriving proprietor of a lumber-carrying business before his thirtieth birthday.

Rejected for military service because of a growing deafness that would force him to use a hearing aid, Morabito nursed his obsession for a major league football franchise. Rebuffed in two preliminary appeals to the National Football League, Morabito met in 1943 with sports editor Bill Leiser of the *Chronicle,* who told him of Arch Ward's secret plans for a new league. Accounts differ as to whether this news came as a surprise to Morabito, but at least he let Leiser think it did.

Leiser, in any event, was impressed.

"Are you prepared to lose money?" he said. "At least at the start?"

"Yes."

"How much?"

"A great deal."

"Have you thought about a coach?"

"Yes."

"Who?"

"Buck Shaw."

Leiser nodded. "I'd be interested in what he has to say when you talk to him."

Morabito nodded back. "I've already talked to him."

This was the stroke that convinced Leiser, for Shaw, the spare, gray, distinguished coach of Santa Clara's nationally-known teams, could bring more in the way of image and reputation to the new league than any other single figure. As a tackle at Notre Dame, he keyed the unbeaten Irish teams in the heyday of George Gipp. As coach at Santa Clara, he had fielded teams with an aggregate won-lost-tied record of 47–10–4 and he produced upset victories in the Sugar Bowl in 1936 and 1937.

Another major addition to the 49ers was a player from Glendale, California, named Frankie Albert, who was so small his first high school coach wouldn't issue him a uniform. Somehow he persisted, and in 1937 he was named Southern California's "prep athlete of the year" by a Los Angeles newspaper. He went to Stanford, where he was promptly lost among the big boys while the team compiled a 1–8–1 record. The next year Clark Shaughnessy, who'd been left without a job when the University of Chicago dropped football, took over as Stanford coach. Having worked with George Halas and Sid Luckman, he decided nothing would be lost in switching to the T. The little guy from Glendale, who could pass, kick, run, and bewilder, was installed as his quarterback. Whereupon Stanford won 10 games in a row.

A man named Jim Lawson was an assistant coach at Stanford. When the 49ers were formed, Shaw picked Lawson as one of his assistant coaches. "By the way, Jim," Buck said. "Have a talk with the little guy." Lawson did, and at war's end Frankie Albert agreed to play for the 49ers.

In this manner, the 49ers became one of the most glamorous football teams ever. They entered the All-America Football Conference with the best-known coach, the best-known quarterback, and, from a glamor standpoint, the best-known city. Buck Shaw was far better known than Cleveland's Paul Brown, and Albert more celebrated than Otto Graham. And, clearly, San Francisco was more renowned than Cleveland.

Cleveland did have a couple of things going for it. If the Browns had to play at Buffalo, they could be home the same night; for the 49ers a trip to Buffalo might as well have been an Arctic safari.

The Browns also had another advantage: defense. In their four years of AAFC competition, the Browns had 27 games in which the opposing team was held to less than 10 points; the 49ers had 11. Cleveland had eight shutouts, San Francisco two.

Yet the glamor was still there. It is incredible that the Browns, with a 47–4 record for the four AAFC years, could have been outscored by anyone. But the 49ers outscored the Browns.

They also handed Cleveland its two worst beatings. In 1946 the 49ers beat Cleveland 34–20. No one ever had scored as many points against Cleveland. In 1949 the 49ers won again. This time the score was 56–28, and the carnage was such that Lawrence T. Shaw, the courtly San Francisco coach, was moved to compassion. As the battle neared its end, he sent in a substitute for Frankie Albert, who had already passed for five touchdowns. Albert was not content with this arrangement. He wanted to pass for a sixth touchdown to make it 63–28. There was no yearning for personal glorification in this; instead, he simply thought the number of 49ers

Runner Joe Perry (left) and linebacker Norm Standlee (below) starred as the '48 team (right) won 12 games and scored 69 touchdowns. Front row, left to right: Joe Vetrano, Forrest Hall, Bob Sullivan, Perry, Frankie Albert, Standlee, Paul Crowe, Nick Susoeff, Art Elston, Visco Grgich, and Verl Lillywhite. Second row: Jim Cason, Eddie Carr, Alyn Beals, Walt McCormick, Joel Williams, Bev Wallace, John Woudenberg, Riley Matheson, Bill Johnson, Bob Mike, and Bruno Banducci. Third row: Hal Shoener, Gail Bruce, Roman Bentz, Clarence Howell, Floyd Collier, Bob Bryant, Norm Maloney, James Cox, Len Eshmont, Don Clark, and John Strzykalski. Fourth row: equipment manager Ziggy Zamlynsky, assistant coach Eddie Erdelatz, head coach Buck Shaw, assistant coach Jim Lawson, and trainer Bob Kleckner.

points on the scoreboard ought to match the white number sixty-three on his red uniform. ("I'm glad we didn't give him number one," Tony Morabito said.)

The 1949 season was to be the All-America Football Conference's last. By this time the league was down to seven teams, round-robin, with Cleveland winding up at 9–1–2 and San Francisco at 9–3–0. The 49ers had to play the New York Yankees in one playoff while Cleveland played Buffalo in the other. No playoffs had caused so great a stir since the argument over who invented the hot water bottle. Interest in the situation was typified by the 49ers, who announced they'd rather not play at all unless they received extra-game salary.

Tony Morabito read them their contracts, threatened to forfeit the game, and announced he'd fine the players 25 percent of their salaries if they refused to show up for practice. The players gave in. They beat the Yankees 17–7, though their hearts weren't in it, and things began looking up. Cleveland had defeated Buffalo, so now it would be San Francisco versus Cleveland for the championship at Cleveland, where the stadium could seat over 80,000.

Those visions of sugar plums disintegrated as the 49ers arrived in Cleveland two nights before the game. Historian Dan McGuire reports what happened then:

"The first thing they saw at the airport was a newspaper banner line announcing that the AAFC had merged with the NFL."

The game was strictly an anticlimax. It was played in snow and slush and only 22,500 fans were interested enough to watch the Browns win 21–7. Each Cleveland player received $266.11; each 49er player, $172.61.

It is a matter of general memory that two AAFC teams → the Browns and the 49ers — were taken into the NFL. In fact, two is not the correct answer. The right number instead is either three teams, or one team, joined the NFL.

The Browns and 49ers did come over into the National Football League, but so did the Baltimore Colts. These Baltimore Colts were like the Baltimore Colts of today. They had just finished a 1–11 season. They were not even assigned to one of the NFL's two revamped divisions, but instead were designated as a "swing" team that would have to play each team once. News reports at the time predicted they would last one year in their new surroundings, then they would either fold or be taken over by another city.

This prediction was to come true. The Colts played out the 1950 season, once again produced a 1–11 record, then went out of business.

Meanwhile, the merger meeting produced a statement from NFL commissioner Bert Bell that while the Buffalo Bills of the AAFC were folding, they would in a sense be combined with the Cleveland Browns. Bell said that Buffalo co-owner James Bruell would possess a "substantial interest" in the new Browns' organization and would retain exclusive rights to present exhibition games in Buffalo.

There was a great shuffling of players back and forth, and when the dust had lifted only one team — the San Francisco 49ers — had come over from the All-America Football Conference absolutely intact. From clubhouse to front office, not a change was made as a consequence of the merger.

The 49ers, along with the Los Angeles Rams, did make one accommodation, though it rankled Morabito. Under heavy pressure from established NFL teams in the east, the West Coast teams had to increase their ticket prices "to make the visits worthwhile." Morabito had been charging $3.60 for the best seats at Kezar Stadium, $2.40 for other reserved seats, $1.80 for general admission, and 50 cents for children under 12. It was symptomatic of that innocent time that the new scale was $3.75, $3.00 and

*Frankie Albert, 5-feet 9-inches and 175 pounds,
ran (below) and passed opponents dizzy in 1948.
In one game against the Brooklyn Dodgers, he
ran for two touchdowns and passed for two more.
His AAFC rival, Otto Graham of the Cleveland
Browns, narrowly defeated Albert for a place on
the all-star team, 46 votes to 44, and they were
named cowinners of the most valuable player
trophy. O. O. (Scrappy) Kessing, the last
commissioner of the AAFC, congratulated the
two star quarterbacks (left) and they received
equal billing on the 1949 record manual (right).*

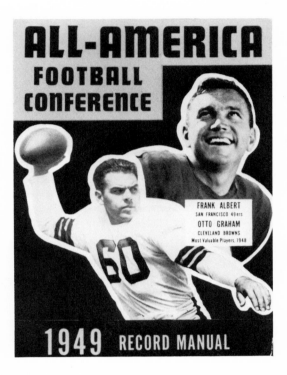

ALL-AMERICA FOOTBALL CONFERENCE

FRANK ALBERT
SAN FRANCISCO 49ers
OTTO GRAHAM
CLEVELAND BROWNS
Most Valuable Players, 1948

1949 RECORD MANUAL

WASHINGTON **REDSKINS** AUG. 26 1950 • KEZAR STADIUM

The 49ers' future was placed in doubt when the team entered the National Football League in 1950, after the demise of the AAFC, and won only three games. The program for San Francisco's first meeting with an NFL team is shown at left; Washington won the preseason game 31-21. Leo Nomellini (right, tackling Dan Towler of the Los Angeles Rams) was a rookie for the 49ers in 1950. He would become one of the game's greatest tackles. By 1951, the 49ers had improved; one of their seven victories that year was a 44-17 rout of the Rams (right, Albert passes under a heavy rush by Don Paul, number 57, and Andy Robustelli).

$2.00 with kids still admitted for half a dollar. That was a sufficient raise to satisfy everybody. Everybody, that is, except Tony Morabito. His smoldering resentment against pressure from "them" remained, and it would surface in some unusual ways. Even with the nominal hike in prices, the 49ers still offered the least expensive tickets in the league, and they would until after Morabito's death in 1957.

In the 1950 player draft the 49ers went for tackles as though they were going out of season. Shaw's first three choices were big tackles, headed by the unforgettable Minnesota All-America Leo Nomellini. Shaw needed tackles because the two top tackles of the team's AAFC years — John Woudenberg and Bob Bryant — were both retiring.

Tackles also were needed for another reason. "Pour it on!" Morabito said to Shaw, as the team prepared for its opening exhibition game against the Redskins at Kezar. "If you get forty points, shoot for eighty." Washington won the game 31–21.

In 1950, the Cleveland Browns swept the National Football League. The 49ers had a 1–4 exhibition and a 3–9 regular-season record. "They aren't big enough or tough enough for the National Football League," said an enemy coach. The observation was not wasted on Shaw.

Still, the glamor had a way of sticking. The 49ers had obtained rookie Gordon Soltau, destined to become a splendid pass-catcher and placekicker, from Cleveland in exchange for a fourth-round draft choice. With the folding of the Baltimore Colts at the end of the 1950 season, the Colts' talent was thrown into a "bonus" draft pool. The 49ers selected a young man to "understudy" Frankie Albert. The newcomer's name was Y. A. Tittle.

Tittle was pressed into regular service almost immediately, because of a shoulder injury to Albert. His major problem was to adjust to the

quick-trap running offense Shaw had built around Joe Perry, who was, without question, the first of the big, *fast* ball carriers. (In those days, 195 pounds was classified as big.) "Where'd you get him?" Tittle asked Shaw. "I go to hand the ball off to him and he's already twenty yards downfield."

If that was Tittle's problem, Shaw had one of his own. The 49ers' dismal showing in their first NFL season — especially when contrasted with the championship performance of the Browns — had put the team's future on the line. Tony Morabito had been right: The city was ready for the National Football League. But was its team?

Actually, the 3–9 record of 1950 could have been 5–7 except for two last-quarter disasters, but football is like drowning — close doesn't count. What made it worse was the fact that San Francisco's 1950 record was completely unexpected. More than a few writers and fans were predicting a Cleveland-49ers showdown for the NFL championship that first season.

But there was even more to the 49ers' losses than stung pride. The simple fact was that two horrible seasons in a row might spell the end of everything.

Nobody asked the Morabitos if they were giving up on their team. Nobody had to, because that wasn't the point. In the old AAFC, the Browns may have won the titles but the 49ers were the better attraction. Now it was a different ball game. At Yankee Stadium in New York in 1950, the 49ers had drawn exactly 5,740 fans. At home, they had exceeded half of Kezar's capacity only once, and then just barely. They'd lost seven games in a row, and these games were precisely the wrong seven — the last two pre-season games and the first five of the regular season.

Half a dozen cities were waiting in the wings for a franchise. For the first time it would not

be up to the 49ers whether or not they stayed in San Francisco. It would be up to the assembled club owners of the NFL.

When the NFL divisional alignment was drawn up for 1950, Jack McDonald of the *San Francisco Call-Bulletin* complained in print that the local team had been placed in the National Conference — or "weaker," of the revised conferences. "The strong and colorful teams are all in the American Conference," he wrote.

It was under these conditions that the 49ers took the field in 1951. In the opening preseason game against Washington, the 49ers won 45–14. Then they lost to the Bears, but that was not unexpected. But then, at Syracuse, the 49ers beat Pittsburgh 24–7; at Minneapolis they shut out the Packers 20–0; at Omaha they punished the Cardinals 37–17. Despite their 4–1 preseason record, the 49ers were still among strangers.

The one way to bridge that gap would be to beat the Browns, who would appear for the opening game of the regular 1951 season at Kezar both as the traditional opponent from the old league and reigning champion of the new.

All things considered, a fine crowd of 48,263 turned out for the Cleveland opener. And the 49ers won! Verl Lillywhite gained 145 yards in 17 carries; linebacker Pete Wismann set up two touchdowns with a pair of interceptions, and Frankie Albert threw a touchdown pass to rookie end Billy Wilson on one of the great textbook plays of all time. *San Francisco Chronicle* photographer Bob Campbell captured the play in two panels. In the first shot Albert is releasing the ball behind the most astonishing pass protection ever recorded on film. In the second, Wilson is about to catch the ball. Also in the picture are Soltau, an eligible receiver himself, and Tommy James, the Cleveland defender. James can't get near Wilson because Soltau's not about to let him. Wilson caught the ball, James fell over Soltau, and the 49ers wound up winning 24–10.

Beating the Browns was one thing; beating the Rams was another. The 1951 Rams were truly a great football team. They had Bob Waterfield, Norm Van Brocklin, Elroy Hirsch, Bob Boyd, Tom Fears, and a choice of aptly-named ball carriers. For the light, swift touch, they had Glenn Davis and Vitamin Smith. For the heavy going, they had Dan Towler, Tank Younger, and Dick Hoerner. The latter three formed a "bull elephant backfield" — three fullbacks — to be used simultaneously against certain defenses too light to stop them.

The 49ers, now with a 2–2 record, took on the Rams at Kezar and beat them 44–17. A subheadline in one of the San Francisco papers summed things up: *Gordon Soltau Scores 26 Pts; Everybody Stars.*

Coming into the final game of 1951, the Detroit Lions were 7–3–1 and playing the 49ers at Kezar. The 49ers were 6–4–1. The Rams were 7–4, but they were playing Green Bay. Any one of three teams (Lions, 49ers, Rams) could have won the division, given the proper combination of results, but the Lions had to be favored. The Lions led the 49ers 17–14 with four minutes to go. Then San Francisco's Joe Arenas took a punt on the dead run and ran it 51 yards to the Detroit 9. Then Tittle bootlegged the ball himself for nine yards and a touchdown. So the Lions lost to San Francisco and Green Bay lost to Los Angeles. The Rams took the conference title and went on to the championship.

With his bootleg run against the Lions in the final game of the season, Tittle had established himself as a worthy successor to Albert. This had its negative side, since it split 49ers fans — and, to an extent, the players themselves — into two camps. In Los Angeles, the Waterfield-Van Brocklin situation was viewed as good for the team. The theory was that two quarterbacks with different styles could keep the opposition off balance. The problem in San Francisco's

Eight players were selected in the 1952 National Football League draft before San Francisco named Hugh McElhenny its number one choice. Among the players chosen earlier were (below, clockwise) Bill Wade, Ollie Matson, Les Richter, Frank Gifford, and Babe Parilli. Few drafts have produced as many great players. McElhenny (right) ran 60 yards for a touchdown the first time he carried the ball for the 49ers.

case was that Albert and Tittle weren't that different. They even shared a mild streak of lunacy. In their 1951 game at Detroit, Tittle's assignment was to protect a 10-point lead in the fourth quarter by staying on the ground. Instead he started throwing long passes. "I wanted more points," he explained to the long-suffering Buck Shaw, "because of what these guys did to me when I was with Baltimore."

With a team that was in title contention until the final game of the season, the 49ers no longer had to wonder about their future. In fact, they would lead the league in attendance the next three seasons.

There were many reasons for the larger crowds and one of them was the player Frankie Albert found between the 1951 and 1952 seasons when Albert decided to play in the Hula Bowl in Hawaii. The Hula Bowl in those days was the strangest of all the bowl games. The visiting team consisted of invited collegians from the mainland. This was fine, but the home team was composed of amateurs, semipros, and — at two or three key positions — professionals. Under these circumstances, Albert found himself at quarterback for the home team. A few hours after the game, Albert placed a collect phone call to Tony Morabito. The collect part of it didn't bother Tony as much as the time of day. Albert had forgotten the time difference, and it was somewhere around 2 A.M. when Morabito groggily answered the phone.

"Tony," said Albert, "I played against somebody today. We need him."

"Who's we?"

"The 49ers."

"All right," Tony said.

"Wait a minute," Albert said. "Don't you want to hear about him?"

Tony sighed. "It must be the greatest running back you ever saw."

"How did you know?" Albert asked.

28

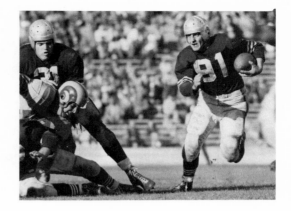

When Frankie Albert played his last game for the 49ers in December, 1952, youngsters waited in line to claim articles of his equipment as souvenirs (left). Star runner John Strzykalski (right) also retired at the close of the 1952 season.

It was a silly question. *Everybody* knew. There was a halfback at the University of Washington who did absolutely incredible things. The fact was the 49ers were not going to have a high draft choice in 1952. Their winning season of 1951 had precluded that. Eight other teams would have a crack at the running back before them.

"He wanders," Morabito said to Albert over the phone.

"I'll room with him," Albert promised. "I'll tie him down."

Morabito nodded sleepily into the telephone. "And who'll tie you down?"

No doubt about it, Albert's "discovery" was no discovery at all. He was already nationally known, and not just for his accomplishments on the gridiron. He was a carefree spirit.

At the draft meetings, everyone agreed he was temperamentally unfit for professional football. Therefore he went unpicked. The Rams had the bonus choice and took Bill Wade of Vanderbilt. The Cardinals went for Ollie Matson, the Packers for Babe Parilli, the Steelers for Ed Modzelewski, the Texans for Les Richter, the Redskins for Larry Isbell, the Bears for Jim Dooley. The Giants, in a dithyramb of self-congratulation, picked Frank Gifford. That took care of all the good choices.

With a look of despair on his face, Buck Shaw of the 49ers chose next. He had done his research well. Now it was time for a sandbag job worthy of Amarillo Slim.

Shaw leveled a finger at the blackboard and said, "I want him."

"Him" was that temperamentally-unfit halfback from Washington, Hugh McElhenny.

One writer, Wally Willis of the *Oakland Tribune,* asked Shaw the inevitable question: *why?*

"Well," said Shaw, "McElhenny has every requisite to become a great running back in this league — speed, power, change of pace, and a straight arm that is a rarity nowadays. But best of all, he puts out on every play, whether or not he's carrying the ball. He's no blocker — but he tries. The team appreciates that effort more than his ability to run away from or over tacklers."

It was left to Albert to introduce him to the rest of the 49ers at training camp. "Gentlemen," Albert said, "I want you to meet a man who took a salary cut to become a professional." McElhenny was not amused.

His first appearance was in a preseason game against the Cardinals. In the huddle, he said to Albert, "Give me the ball."

Albert grinned. "Do you know the plays?"

Again McElhenny was not amused. "Make one up," he suggested.

That made sense to Albert. So he made up a play in the huddle — a wide pitchout. McElhenny took the ball and went 60 yards for a touchdown. On the sidelines Buck Shaw moistened his finger and began to consult his playbook. He turned to his assistants. "What the hell was that play?" he wanted to know.

The headlines had an answer. Three weeks into his rookie season, they were already calling McElhenny a name that he would keep for his career — the King.

Detroit was destined to win the NFL championship in 1952 but not with help from San Francisco. Two of the 49ers' first three regularly-scheduled games were against the Lions. The 49ers won the first 17–3 and the second 28–0, the first shutout against a Lions' team since 1948. The second game drew a record 56,822 fans at Kezar Stadium.

McElhenny scored a touchdown in that game — cracking tackle from seven yards out and literally running over a defender, Don Doll. Had he been allowed to do so, the King might have thrown that one back under the fish-and-game rules. With him, anything under 60 yards was suspect. The 49ers were playing that game

31

with only 28 able-bodied members. One 19-year-old rookie from San Diego High School, Charley Powell, was pressed into starting service at defensive end. "Your job is to hit Bobby Layne," 49ers line coach Phil Bengtson explained to him. Charley Powell took Bengtson at his word. Layne didn't complete a pass till the fourth period.

The next stop for the 49ers was Wrigley Field. The 49ers had lost to the Bears in every previous meeting — preseason or regular season.

The events that unfolded then surprised the hostile Chicago crowd and pictures of them still festoon the walls of the 49ers offices. It was not just a question of beating the Bears. The San Franciscans tore them apart. McElhenny returned a punt 94 yards for a touchdown. From scrimmage the King gained 114 yards in 12 carries. The 49ers won 40–16 before a spillover turnout that rose to give McElhenny a tumultuous standing ovation as he left the field for the last time in the final quarter.

A genial new entry in the league, named the Dallas Texans, became the 49ers' fifth straight victim. This set the stage for the November 2 rematch with the Bears, this time before 58,255, the season's top crowd at Kezar Stadium. The 49ers held a 17–10 lead in the fourth period. Frankie Albert was back to punt with fourth down and two yards to go and the ball at the San Francisco 32-yard line.

A lot of things *can* go wrong on punts: a bad snap from center, a fumble, a squibbed kick, a missed blocking assignment. None of these happened. Instead, Albert decided to *run* with the ball.

He had spotted an inordinate gap between the Bears' right tackle and right end. To a man of Albert's flair, the invitation was irresistible. How could the surprised end close the hole in time? However, the defensive end was the veteran Ed Sprinkle, and nothing surprised him.

He had stationed himself wide on purpose, literally to psych Albert into the astounding gamble. It failed, of course. When Albert reached the gap, there was no gap. Instead, he rushed smack into Sprinkle's tender embrace. The 49ers gave up the ball, the Bears moved to the tying touchdown, and later, on a George Blanda field goal, Chicago won the game 20–17.

"Frank has won a lot of games for us with his daring," coach Shaw said after the game. "He's gotten away with that same play many times."

But 1952 was to be the last season for Frankie Albert. Like Johnny (Strike) Strzykalski, he announced his retirement. In Albert's case, it was a question of whether he had been to the well once too often with his uncanny inventions. The 49ers were to lose four of their next six games following the Albert-Sprinkle contretemps, finishing with a 7–5 record. Adding to the 49ers' problems was a tragedy involving team captain Norm Standlee. Albert's old Stanford colleague was stricken by polio after a game at Los Angeles. He recovered, but it was many months before he walked again.

As for Hugh McElhenny, he made every all-pro team and was *Sport* magazine's "pro player of the year." Among other records, he had the league's longest run from scrimmage that year (89 yards against Dallas). In addition to his kick returns, he recorded 684 yards in 98 carries and an additional 367 yards on 26 pass receptions.

All this made McElhenny a marked man. The 49ers won the opening game of the 1953 season against Philadelphia, but the highlight was a 15-minute player brawl on the field, with McElhenny the chief target. Joe McTigue's 49ers band, accustomed to piping sprightly airs from the sidelines, attempted the National Anthem to simmer things down. When that didn't work, the clarinet section poured onto the field and started poking Eagles with their instruments.

San Francisco traded with the Pittsburgh Steelers for running back John Henry Johnson (far left). Massive tackle Bob St. Clair (left) was a 49ers' rookie in 1953. The fanatical play of Hardy Brown (right) at middle linebacker was an important element in the defense in the mid-1950s. Y. A. Tittle, successor to Albert, retreated to pass behind the blocking of Joe Arenas, number 22, and Leo Nomellini in a preseason game against Los Angeles (pages 34-35).

The second game of the season, against the Rams at Kezar, also was won by the 49ers 31–30. There are graybeards who still don't believe that game. Los Angeles was leading 20–0 in the second quarter when Norm Van Brocklin came down with a case of Frankie Albert fever. Like Albert, the Los Angeles quarterback was also a punter. When it came time to kick on fourth down at his own 28, did he kick? No. He *passed*.

It almost worked. Fortunately for the 49ers, Night Train Lane, downfield and in the clear, dropped the ball. The 49ers eventually took a 28–27 lead but with three minutes remaining Ben Agajanian kicked a field goal for Los Angeles.

Behind 30–28, the 49ers had the ball at their own 20, and the Rams braced for the long pass from Tittle. But the Bald Eagle from Marshall, Texas, by way of Louisiana State and the Baltimore Colts, had Hugh McElhenny.

So instead of throwing long, Tittle gave the King a little semi-screen pass behind the line. Leo Nomellini threw a big block, and the rest was up to McElhenny. He came to rest 71 yards later at the Rams' 9-yard line. Tittle ran down the clock. Then with five seconds left he called on Soltau on fourth down. Soltau kicked a field goal to give the game to the 49ers.

The second Rams game, which attracted 85,856 fans to the Los Angeles Coliseum later in the season, was another last-minute 49ers' triumph. They won 31–27 on a 17-yard Tittle-Soltau pass to climax an 85-yard drive. The difference was that this time Tittle was wearing a mask. His cheekbone had been shattered in three places as the 49ers lost to Detroit in their third game of the season.

Tittle's replacement, Jimmy Powers, worked well in his two games before Tittle's return, but one of those games was a rematch with the Lions, and the Lions were it in the Western

Conference that year. They won again and went on to a 10–2 record, one game better than San Francisco's 9–3.

It was a season that saw Joe Perry gain 1,018 yards, for which a grateful Tony Morabito gave him a bonus check for $5,090 ($5 per yard). It also saw the arrival in San Francisco of a magnificent new lineman, offensive tackle Bob St. Clair, who weighed 260 pounds and stood 6-foot 9-inches. And in the wake of 1953, the 49ers were to obtain a top ball carrier in a trade with Pittsburgh. His name was John Henry Johnson. They sang "John Henry" songs about him, and the 49ers' starting backfield for 1954 — Tittle at quarterback, Perry at full, Johnson and McElhenny at the halves — came as close as you could come to the Chicago Cardinals' foursome of Christman, Harder, Angsman and Trippi in the late forties. If it stayed healthy.

Tittle was sidelined early in 1954 with a broken left hand. In the sixth game of the season, McElhenny — having piled up 515 yards in 64 carries for an eye-popping eight-yard average — suffered a shoulder separation and was out for the balance of the season.

Almost unnoticed in 1954 was Joe Perry's feat of becoming the first ball carrier ever to gain more than 1,000 yards from scrimmage in two consecutive seasons. This time, he picked up 1,049. This feat has been repeated by others. But the others, for all their undoubted talent, have 14 games per season to do it in under modern schedules. Perry only had 12.

It is not recorded whether Tony Morabito issued Perry a check for $5,245. Tony had other more serious things on his mind. Despite a 7–4–1 record for the team in 1954, he had to wonder if nine years without a title dictated a change in coaches. Personally, he was living on borrowed time, and he knew it. In March of 1952, he had suffered a massive coronary. A priest had been summoned to administer the

Critics called Frankie Albert too young — at age 36 — and too inexperienced for the job when he was named head coach of the 49ers in 1956. Albert was confident, however, that he had an exceptional array of playing talent to coach, including the two towering linemen standing with him at left, Leo Nomellini (number 73) and Bob St. Clair. The board of stockholders of the team posed in a 1957 photo at right. They were, front row, left to right, Vic Morabito, Tony Morabito, and Dr. William O'Grady, and back row, left to right, Lawrence Purcell, Albert Ruffo, Franklin Mieuli, and James Ginella.

last rites. Yet he survived. As he recovered, his doctors told him: "Sell the 49ers. Get out of football. You don't have the heart to survive this kind of tension." Tony agreed. Yet somehow the club never got sold. Buyers came and buyers went.

"Damn it," Dr. Bill O'Grady said to him, "you're never going to sell this club."

"Damn it," Morabito responded, "I'd be worse off if I got out of football. Did you ever think of that?"

So there were now the two problems: the professional and the personal. Tony solved (if "solved" is the right word) the professional problem by asking Buck Shaw to step down as coach. The case against Shaw was that he was too easy on the players. The counter-argument was that it was their very freedom of spirit that had infected the football world and made the 49ers the most colorful team in football and the best visiting-crowd draw in the league for three seasons. The case for Shaw was that his nine-season record was 71–39–4 and that injuries were not his fault. The counter-argument was that the record would have been even better if he had gone for bench strength to guard against injuries.

As for the personal problem: Tony Morabito did not sell the 49ers.

Red Strader, or Norman P. Strader, according to his birth certificate, was the coach for 1955. He and Morabito had been foes, often on the small, picky level, when Strader coached the New York Yankees in the All-America Football Conference. But Strader was a local product, having played at St. Mary's in the 1920s and having coached there beginning in 1939. He had the things Shaw seemed to lack — a gift for organization and discipline.

"What the hell is this — a military school?" one 49ers veteran grumbled at preseason training. The sight of Strader, personally patrolling the dormitory halls at curfew time, was something new.

An early foot injury to McElhenny in a pre-season game against Pittsburgh didn't improve things. Neither did having three touchdowns called back because of penalties in a league game.

Strader had selected Frankie Albert and Red Hickey as two of his assistant coaches, unaware that not one but both would become 49ers head coaches after him. At least he did not have to wait long for the discovery to set in. Asked by the Morabitos to defend the team's 1955 record of 4–8, Strader had a frank response.

"You want to know how many other games we might have won," he said. "I'm trying to figure out how we won as many as we did."

Whereupon Tony Morabito startled professional football by firing Strader after that one season. He named Albert coach of the 49ers. At 36, Frankie was the youngest — and least experienced — coach in the league.

His 1956 debut was not auspicious. The 49ers were 1–6 when they hit Green Bay. An 86-yard touchdown run by McElhenny won the game by one point and may have saved Albert's job. The unsung Joe Arenas had a hand in things too. Against the Colts, in the final game of 1956, he did what came naturally, returning a kickoff 96 yards and a punt 67. In Albert's first year, the 49ers won 5, lost 6, tied 1. They drew a record attendance (522,339 for the 12 league games) but that went almost unnoticed.

"We wouldn't for one minute think of throwing this young fellow to the wolves," Tony Morabito had said of Albert, when he named him to take Strader's place. "We picked him chiefly because of his quality of leadership — and that is something so intangible it can't be defined. But he has it. We've observed him for eleven years and we liked what we saw."

At the time of Albert's signing, sports editor

Three gifted receivers were on hand to catch the passes of Y. A. Tittle as the 49ers began the 1957 season. They were veterans Gordy Soltau (far left) and Billy Wilson and a tall rookie, R. C. Owens (right), who had an uncanny ability to outleap defenders for the ball.

Curley Grieve of the *San Francisco Examiner* wrote:

"Frank Culling Albert, who never had a nickel's worth of experience as head coach, yesterday was named boss of the San Francisco 49ers in a spectacular if risky move . . .

"Selection of a raw rookie as head coach . . . easily could be termed the biggest gamble taken by a pro club since the All-America (Football) Conference and National Football League laid aside their war clubs and joined hands.

"In addition, it is sure to stir up a public debate as heated as any inspired by Frankie as a player, when his unorthodox signal calling — including his memorable fourth-down call against the Chicago Bears that cost the 49ers a championship — was always a subject of controversy."

That was a bit of an exaggeration. Costly as Albert's run from punt formation was in that 1952 game against the Bears, it wasn't quite as bad as Grieve made it look. Yet in fairness to the same writer, he also reported in this story that Frankie Albert was the one man the 49ers players wanted to coach them. But Albert was on trial, no matter what was said. He was still on trial in his second season — 1957.

The 49ers averaged 60,000 fans per game in 1957. It was an amazing season.

It started, innocently enough, with a preseason victory at Seattle over the Cardinals, in which an unheralded rookie named R. C. Owens made a leaping circus catch of a pass for a touchdown. Owens caught three passes for 109 yards that game.

A 58–27 loss to the Rams in another preseason game followed. The 49ers had three quarterbacks: Tittle, Earl Morrall, and a bright young rookie who had rocked the college football world at Stanford, John Brodie.

San Francisco needed a linebacker. Pittsburgh needed a quarterback. San Francisco offered Morrall to Pittsburgh in exchange for linebacker Marv Matuszak. In offering a backup man for a front-liner, the Morabitos were dealing hard. They also demanded Pittsburgh's first draft choices for the next two years. Buddy Parker, the coach of the Steelers, screamed that he was being done in. "We don't want you to feel that way," said Tony Morabito, silkily. "If you want somebody else we'll throw in (tackle) Mike Sandusky." It was an offer Parker could not refuse. The trade was made.

In the first game of the season the 49ers found a way to lose to the Cardinals, 20–10. And next week they would have to face the mighty Rams.

In practice sessions for the Rams game, Tittle found himself running out of enthusiasm. In one scrimmage, he simply threw the ball a country mile away, from pure disgust. Incredibly, he saw a repeat of the preseason play in Seattle. At the goal line, R. C. Owens jumped up from among three defenders and came down with the ball.

"That's it! Alley-Oop!" cried assistant coach Red Hickey. To Albert, he said, "Let's practice that some more."

"*Practice* it?" said Albert. "How do you practime something like that?"

"You're missing the point," Hickey said. "The boys enjoy it. It improves their morale. We ought to work on it fifteen minutes a day."

That was the beginning. Somehow a play designed strictly to make the players feel better became the play that beat Los Angeles in the next game. Then, at Chicago, it was Tittle-to-Owens again and a 21–17 win. This one was a variation on the Alley-Oop. Owens couldn't go up — he'd been knocked down by three Bears. So he stayed down instead. Tittle threw a low line drive to him and R. C. caught it on his knees for the winning points. The Bears had led 17–14 with 4:29 to play. The win impressed no one. "That's the worst football team we've seen yet," one of the Bears said.

The 1957 season was one of both sadness and spectacular games. Distraught with grief after being told of the death of owner Tony Morabito during the game, the 49ers came from 10 points behind to defeat the Chicago Bears 20-17 (left, Billy Wilson catches a pass in front of the Bears' Vic Zucco). A record crowd, the largest in professional football history, watched the 49ers and Rams at the Los Angeles Coliseum (right, the Los Angeles Times *sports page the following day). With his team trailing the powerful Baltimore Colts by three points with less than a minute left in the game, rookie quarterback John Brodie passed to Hugh McElhenny in the endzone (far right) for the winning touchdown.*

Now the "worst football team" beat Green Bay in Milwaukee 24–14, and returned to San Francisco to face the Bears again. What resulted was the 49ers' victory recounted in the introduction of this book. The San Franciscans were driven to a fury of dedication by the news of Tony Morabito's heart attack in the stands and his resultant death thereafter.

Dan McGuire has recorded what took place:

"Midway in the third period, Dr. Bill O'Grady brought the dreaded news from the hospital. There was a moment of stunned silence, then the bench became a madhouse of crying, shouting player."

Distraught with grief, the 49ers chose the sole emotional outlet available to them and savagely attacked the Bears, turning a 17–7 halftime deficit into a 21–17 San Francisco victory.

The following week a Tittle-to-Owens Alley-Oop with seconds remaining brought a 35–31 victory over Detroit at Kezar. The 49ers had trailed 10–0, led at halftime 14–10, stretched it to 28–10. Then Tobin Rote threw three fourth-quarter touchdown passes to put the Lions in front 31–28 before the Tittle-Owens feat.

Halfway through the season, the 49ers had a 5–1 record but three other teams — the Lions, Colts and Rams — were challenging for the Western Conference title.

Crowds throughout the league were big, though none were bigger than those of the 49ers. At Los Angeles, they attracted an all-time record 102,368 — and lost. At Detroit the next week, they set a local record 56,915 and lost again. At Baltimore they almost won, but with less than a minute left Johnny Unitas hit Alan Ameche with an eight-yard scoring pass for a 27–21 Colts' victory.

Then it was on to New York, where the favored Giants were battling for the title in the Eastern Conference. The 49ers rode the arm of Tittle and the linebacking of Karl Rubke, Matt

Hazeltine, and Matuszak to a 27–17 victory. Playing in Yankee Stadium (which four seasons later would become his home), Tittle ran five times for 49 yards and completed 11 of 16 passes for another 143, and the Giants, encouraged by the 49ers' defenders, lost the ball six times on fumbles.

There were only two games left, both at Kezar. For the game with the Colts, crowds began to form in front of the ticket windows the previous afternoon, and a near-riot ensued when the gates finally were opened. Many fans were arrested for disturbing the peace. Thousands were turned away.

Those who got in witnessed another 49ers special. The Colts, with a 7–3 won-lost record to the 49ers' 6–4, gave their special regards to Tittle, who wound up with a personal rushing loss of 52 yards.

With just over a minute remaining, Baltimore leading 13–10 and the ball on the 42, Tittle threw a short pass to McElhenny over the middle. Two Colts tacklers lunged for the King and wound up tackling each other. The Colts finally pushed him out of bounds on the Baltimore 15.

Two plays later, Tittle disappeared. At the moment he got rid of the ball the Colts got rid of him. The pass fell incomplete and Tittle went down under half a ton of young manhood. They had to dig for him. Teammates carried him off the field — muscles were pulled in both his legs — and rookie John Brodie came on to take his place.

Two plays later, Brodie disappeared, this time under a full ton of young manhood. But this time it was his teammates, for Brodie had found McElhenny in the endzone for the winning touchdown. The final score was 17–13.

Going into the final Sunday of the season, three teams — Baltimore, Detroit, and San Francisco — had 7–4 records. The Rams stunned the Colts 37–21, while Detroit beat the Bears 21–13.

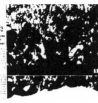

The 49ers figured to beat the lowly Packers, but Brodie would have to lead San Francisco, since Tittle was still hobbling.

The 49ers took a 10–0 first-period lead, but Bart Starr's passes gave Green Bay a 20–10 lead at halftime.

In hobbled Tittle. One march resulted in a 28-yard Soltau field goal for 20–13; an interception by Val Joe Walker set up a Joe Perry touchdown for a 20–20 tie; and Tittle's passing and Perry's running combined for a final touchdown drive as the 49ers pulled it out 27–20.

That left San Francisco and Detroit tied for the division championship and a playoff game was scheduled at Kezar.

Records show that Tittle connected on 176 of 279 passes for a completion percentage of 63.1 during the regular season. He started the playoff game against the Lions the same way, with a 34-yard Alley-Oop to R. C. Owens for a touchdown. Then McElhenny took a short pass and buzzed 47 yards for another score. Billy Wilson caught another pass for a third touchdown, and Soltau kicked a 25-yard field goal for a 24–7 San Francisco halftime lead.

The national telecast of this game attracted an enormous audience which saw the 49ers pouring it on. On the first play of the second half, for instance, McElhenny took a pitchout, stopped just long enough for Lou Palatella to throw a good block, then journeyed 71 yards to the Detroit 9-yard line.

There the Lions, led by linebacker Joe Schmidt, held their ground, so Soltau kicked a field goal and it was 27–7.

What happened after that didn't hurt the telecast's ratings, but it didn't do much for the 49ers. They had gained a first-place tie in their division, the highest they had ever finished. They also lost the football game 31–27. Suffice it to say that as televised epics go — and this still in the formative years of coast-to-coast television —

this one may stand for all time in sports history.

A curtain of sympathy descends over the next decade-plus of 49ers activity. A tie for second place in 1960 was the best they could show. They were using a new formation (one devised by Red Hickey, assistant coach under Albert and head coach beginning with the 1959 season). The formation, called the Shotgun, won three of the last four games in 1960 and four of the first five in 1961, featured by an absolutely stunning 49–0 victory over the Lions at Detroit. Then the Bears found a way to stop it.

Hickey departed after the first three games of 1963 and was replaced by *his* assistant, Jack Christiansen, the 49ers completing that season with a 2–12 record.

Hickey was to have a record of 27–27 as 49ers coach. His tenure included an engaging 1959 season featuring a 34–0 win over the Rams, an Alley-Oop with a minute to go that beat the Bears 20–17, and two wins over the Lions (both starring the explosive running of J. D. Smith). And there was a memorable game at Cleveland that year in which Brodie (substituting for an ailing Tittle) threw two touchdown passes and McElhenny added a third score as the club hung on for a 21–20 victory over the Browns. The 49ers' defense that day was led by a youngster named Charlie Krueger, who would become known as the "textbook tackle." Rival teams would soon be showing 49ers films to their defensive linemen so they could see how Krueger went about things.

But a strange and uneven quality managed to pervade the season. At one point, the 49ers were in first place. They led Baltimore by one game, only to lose to the Colts 48–14, a game in which San Francisco managed only 35 yards rushing and three first downs.

One of the things that afflicted the 49ers, beginning in 1960 and ending with Christiansen's departure as coach following the 1967 season,

The 49ers would meet the Detroit Lions in a playoff that day for the Western Conference championship, but their fans—believing the playoff to be a sure thing—stormed the Kezar Stadium booths (top left) for tickets to the championship game to be played one week later against the Cleveland Browns. But a ticket to that game (right) would become nothing more than a souvenir. The Lions made an incredible comeback and won the playoff game 31-27. Unsung Tom Tracy took off on a 58-yard touchdown run (below left), followed by Gene Gedman's two-yard touchdown plunge (below) that tied the game 27-27. Jim Martin's extra point and ensuing field goal (not shown) made it 31-27. San Francisco would not reach the playoffs of pro football again for 13 years.

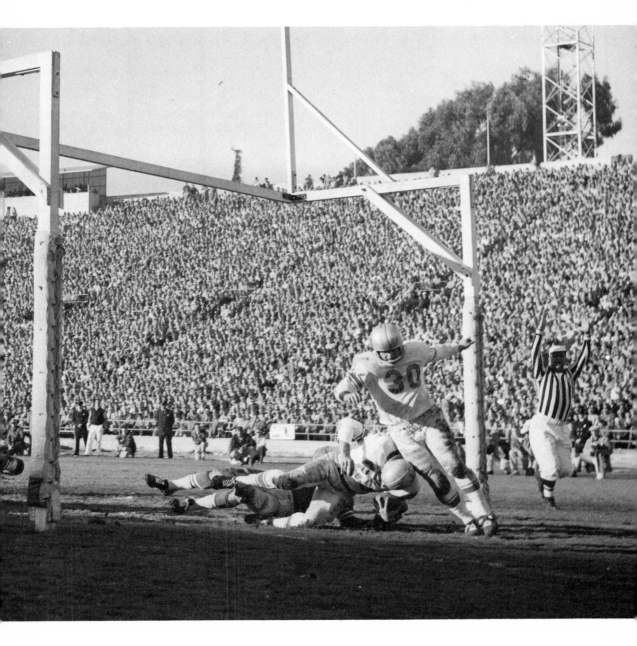

was something that beset the entire Western Conference of the NFL. That something was called Green Bay.

Under Vince Lombardi the Packers won six conference championships in eight seasons (and 19 of 26 decisions the other two years). It would take a lot of help to finish ahead of a club like that, and the 49ers didn't get that help, not even that afternoon when Jim Marshall of Minnesota recovered a 49ers' fumble and went 66 yards the wrong way with the ball (two yards farther than Roy Riegels in the Rose Bowl a few years earlier). Asked why he had not tackled his man as he rambled past the Vikings' bench, Minnesota coach Norm Van Brocklin said, "I don't think fast enough and I don't run fast enough."

Gone by then, retired or traded, were Perry, Soltau, McElhenny and Tittle. And in the spring of 1964 Vic Morabito followed his brother Tony in death from a heart attack. The parallels were sad. Both were far too young (Tony was 47, Vic 44) when death came. Each had a history of previous heart trouble. For each, the end came at St. Mary's Hospital, barely three blocks from their beloved Kezar Stadium. In what Wells Twombly rightly called "a classic immigrant's tale," they were half-brothers — and cousins as well. When Tony's mother died, his father sent to the old country for her sister to come to take care of the household. There was a second marriage and another son.

Two weeks after Tony's death, Vic had issued a statement: "The San Francisco 49ers are not for sale. They never will be."

Then, in 1964, there were two widows, the elder Josephine and the younger Jane. "If anything happens to me," Vic had told them privately, "you'll sell out, if you have any sense." But they did not sell out. Vesting operational management of the team in Lou Spadia, Josie and Jane decided to hold on to the club.

Spadia had been with the 49ers from their first season in the old AAFC, and he had come a long way. There were memorable moments as he learned the ropes, such as the time Tony got him on the intercom and said, "Phone Marshall and tell him I've got Johnny Powers's contract all set."

Obediently, Spadia put in a long-distance call to Washington Redskins' owner George Marshall and passed along the good news. But it didn't make Marshall happy. "I couldn't understand what he was upset about," Spadia reported back to Morabito, "but he sounded like he thought you were some kind of lunatic."

"You're the lunatic," Tony told him. "I meant Leahy." The latter, whose first name was Marshall, was the 49ers' lawyer.

But Spadia's touch was to become more and more evident — and less and less subject to error — as the years wore on. When, following the 1967 season, he heard that Dick Nolan might be available as a coach, he reached for the telephone again. This time Spadia got the right man.

The right man had six children and a reputation. After a distinguished career as a back at the University of Maryland, he had been drafted by the New York Giants. He had an intense, nonsmiling face, featured by cantilever eyebrows and a rock-hard jaw. He also had a Giants' teammate named Tom Landry. Nolan went with Landry to Dallas as a player-coach in 1962, then became defensive backfield coach, then during the rise of the Cowboys, overall defensive coach under Landry.

Jack Christiansen had a 26–38 won-lost record as 49ers coach, but in 1967 the 49ers won only two of their last eight games, and the natives were restless.

Under Nolan in 1968 the team was 7–6–1 and then, with the defensive unit decimated by injury, 4–8–2 in 1969. But there was the scent of something new. For one thing, there was a new training base at Santa Barbara; for another

Like his brother, Vic Morabito was, in 1964,
the victim of a fatal heart attack. The Morabito
widows retained control of the team, but vested
administrative authority in Lou Spadia.
Jane (far left), widow of Vic, and Josephine,
widow of Tony Morabito, pose against a backdrop
of their city. A new era of 49ers greatness
was on the horizon when Dick Nolan became
head coach in 1968. He would build a
championship team around veterans John
Brodie (left); Charlie Krueger, whose battered
helmet showed the wear and tear of more than
a decade in the front lines of pro football;
Ken Willard, and (below) one of the league's
greatest cornerbacks, Jimmy Johnson. Nolan
ran off a string of excellent draft selections.
Star receivers Gene Washington (pages 46-47)
and Ted Kwalick were 1969 first-round choices.

Running back Vic Washington (left), joined the 49ers in 1971 after three seasons in Canadian professional football. Young tight end Ted Kwalick (right, being covered by Ron Smith of San Diego) caught 52 passes in 1971.

there was a new 49ers' philosophy: defense.

The merger of the National and American Leagues came in 1970. There would be not just a Super Bowl at season's end, but one overall league, commanded by commissioner Pete Rozelle. Leagues would officially become conferences, conferences would officially become divisions. There would be four steps to a title: (1) either win or "wild-card" your way into the divisional playoffs, (2) win the divisional playoff, (3) win the conference playoff, (4) win the Super Bowl.

In their opening league game of 1970, Bruce Taylor, a rookie cornerback and kick-return specialist, returned three punts for 61 yards — just two yards short of the entire team's punt-return yardage the previous season. Second-year man Gene Washington caught 6 passes for 95 yards. Brodie completed 17 out of 21 passes for 178 yards. The 49ers beat Washington 26–17.

The second game was against Cleveland. Ken Willard was the big runner and a 69-yard Brodie to Jimmy Thomas pass made the difference. San Francisco won 34–31. All this bespeaks offense, and Dick Nolan had a theory about offense: It wasn't just what you did with the ball; more subtly, it was that if you had the ball, the other team didn't. To emphasize the point, a Dave Wilcox interception gave the 49ers the ball with over six minutes to go. No score resulted, but by the time San Francisco finally gave up the football, there were only 27 seconds remaining to be played.

A 21–20 loss to the Atlanta Falcons followed. Bruce Gossett missed a 19-yard field goal with six seconds remaining, but he more than made up for that the following week by kicking two field goals against his former teammates, the Rams, during a Brodie-inspired 20–6 49ers' win.

Then came a 20–20 tie with New Orleans. Gossett kicked four field goals as San Francisco

downed Denver 19–14. The following Sunday, Bruce Taylor had a 70-yard touchdown runback of an intercepted pass; Gossett had four more field goals, and the 49ers beat the Packers 26–10.

Against the Bears, Brodie completed 21 of 28 pass attempts. He threw three touchdown passes, one of which was to Gene Washington for 79 yards. Gossett was no flash in the pan and neither was Taylor. He returned a punt for 76 yards as the 49ers defeated Chicago 37–16. The following week, Taylor picked up 133 yards on six punt returns as the 49ers beat the Houston Oilers 30–20.

The next week, Brodie completed 18 of 25 passes, but the 49ers lost to Detroit 28–7. The 49ers' playoff hopes got more tenuous with the next game, a 30–13 loss to the Rams, and once again the Kezar faithful started reaching for their missiles.

But the combination of Brodie-to-Gene Washington and an extraordinary defense which, led by Earl Edwards, sacked the Atlanta quarterback five times in the fourth period, produced a 24–20 win over the Falcons. The 49ers followed with a 38–27 win over the Saints. Brodie hit Washington for touchdowns three times. Brodie connected on 15 of 22 passes for 227 yards, and Bruce Taylor had a wild runback play (92 yards to score with a missed field goal attempt).

It came down now to the final game of the season. A Rams' victory at New York coupled with a 49ers' loss at Oakland would give the division title to Los Angeles. The Rams won — the time difference made the news known even before the 49ers-Raiders' kickoff.

Oakland, a heady intruder into San Francisco's territory, was a winning team. Oakland and San Francisco had never met before in a league game. And San Francisco had never won a divisional title.

It rained like crazy, but there wasn't an empty

seat in the Oakland Coliseum. At the beginning of the game that is. By game's end, there were plenty. The 49ers took the Raiders apart 38–7.

The Raiders turned the ball over nine times that day. After the game, coach Nolan singled out safety Mel Phillips as the game's unsung hero but in the same breath, he confessed it was hard to single out anybody. "When the defense gets the ball for you nine times and the offense scores four touchdowns. . . ." His voice trailed off.

There was no question who would get the game ball. For the year of the 49ers' first divisional crown, John Brodie was the NFL's most valuable player, and Bruce Taylor rookie of the year. But there is another category: coach of the year. The game ball went to Dick Nolan.

Writing in the *Examiner,* Wells Twombly had this to say:

"It takes magic to lay a hex on someone. It takes the same occult art to remove it. After a quarter of a century, the San Francisco 49ers finally were free to win a divisional championship. It was downright spooky, as if the shaded hands of Vic and Tony Morabito, two club owners who lived and died for their team, were guiding the ball in its curious flight. It came down to this final game against the Oakland Raiders. Now there was no other way. It was win or else. In previous seasons, the 49ers would have swooned. But not this time.

"Nothing went wrong for the 49ers yesterday afternoon at the Oakland Coliseum. Receivers caught passes they should have dropped in the slop and the sleet. The Raiders lost the ball at the most amazing times. The story is that someone put a jinx on the 49ers. Never, never would they win their division. But curses last just so long. Who says the Morabito brothers weren't out there, helping the team they created and died for? It certainly looked that way."

"I've got the best of both worlds," said Charlie Krueger. "I'm in San Francisco and I'm with a winner."

"'Wait 'til next year,'" wrote columnist Prescott Sullivan. "It was a prayer as well as a slogan. And now, after a quarter of a century, that year has come, and the enduring faith of the peasantry has been rewarded."

So rewarded was the peasantry, indeed, that the glow of the 49ers' first divisional title, made even brighter by a 17–14 playoff win over the Vikings, held fast despite what then happened: The 49ers lost the NFL championship to the Cowboys 17–10. Mentor Landry reminded pupil Nolan all afternoon that ball control is the name of the game.

The glow held fast through 1971 as well. This time the 49ers clinched the NFL's Western Division with a 31–27 triumph over the Lions in the final game. It was the same score by which the Lions had won in that playoff game of 1957.

Again the 49ers went on to win their first playoff game. The deciding touchdown came when Bob Hoskins, a reserve defensive lineman and member of the special teams, recovered a bad snap from center that went through punter Mike Bragg's legs. It was a rain-soaked, sloppy encounter, but a nail-biter nevertheless. Final score: 49ers 24, Redskins 20. Next week: Dallas again for the NFC championship.

Again, the Cowboys won. This time the score was 14–3. It was a game for defenses: Cedrick Hardman led the 49ers' charge that sacked Dallas quarterback Roger Staubach six times, but the Cowboys intercepted Brodie three times. In the end, it was Staubach's scrambling that made the difference.

In 1972, there was another replay. The 49ers were champions for the third year in a row. The clincher this time was an eerie 20–17 win over the Vikings at Candlestick. There were two fourth-quarter 49ers touchdowns, the second a

short Brodie pass to Dick Witcher with 19 seconds remaining in the game.

But this time the script was to change. Dallas did not beat San Francisco in the second playoff game, the conference championship game.

Dallas beat San Francisco in the first playoff contest, the divisional game.

The 49ers shouldn't have lost. They held a 15-point lead at 28–13 after three periods, but the Cowboys were dominant in the final quarter and escaped with a 30–28 victory.

At the beginning, it looked easy for San Francisco, perhaps too easy. Vic Washington returned the opening kickoff 97 yards for a touchdown. A Tommy Hart fumble recovery and a Skip Vanderbundt interception led to two more 49ers touchdowns in the first half, and Larry Schreiber made his third one-yard scoring plunge in the third period. It was 28–13 then.

But Roger Staubach, replacing Craig Morton as the Dallas quarterback, got the Cowboys close enough for a fourth-quarter field goal, then passed to Billy Parks for a touchdown.

Then the Cowboys recovered an onside kickoff, and within two minutes there was Staubach, defying clock and 49ers alike, passing to Ron Sellers for 10 yards and the winning score.

But one fact remained: Of all 26 teams in the National Football League, the 49ers were the only one to win their division three straight years. In each of those seasons, the 49ers had won their title on the last day of the schedule.

Thus their followers have come to display an admixture of joy and patience unmatched anywhere in professional football. For in San Francisco it can be said that happiness is a 49ers' fan waiting not for next year, but simply for next Sunday.

The Memories

The cover for their first game versus the 49ers notwithstanding, the Chicago Rockets never really got off the ground. They symbolized hard times of most AAFC teams.

Halfback John Strzykalski was one of the charter 49ers who joined the team when it began play in the All-America Football Conference. Above, he is upended in a 1947 game by Lou Sossamon of the New York Yankees in Ernest Sisto's prize photo.

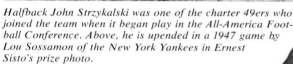

End Alyn Beals (battling with Rex Bumgardner of the Buffalo Bills above for a pass) was named All-AAFC in the inaugural season, 1946.
Lefthanded quarterbacking genius Frankie Albert (left) completed 29 touchdown passes in 1948 and was named outstanding player in the AAFC.

Only Jim Brown and Jim Taylor gained more yards carrying the football than Joe Perry. The 49ers signed him after watching him play for Alameda Naval Air Station. In 1953 and 1954, he had back-to-back seasons with over 1,000 yards, the first runner ever to achieve that record.

Y. A. Tittle (right) passed for over 18,000 yards in 10 years with the 49ers. The old Baltimore Colts originally signed Tittle, but when they disbanded in 1950, their players were pooled and the 49ers obtained him.

Billy Wilson (right) was called hardest end in league to cover by Emlen Tunnell.

Charley Powell (above) played in the San Francisco defensive line at age 19. He was also a professional boxer and once fought Muhammad Ali. Early emblem of team pictured giddy 49er firing off in all directions, just missing brain and boot.

Leo Nomellini (top left) set a league record by playing in 174 consecutive games and was named the greatest defensive tackle in the first 50 years of the game by a Hall of Fame selection committee. Gordy Soltau (far left) was a Navy frogman turned receiver and kicking star. He was acquired from Cleveland in 1950 in one of the greatest trades in the 49ers' history. Few backs before Gale Sayers could maneuver in the open field in the manner of Hugh McElhenny (left). If tacklers missed him once, they could not rest, for he would probably be back their way again before the play was over.

When his jaw was fractured in a preseason game in 1954, Joe Perry played on wearing a face mask designed especially for him.

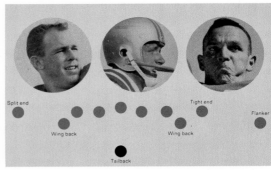

The shotgun offense was unveiled by coach Howard (Red) Hickey in 1960. Pulling the trigger were quarterbacks (left to right) John Brodie, Bill Kilmer and Bobby Waters.

At 6 foot 9 inches, Bob St. Clair (above) was one of tallest NFL players of all time. He was a perennial all-pro tackle. Abe Woodson (right) led the league in kickoff returns three times, an NFL record.

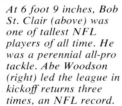

Salvaged from the waiver list, then tried unsuccessfully on defense, J. D. Smith (above) became a 1,000-yard rusher as running back. Tommy Davis (right) holds most 49ers kicking records. Jim Johnson (below) has been a starter at cornerback for 12 years.

John Brodie (right) did what neither Frankie Albert nor Y. A. Tittle ever could: lead the 49ers to a championship—three of them, in fact, in 1970, 1971 and 1972. John Thomas (below), Bruce Bosley were great sixties guards.

Ken Willard runs behind the blocking of center Forrest Blue in San Francisco's victory over Minnesota in 1970 playoff.

It had been their home for 25 years, but the 49ers left Kezar Stadium (above) in 1970 and moved into a restructured Candlestick Park for their silver anniversary season in pro football.

Dave Wilcox (above) has been an annual all-pro at left linebacker for San Francisco. Gene Washington (right) piled up impressive yards-per-catch figures as the last great deep receiver for John Brodie. A rookie in the 1950s still playing in the 1970s, mighty defensive tackle Charlie Krueger (left, bearing down on Donny Anderson of the Green Bay Packers) declared himself a "dinosaur" of pro football—a holdover from the sport's distant past.

HALL OF FAME

Hugh McElhenney, halfback, 1952-60. Inducted in 1970.

Leo Nomellini, defensive tackle, 1950-63. Inducted in 1969.

Joe Perry, fullback, 1948-60, 1963. Inducted in 1969.

Y. A. Tittle, quarterback, 1951-60. Inducted in 1971.

The Great Games

October 9, 1949

Ripe in the history of the Cleveland Browns is the memory of their mammoth placekicking specialist Lou Groza. Not so vivid, and it's a pity, are memories of Joe Vetrano of the San Francisco 49ers. Groza was known as "the Toe." Vetrano, at 5-foot 9-inches and 170 pounds, had his own proud nickname: "Little Toe." But at one point he owned the all-time pro mark of 107 consecutive extra points. In effect, he had out-Groza'd Groza.

In fact, the only threat to "Little Toe" was "the Knee." The latter was the nickname for Bill Pacheco, a ukulele-playing, barefooted place-kicker from Honolulu. Dan McGuire, in his history of the 49ers' early seasons, records that at the age of 32, "the Knee" did not anticipate bodily contact, but he showed up at the San Francisco team's 1949 training camp firmly convinced he was the world's greatest placekicking specialist.

Asked to fill out the club's publicity questionnaire, "the Knee" was nothing if not candid:

Your favorite sports hero: Myself, naturally.

Hobbies: Reading newspaper clippings about myself.

Accomplishments: Doing the hula when I kick a field goal or extra point.

"The Knee" presented a Hawaiian shirt to "Little Toe." "This is a token of my admiration and esteem for you," "the Knee" explained. "Please don't be jealous when Shaw selects me to do the placekicking."

Four hulas and five days later, "the Knee" was en route back to Hawaii, where he opened a night club in partnership with his wife, played the ukelele and guitar, and sang songs in four different languages.

It would have been astonishing if "the Knee" had made the team — no less astonishing, however, than the fortunes of "Little Toe" himself, who arrived in a package deal. A number of clubs had been after Johnny Strzykalski, who

was playing with the powerful Fourth Air Force team from March Field when Shaw and Tony Morabito first saw him in 1945. The 49ers made an offer. Johnny Strike made a counter offer. "I'll play for you," the mighty halfback from Milwaukee said, "if you'll sign my buddy, too."

"Who's your buddy?" Morabito asked.

"Joe Vetrano."

"I never heard of him."

"Are you saying no?"

"I'm not saying no. I'm just saying I never heard of him."

So Vetrano came to the 49ers, and on the afternoon of October 9, 1949, he scored the most exciting touchdown in an afternoon that was a blizzard of touchdowns. Before a Kezar Stadium throng of 59,770, the 49ers were to beat their perennial tormentors, the Browns, 56–28.

Those were the days before uniforms were numbered by position, and Vetrano was a halfback who wore number 82. Not that he did all that much halfbacking. He played behind Johnny Strike, whom coach Shaw had called "the best right halfback in football," and Joe Perry, who didn't convert to fullback until Norm Standlee was shifted to defense; and other assorted swifties such as Eddie Carr.

This didn't mean that "Little Toe" was inactive. His work as placekicker for the 49ers was not merely a social amenity: For a team that averaged 35 points a game its last two seasons in the All-America Football Conference, "Little Toe" found himself shuttling like a loom.

His great moment in the Cleveland game, though, came just after Strzykalski ran a kickoff back to the Browns' 49. Players came on and off the field for the ensuing scrimmage sequence, and on the first play number eighty-two came bursting over his own right tackle.

On the Cleveland side of the field, coach Paul Brown blinked and reached for his pro-

Browns 7 14 0 7 28
49ers 21 14 7 14 56

gram. It was Vetrano, all right — eighty-two. He had a speed and a drive no one had suspected. He also had suddenly grown three inches and put on 25 pounds. In addition, he appeared to have acquired a magnificent tan.

Members of the Cleveland secondary were just as fascinated as their coach. They stood there and watched the ball carrier go 49 yards untouched for a San Francisco score.

To this day, there are those who were in the stands that afternoon and remain convinced they saw "Little Toe," unbelievably larger than life, streak 49 yards for a touchdown. The truth is that Vetrano and Joe Perry, acting on one of those forever-unexplained impulses that have made the 49ers the most interesting team in football, had swapped jerseys on the sidelines two plays earlier.

The record cited above — a capacity crowd of 59,770 for Kezar Stadium — tells only part of the story. The 49ers' management estimated it had to return orders for another 40,000 tickets, so eager were fans to see the 49ers, who by beating the Browns, could take over first place in the standings.

The 49ers hadn't beaten Cleveland since their first meeting in 1946, but who had? In their four seasons, the Browns had lost only three games, and were unbeaten in their last 29 starts.

Adding to the game's appeal to fans was the Browns' last appearance at San Francisco, in the next-to-last game of 1948. In 1948, the Browns were en route to a 14–0 record — 15–0, if you count their 49–7 championship-game victory over the Buffalo Bills. In beating San Francisco earlier in the 1948 season they had held the 49ers to seven points, a tribute to the Cleveland defense. The 49ers weren't accustomed to scoring so little. The week before, San Francisco had scored 44 points against the Chicago Rockets; the week after, they scored 63 against the Brooklyn Dodgers. In fact, coming

into the 1948 game at Kezar, the 49ers had lost only the game in Cleveland. In the rematch San Francisco was a six-point favorite.

The explanation of the odds was legitimate enough: Otto Graham, the celebrated Cleveland quarterback, had injured his leg the week before. No one seemed to know how severe the injury was.

As uncertain as the status of Graham was the health of the AAFC itself. If the league was to survive, somebody had to beat Cleveland and that logical somebody was the 49ers.

As the big game unfolded, the 49ers fell behind 10–0, then scored two second-period touchdowns to lead the Browns 14–10 at halftime. The most memorable play that half was a 29-yard run by Johnny Strike. In those days, you could get up after being knocked down. So he did. He spent more time on the ground than on his feet, and ultimately it took the entire Browns' team to give him a decent burial.

But in the second half, the Browns outscored the 49ers three touchdowns to two and won the game 31–28. Had the 49ers won, each of the clubs might have made $50,000 from a playoff, or so Tony Morabito estimated. "But I'm almost glad the playoff is out," he said. "To me, it's worth that much to make the wise guys shut up."

Bud Spencer, sports editor of the *San Francisco News*, found nobility in that day's struggle — and with good reason. It was a hell of a game. "Whatever happened to the weisenheimers who whispered it was San Francisco's turn to win over Cleveland?" Spencer wrote. "As it turned out, it was a game of games, strictly for keeps, and a rugged afternoon for the finer qualities of manhood."

Thus the case can be made that the 49ers, who had discovered so many other unusual things in their All-America Football Conference lifetime, found a game they were just as happy to lose.

On the afternoon of October 9, 1949, the Browns once again were the visitors at Kezar. This time the odds favored Cleveland.

By the fourth quarter, a patriarch who was sitting in the pressbox — none other than Glenn S. (Pop) Warner himself — had turned to those surrounding him and said, "For this one day, this is the greatest football team I have ever seen."

He meant the 49ers.

It was, as Prescott Sullivan observed, "the pent-up fury of three years of frustration." Nobody had ever done this to the Browns. In one really poor earlier effort — against the 49ers in 1946, as a matter of fact — the Browns had five touchdowns scored against them. In this game, Frankie Albert produced five touchdowns, all by passing.

Perry, Strzykalski, and Carr each scored twice, Alyn Beals and Nick Susoeff once each. Hal Shoener, a defensive end from Iowa who was hailed by his 49ers teammates for having two arms and six elbows, twice escaped blockers and hit Otto Graham for fumbles that resulted in turnovers.

Otto didn't do all that badly. He threw for three touchdowns. But Shorty Albert, as Frankie was known to his colleagues, had five. The comparison of counterparts extended down the line. Cleveland's great Marion Motley got 89 yards in 13 carries. But San Francisco's Joe Perry got 156 yards in 11 carries.

Albert completed 16 of 24 passes for 242 yards. In addition to his five touchdown throws which set a league record, he had another that went 42 yards to the 1-yard line, leading to a touchdown on the following play.

As Sullivan wrote in the *Examiner,* it was indeed the pent-up fury of three years of frustration. But fury begets fury, and so it was in that 1949 game, which was one of the most physical games ever.

Only one All-America Football Conference team was good enough to beat San Francisco regularly. That team was the Cleveland Browns, perennial AAFC champions. Finally, the 49ers took out their frustrations and buried the Browns 56-28 on an October afternoon at Kezar Stadium in 1949. The first touchdown of the game came on a pass from Frankie Albert to John Strzykalski (below). The program for the game is shown at left.

"Physical," in the laundered language of pro football today, is a euphemism that didn't occur to anyone who witnessed or participated in that '49 game. "Vicious" — yes. "Brutal" — yes. The partisan home crowd booed the Browns for piling on, play after play, and no one has the right to dispute the fans' reaction. Still, the 49ers gave as good as they got, and when they piled on it was an occasion for cheering. For an early season game whose outcome was decided almost at once, the violence of this one was unusual. On one play, hardly atypical, *both* teams were penalized for unnecessary roughness. And this was in the era before facemasks or rapid whistles, when, if you threw three punches, the officials tended to overlook at least the first two.

Eddie Carr, playing both ways on defense and offense, started things in the first period by intercepting a Graham pass intended for Special Delivery Jones. It happened deep in enemy territory. Cleveland had to kick, and Alyn Beals (the end from Santa Clara who would establish a new AAFC scoring record by day's end) snatched an Albert pass from the fingers of defender Weldon Humble for a 15-yard gain. Two plays later, Albert passed to Stryzkalski, who caught the ball on the 5, ran over Les Horvath, and tumbled into the endzone.

Two minutes later the 49ers scored again. An electrifying Albert-Beals pass covered 42 yards, and Strzykalski bulled over from the 1. Scarce minutes later Special Delivery Jones fumbled. Shoener recovered at the Cleveland 27, and on the next play Albert threw the ball to Perry, who made a spectacular one-handed catch at the 5 with Warren Lahr draped over him like a Dali watch face. Perry simply carried Lahr into the endzone with him. Indeed, to his amazement, the Cleveland defender traveled faster on Perry's back than he was accustomed to cruising on his own.

Thus with the game not yet 12 minutes old,

San Francisco had a 21–0 lead. It was reduced, shortly, to 21–14. Graham's two friends at the ends, Mac Speedie and Dante Lavelli, each caught passes for touchdowns. Lavelli's came after Albert had been intercepted by Alex Agase on the 49ers' 11-yard line. Why Albert was passing from that deep in his own territory with a 21–7 lead is a question best answered by faith. Frankie had an abiding trust in the unexpected — a quality that was to become and remain the hallmark of the 49ers over the years.

Later, Shoener hit Graham so hard that Otto coughed up several things, including the ball. Bob Mike fell on it for San Francisco at the Cleveland 15, and on the next play Albert hit Beals in the endzone for a touchdown. Accounts of this play differ. According to one account, Beals was standing alone. According to another, he outjumped Lahr for the ball. No one ever asked Lahr which version he preferred.

That made it 28–14 in San Francisco's favor. Then Graham took the Browns 74 yards in two plays — one a 61-yard pass play to Dub Jones, then another pass to Speedie for the score.

But Perry raced back 31 yards with the Cleveland kickoff. Verl Lillywhite gained 8 yards, and took an Albert pass for 15 more. Beals caught one for 9, Carr another for 5. Lillywhite cracked the middle for 12. With the ball on the Cleveland 8-yard line, Albert, faking a bootleg play, suddenly passed to Nick Susoeff in the endzone. That made it 35–21, San Francisco, at the half.

In the third quarter it became 42–21. Perry bolted 19 yards, then Strzykalski went another 6. With the ball on the Cleveland 24, Albert rifled a pass to Carr in the flat for another touchdown play.

The business of trading touchdown for touchdown is fine, but at this point the Cleveland Browns had the distinct sensation they were trading one touchdown for two touchdowns. They had trailed at 28–14 and were now trailing

42–21. Back they came with a 12-yard Motley touchdown smash to make it 42–28. But by now the fourth quarter had begun.

The 49ers wasted no time. Back came "Little Toe's" number eighty-two on that incredibly swift 49-yard burst off tackle for a touchdown. That was the play "Little Toe" became "Little Joe" (Joe Perry was the gentleman with the ball). Then Carr intercepted Graham again and, after Perry — clearly identified this time — had picked up 25 yards around end, Carr took the ball over from 5 yards out for the final San Francisco touchdown. That made it 56–28.

Albert was not satisfied. When the 49ers got close again, they lined up for a field-goal attempt by Vetrano with Albert holding. But Albert had other plans. He took the ball from center, rolled out, and fired into the endzone. Nobody was there to catch it. The question is whether he ever told Vetrano about it.

A similar incident occurred later in 1949. In the Cleveland game, Vetrano ran his record of consecutive points-after-touchdown to 79.

Later, the 49ers were playing the Los Angeles Dons. The 49ers-Dons rivalry never became as fierce as the 49ers-Rams' competition of the NFL years to come. In fact, in all their years of head-to-head play, the Dons never won. But at this point, Vetrano was closing in on 100 consecutive conversions.

Walt Daley, of the *Call-Bulletin,* reported:

"Vetrano, who split the uprights five times yesterday as the 49ers romped over their favorite punching bags, the L.A. Dons, 41–24, was undoubtedly robbed of his century boot by Albert's call after the fifth 49ers' touchdown at the Coliseum in Los Angeles, before a scant 18,000 fans.

"The men lined up for the extra-point try in proper fashion, but Albert chose that moment to pull a fake and passed to Al Beals instead, unsuccessfully."

Vetrano finished the game with a total of 99, and writer Daley could not be sure whether the odd play that robbed him of 100 should "be charged to Frankie Albert's diabolical sense of humor or to a mere temporary mental lapse on the part of the great T-formation signal caller." It is an open question. When you have a team with two players, one white and small, the other black and large, who switch shirts on impulse, who is to say where diabolical humor ends and mental lapse begins?

Cleveland	7	14	0	7 —	28
San Francisco	21	14	7	14 —	56

SF — Strzykalski 16 pass from Albert (Vetrano kick)
SF — Strzykalski 1 run (Vetrano kick)
SF — Perry 27 pass from Albert (Vetrano kick)
Clev — Speedie 39 pass from Graham (Groza kick)
Clev — Lavelli 25 pass from Graham (Groza kick)
SF — Beals 15 pass from Albert (Vetrano kick)
Clev — Speedie 13 pass from Graham (Groza kick)
SF — Susoeff 8 pass from Albert (Vetrano kick)
SF — Carr 24 pass from Albert (Vetrano kick)
Clev — Motley 12 run (Groza kick)
SF — Perry 49 run (Vetrano kick)
SF — Carr 5 run (Vetrano kick)

October 19, 1952

"As we came out of the dressing room after a short practice today, some of the 49ers were drifting in. I said hello to John Brodie (their quarterback), to Dick Voris (one of their coaches who used to be with us), and to Hugh McElhenny (who worked on San Francisco broadcasts). I started thinking about the first time I played against Hugh McElhenny. It was a preseason game in 1958, and I was on the punting team, and he was returning punts for the 49ers. He'd already been a pro for seven years, and I guess I'd been hearing about him all my life. He had played for the University of Washington before he joined the 49ers, and he was a legend, one of the all-time great football players. We punted to him, and I started running down the field, supposedly to tackle him, and I found myself thinking, 'How absurd for a dumb ass like me to tackle a man like Hugh McElhenny. That would really be a dumb thing to do.' It seemed inconceivable, a young upstart dum-dum from Idaho trying to knock down the King . . ."

"He had the finest coordination and balance of any back I've ever seen. Don't forget he was a hurdles champion in high school. When you saw him coming at you, it put chills down your spine."

"I played against him in college last year. He wasn't this great."

These unsolicited testimonials were taken, in order, from Jerry Kramer, the great Green Bay guard; Don Paul, the famous Rams' linebacker whose art was to frighten, not be frightened; and Tommy O'Connell, a reserve quarterback in his rookie season with the Chicago Bears in 1952. For all its brevity and understatement, O'Connell's observation, made the afternoon of October 9, 1952, may be most to the point. It was uttered a few minutes after that day's game beween the Bears and the San Francisco 49ers at Wrigley Field in Chicago, and no self-respecting fan — of either team — will ever forget it.

The Morabitos had special reason not to forget it, and that reason had comparatively little to do with Hugh McElhenny. It dated back instead to their earliest dealings with owner-coach George Halas of the Bears.

Early on, according to the Morabitos' version, Halas had discouraged them from even thinking about fielding a professional football team. Subsequently, again according to their version, he had promised them a National Football League franchise. Somehow the promise had misfired. The rival All-America Football Conference was born, and the 49ers spent four glorious years in that debtors' prison. Finally, with the acceptance of San Francisco into the NFL in late 1949, the 49ers had made it. Or so they thought.

"We're in the National Football League," Tony Morabito breathed, at the ensuing organizational meeting. "A member. I never thought I'd see the day."

George Preston Marshall of the Redskins smiled at him charitably. "You still haven't seen the day," he said.

"What do you mean?" Morabito demanded. "We're members of the National Football League."

"You're not a member of the National Football League," Marshall intoned, "until you beat the Bears."

Morabito was stung. "The last time I looked up your record," he said to Marshall, "you lost to them 73–0."

"We beat them the game before that," George Preston Marshall said.

History fails properly to record one of the essential features of the merger between the NFL and AAFC. In the AAFC's final season of 1949, average attendance at its games was 26,329. (The 49ers led the pack with an average turnout of 38,240.) Yet in the National Football League that same year, the average turnout was 27,285, only 956 per game better than the

49ers 14 7 10 9 40
Bears 2 7 0 7 16

average crowds that watched AAFC games.

Among other things, Morabito's 49ers of 1949 drew more than 10,000 more people per game than did Marshall's 1949 Redskins. For Marshall, even in jest, to deny Tony what he had spent his adult lifetime delivering — membership in the NFL — had to rankle, and it did.

"I would like to beat the Bears," Tony said to coach Buck Shaw.

"So would I," said Shaw.

The 49ers would play the Bears twice in 1950. The Bears won the first game 32–20, the second 17–0.

They would meet twice again in 1951, first in a preseason game (Bears 24–7), then in regular season at Kezar (Bears 13–7).

"I no longer want to beat the Bears," said Morabito to Shaw.

"No?" said Shaw.

"No," said Morabito. "I want to kill them!"

This was arranged, commencing with the opening kickoff on October 9, 1952, at Chicago. With Y. A. Tittle in gentle command, the 49ers began to drive down the field. Tittle got 19 yards with a pass to Gordy Soltau and another 19 with a short toss to McElhenny. San Francisco reached the Bears' 1-yard line, from where Joe Perry carried it over for a 7–0 49ers' lead.

One touchdown does not win a game, and the crowd at Wrigley Field bellowed in glee on a following sequence, when the Bears trapped Tittle in his endzone for a safety. But the next time the Bears got the ball, Lowell Wagner, a gifted 49ers' halfback, clutched a pass in midair after Hardy Brown, his linebacking colleague, had tipped it. Wagner ran the interception 20 yards to Chicago's 39-yard line. The 49ers got to the 30, then McElhenny, in one of his weird runs, took it 25 more yards to the 5. Perry carried for the final 5 and the second 49ers' touchdown, and San Francisco owned a 14–2 lead at the end of the first quarter.

Once again the Bears challenged. Bob Williams, their quarterback, had some good moves, and a 56-yard Williams-to-Schroeder pass put the ball on the San Francisco 8. Fred Morrison plunged the short distance for a touchdown, and the score was 14–9.

Later, on fourth down, Morrison, who also did the Bears' punting, was called on to kick from the 49ers' 41-yard line. Back to receive for the 49ers were Joe Arenas and the rookie McElhenny. Arenas reasoned that from 41 yards away Morrison would be trying for the coffin corner. Cannily, he moved forward, toward the Bears, and outward toward the threatened sideline. At the same time, he signaled McElhenny to move toward the center of the field. So McElhenny moved in three steps and caught the punt on his own 6-yard line.

What happened then must challenge all football history. It is customary, for instance, to credit blockers for the success of a long run, but in this case no such credit is deserved. There were no blocks thrown. Instead, most of the 49ers simply stood there, nodding to one another in admiration. There may have been two or three *missed* blocks. If there were, they simply further enlarged McElhenny, upon whom a host of Bears were descending. He was simply standing there with the football.

There were Bears to the left of him, Bears to the right of him, when he finally made his move — straight up the center of the field, so swiftly that the screech of braking cleats, as the Chicago tacklers tried to change direction, could almost be heard on the shores of Lake Michigan half a mile away.

The King made a 90-degree left turn at his 23-yard line and raced to the sideline. There he made a 90-degree right turn and continued toward the distant goal line. It was surrealistic. With the exception of the ancient Clyde (Bulldog) Turner, who was trying to chase him —

The 49ers learned that they would never be fully accepted as members of the National Football League until they could beat the mighty Chicago Bears. In 1952, they did, and by 34 points. Y. A. Tittle (left) and rookie star Hugh McElhenny (below) were too much for the Bears' defense. At right, San Francisco's Ed Henke, number 89, and Leo Nomellini move up to tackle Bob Williams of Chicago.

probably more out of reflex than anything else — the playing field seemed devoid of anybody save McElhenny. His 49ers teammates — who had also been left far downfield when the cork blew out of the bottle — began shaking hands with one another. Mysteriously, one account persists that Bob Toneff, the 252-pound 49ers' tackle from Notre Dame, was "in front of McElhenny all the way."

"I didn't think it was that long a run," the King said when informed that his gallop had covered 94 yards. "If I'd known I was starting on my own six, I would have let the ball roll into the endzone."

Bruce Lee of the *San Francisco Chronicle* wrote that it was "as great an exhibition of open-field running as has ever been seen on any football field." But Lee was not talking of that 94-yard run alone. The King was to gain 114 yards in 12 carries that game, winning a standing ovation from the multitude when he finally came off the field for the last time. He had two other punt returns for another 26 yards, giving him an average of 40.3 that still stands as a 49ers' one-game record. Indeed, playing for a team whose punt-return men over the years have included such undeniable greats as Joe Arenas and Abe Woodson, McElhenny's 94-yarder still stood as a record 21 years later.

From scrimmage, he would have a 71-yard run in the fateful San Francisco-Detroit division playoff game of 1957, but that is not classified as the 49ers' longest in that category. Over the years, they have seen runs of 82, 86, even 89 yards from scrimmage.

McElhenny made all three of them, too.

One effect of his long punt return in the Bears' game was to give the 49ers a 21–9 halftime lead. By now they were sniffing victory — a victory that would give them 12 wins in a row, counting their preseason games. But victory over the Bears, as sweet as it would be for the Morabitos

and their team, would not be enough this day. The 49ers did not have it in mind simply to beat the Bears. They wanted to destroy them.

Accordingly, in the third period Frankie Albert, taking over from Tittle, who had wrenched his back, marched the club 46 yards for another 49ers touchdown. Per custom, Joe Perry carried for the final 3 yards and the score. Not per custom, he didn't piggyback an enemy tackler with him this time: Instead, he carried two of them, Ed Sprinkle and Jim Dooley. To somebody who likened Perry to a racehorse, coach Shaw once said: "Yes. And his handicap is five hundred and twenty pounds."

The applause for McElhenny was less an expression of sportsmanship than of sheer awe. When they weren't futilely attempting to tackle McElhenny, the Bears were beating up on the 49ers, and vice versa. By the time Soltau kicked a 39-yard field goal, making the score 31–9. after three periods, two San Franciscans had been thrown out of the game for throwing punches. "I'm bruised all over," Soltau confided to a teammate. "Isn't it wonderful?"

A pass interception led to the final Bears' touchdown in the fourth period, but the 49ers still had some more scoring to do. First they got their safety back when Ed Henke and Bob Momsen hit Williams in his endzone. Then Stanford's Bobby White capped a 71-yard San Francisco progression with a 4-yard run off tackle for a touchdown.

In the final minute of the game the San Franciscans became playful. Leo Nomellini, possibly addled by too much contact, announced that he was another McElhenny. Obligingly, his teammates stationed him in the backfield and gave him the ball on the next play. Hemingway was right. The earth does move. Leo the Lion trundled for a five-yard gain. He was still charging when he discovered he no longer had the ball. It went in the books as a 49ers' turnover.

In remaining as the only unbeaten team to that point in the NFL in 1952, the 49ers were not only leading the league, they were joining it. As the man said, you had to beat the Bears. *Beat* them? It was 40–16. Many a moon had set over Wrigley Field since anybody had handled the Monsters of the Midway with such ease.

Possibly no other game in San Francisco's football history provided such a range of memories for old-time 49ers fans. The score itself was something to treasure. The Bears might defeat the 49ers in future years — in fact they defeated them two weeks later to end the 49ers' winning streak at 13 — but the myth of the Bears' supremacy was gone.

More than a decade later, somebody asked Leo Nomellini about the game.

"They should have given me the ball more," Nomellini said.

"But McElhenny . . ."

"I carried it once and I got five yards."

"But you fumbled, Leo."

"So? I've seen McElhenny fumble."

Not on October 9, 1952.

San Francisco	14	7	10	9 — 40
Chicago	2	7	0	7 — 16

SF — Perry 1 run (Soltau kick)
Chi — Safety, Tittle tackled in endzone
SF — Perry 5 run (Soltau kick)
Chi — Morrison 2 run (Blanda kick)
SF — McElhenny 94 punt return (Soltau kick)
SF — Perry 3 run (Soltau kick)
SF — FG Soltau 39
Chi — Schroeder 36 pass from Romanik (Blanda kick)
SF — Safety, Williams tackled in endzone
SF — White 4 run (Soltau kick)

October 4, 1953

In the old All-America Football Conference, Los Angeles never beat San Francisco. Few fans believe that. In the National Football League, San Francisco never beat Los Angeles. Few fans believe that.

In the latter instance, though, they're close.

In league play in the AAFC, the 49ers were 8–0 against the Los Angeles Dons. In preseason play, the 49ers were 3–1.

In league play in the NFL, through the 1973 season, the 49ers were 17–29 against the Los Angeles Rams. In preseason play, the 49ers were 6–16. In league play, at that point, San Francisco had lost seven games in a row to the Rams. In preseason play, San Francisco had lost 10 in a row.

In 1953 the Rams came to Kezar Stadium as favorites. The two teams met six times before in NFL league competition, and Los Angeles had won five of the six.

A lot of people are convinced the game of October 4, 1953, was the greatest of all between the two teams. The 49ers believe they won it, though to this day the retired Buck Shaw isn't quite sure how. And to this day the Rams' coach, Hampton Pool, isn't convinced his team lost.

This game for the 49ers against the Rams differs almost completely from their game against the Bears the year before. There was only one link between the two. Hugh McElhenny was working both days.

McElhenny made runs of 93 and 71 yards against the Rams, but the former was called back. It was a punt return for an apparent touchdown but Bob St. Clair was caught clipping Rams end Andy Robustelli. Ordinarily one denies such an offense and stoutly defends the teammate accused of it, but McElhenny had a different philosophy. "Of course he clipped him," he said, in response to a reporter's question. "Are you crazy? Do you think I could

have gone all the way if he hadn't? He got called for it, that's all. It's a chance you take."

The play may have sapped the King. When he went 71 yards in the final moments and set up one of the wildest endings in memory, he was tired, he later confessed. Woodley Lewis, a Rams' defensive back, caught him on the Los Angeles 9-yard line. "If I'd been fresh, I don't think he could have touched me," the King said.

Coach Pool of Los Angeles was impressed. "McElhenny?" he said. "I don't know. I have been in this game a long time, but I never saw anything quite like him." Pool had warned his players in advance that they could not let up on McElhenny. This advice was on a par with telling a baseball team to watch out for Walter Johnson's fastball.

Coach Shaw also had some pregame advice for his players. It consisted of ordering extra practice sessions to sharpen the 49ers' defense against Los Angeles's passing attack. "It paid off," he said after the game, in which Norm Van Brocklin, throwing for the Rams, was limited to 20 completions out of 34 passes and a mere 272 yards. From those figures, one can speculate what the San Francisco pass defense was like before Shaw ordered the extra workouts.

The 49ers were behind 20–0. The natives were becoming restless. Sporadically, beer cans and cushions sailed onto the playing field from the stands at Kezar.

In the first period, Van Brocklin connected with Bob Boyd for a touchdown, and, after an ensuing interception, Ben Agajanian kicked a field goal. In the second period, Van Brocklin completed a short pass to Elroy Hirsch for another touchdown, followed by another Agajanian field goal.

So it was 20–0 Rams, and at this point a shade came over Van Brocklin's brain, much as it had over Albert's the preceding year. Back to punt on fourth down with the ball on the

Rams' 28. Van Brocklin elected to pass instead. In one sense the decision was not as wondrous as Albert's had been: This play was planned in advance, and Night Train Lane was in the clear only to drop the ball when it reached him. So the 49ers had a first down on the Rams' 28.

In five plays, Y. A. Tittle moved San Francisco across the goal line. He bootlegged the ball himself for eight yards during the sequence, then produced the touchdown with a final short pass to Billy Wilson. That made it a respectable 20–7 at halftime. From the opening kickoff of the second half the 49ers moved 68 yards to a touchdown in 14 plays (all but two of them passes) making it 20–14. The scoring play was delicately timed and deliberate. It began with a simple Tittle-to-McElhenny pitchout. Drilled for this exercise, seven Rams leaped on McElhenny, but he had already lateraled to Joe Perry. The remaining four Rams leaped on Perry. He carried them into the endzone with him and then gave one of them the ball as a memento.

From the ensuing kickoff, the Rams drove 90 yards in 11 plays. Tank Younger scored the touchdown. A few plays later an unsung defensive back, Lowell Wagner, fell on a Van Brocklin fumble. The 49ers worked the ball back to the 11-yard line. Then, with the usual tackling crew draped over his shoulders, the human conveyor belt, Joe Perry, scored, making it 27–21. The Rams still led at the end of the third quarter.

If a reversal was to come, it would have to come in the final period. It began when Rex Berry intercepted a Van Brocklin pass at the Rams' 48 and returned it to the 30. In seven plays, Tittle brought the 49ers a touchdown. A rookie 49ers' halfback, Bill Mixon of Georgia, did the honors from 4 yards out. That tied it at 27–27, and moments later Soltau kicked the extra point for a 28–27 San Francisco lead.

Then the Rams took the ball and worked to fourth down and inches to go at the San Fran-

cisco 11. The clock showed three minutes left in the game. Coach Pool had about as good a set of alternatives as you can have when you trail with three minutes to go. He sent in Ben Agajanian. If Ben made the field goal, then the Rams would be in front and could kick off deep to the 49ers. If he missed it, the 49ers still would be on their own 20, and there would be time for the Rams to regain possession.

Agajanian made the field goal and the Rams led 30–28.

The following kickoff traveled into the endzone and the 49ers had the ball on their own 20.

San Francisco went into its huddle, and Tittle called for a sideline pass to stop the clock. The Rams' defense was deployed deep against the home-run pass, and Colonel Slick (one of Tittle's nicknames) had to utilize the playbook and the clock together for short spurts that would get San Francisco within field goal range in the final seconds.

The 49ers broke from the huddle, and now a shade came over Tittle's brain. A glorious shade it was. He switched the call with an audible at the line of scrimmage. He knew the Rams defense would be deep. But *that* deep?

Instead of a sideline pass, Tittle threw a little semiscreen to McElhenny, who was not quite at the line of scrimmage when he caught it. One Ram had a shot at the King and in the bewilderment of the moment failed to bring him down. Leo Nomellini threw a tremendous block. Team captain Bruno Banducci threw another. Downfield, Billy Wilson turned from likely receiver to blocker and leveled his man.

The King pulled to the sideline and covered 71 yards before the disbelieving Woodley Lewis could nudge him out of bounds. It was first down for the 49ers on the Rams' 9-yard line.

The clock was moving again, but Tittle sniffed a touchdown. He called on the obvious man. Too obvious. It was Joe Perry, and the entire Rams

Hugh McElhenny had no peers as an open-field runner. One of his finest games came in 1953 against the rival Los Angeles Rams. A 93-yard punt return by McElhenny had been called back because of a penalty. Later, the run shown in the sequence of photos below set up the game's controversial winning field goal. The "magic eye" camera of the San Francisco Examiner captured McElhenny as he weaved through the Rams for 71 yards. Leo Nomellini and Gordy Soltau were among the blockers for him; the Rams' defenders trying to catch up with him included Norb Hecker, Jack Dwyer, Dick (Night Train) Lane, Bud McFadin, Woodley Lewis, and Tom Fears. Sport magazine made McElhenny a cover subject (right) and named him player of the year in the NFL.

team hit him for a three-yard loss. Very well. Tittle would vary things. He handed off to the rookie Bill Mixon, and regained the three yards. Third down now. Clock still moving. Tittle still had some ideas left. This time he would bootleg the ball. He did and gained 4 yards to the Rams' 5-yard line. In his zeal, the Bald Eagle had overlooked only one thing. He had failed to get the ball in front of the goal posts for the Soltau field-goal attempt. As the 49ers faced the goal posts, the ball was off to the right.

By now, the clock showed less than a minute to play, and still the second hand moved. Soltau came on to kick the field goal. In later years he would say that he didn't mind kicking from an angle. It would appear, however, that he had not yet communicated that attitude to Tittle. Y. A. kept the 49ers in the huddle for the full 30 seconds of the remaining 35. In so doing, he was penalized 5 yards for taking too much time. The penalty increased the distance from 5 yards to 10, but reduced the angle. This strategy came as a revelation to coach Shaw. According to Bill Mulligan's story in the *Examiner* the following day:

"Shaw confessed he almost had heart failure after he had sent in word for Gordon Soltau to try for a field goal in the last 30 seconds with the 49ers trailing 30–28 and the ball on the Rams' 5."

"Y. A. took so much time in the huddle I thought we would never get the kick away before the final gun," Shaw said.

Tittle said he was completely confident, not only of getting off the field goal attempt, but that it would be good.

"I had my eye on the clock and when I turned my back to hold the ball for the placement, I was ticking off the seconds.

"That is the result of long experience. I did not want the Rams to have any more seconds on the play after the kickoff than possible. Also I

felt that Gordy would make good on the kick. The pass from Bill Johnson was perfect and I made a good hold. The Rams did not charge fast at all."

Another version might be that Tittle wanted the delay of game penalty to give Soltau the better angle, then realized that (a) the stadium clock might be wrong, and/or (b) the officials on the field might fail to note how much time he'd taken. After planning to take too much time, Tittle had second thoughts.

No matter. As it worked out, five seconds still remained when Soltau kicked the winning field goal.

The referee's arm shot up indicating the score. The Rams took exception to the decision, but did not press their case and that perhaps is the greatest tribute of all to the thrust of the game. It was easier to accept the field goal than to dispute it. A recount could only have made it worse.

Phil Bengtson, then the 49ers' line coach, called it "the greatest game I ever saw, either as player or coach."

One thing is certain. It had to be the greatest 49ers' triumph over the Rams, if only for the fact that no one, not even the man who kicked the final field goal, knows for sure who should have won the game.

Los Angeles	10	10	7	3	— 30
San Francisco	0	7	14	10	— 31

LA — Boyd 66 pass from Van Brocklin (Agajanian kick)
LA — FG Agajanian 22
LA — Hirsch 2 pass from Van Brocklin (Agajanian kick)
LA — FG Agajanian 37
SF — Wilson 2 pass from Tittle (Soltau kick)
SF — Perry 11 pass from McElhenny (Soltau kick)
LA — Younger 1 run (Agajanian kick)
SF — Perry 11 run (Soltau kick)
SF — Mixon 4 run (Soltau kick)
LA — FG Agajanian 18
SF — FG Soltau 13

November 3, 1957

The morning of November 12, 1973, was a dreary Monday, for everybody but R. C. Owens, who showed up for a champagne breakfast on the Golden Gate Bridge. The meal, served by a fetching handmaiden, was to commemorate R. C.'s thirty-ninth birthday. "I figured it was time I popped up," he explained.

As recorded earlier in this history, there was a time — in that unbelievable 1957 season of San Francisco football — when he popped up on the play born of initial disgust on the part of quarterback Y. A. Tittle that became known as the Alley-Oop.

It was the season in which the 49ers and Lions would tie for a division title — the furthest San Francisco had advanced in league play up to that time. (You couldn't count that AAFC playoff with Cleveland in 1949. The Browns had won 9, lost 1; the 49ers had won 9, lost 3.) The Lions and 49ers each were to win 8, lose 4, in regular-season play, and the game that made a playoff possible was the November 3 game at Kezar Stadium.

"Fans collapsed everywhere," reported Bob Brachman in his *Examiner* story, "and the siren on the stadium ambulance, which had kept up a steady screeching during the afternoon in response to repeated emergency calls, let go with one final blast and headed in the direction of the pressbox, where one observer had fainted dead away, overcome by emotion."

Ordinarily, pressbox observers tend to faint at card tricks, but this swoon had to be genuine. To this day, the argument rages about the time R. C. jumped up between two of the most gifted defensive backs in the game — Detroit's Jack Christiansen and Jim David — and . . . ?

Well, first things first. R. C. Owens was no total star that day. Not, at least, if you believe the statistics, which show him to have been no better than the fifth best 49ers' receiver in the game that day behind Billy Wilson, Clyde

Conner, Gene Babb, and Hugh McElhenny.

Quarterback Y. A. Tittle passed for two touchdowns and took it over on his hip for another; he carried the ball on two unnerving runs of 26 and 13 yards, both of which led to scores; he eclipsed Frankie Albert's club record with 21 out of 28 pass completions in a game; and he wiped out Albert's lifetime team record with his eight-hundred and forty-third pass completion.

Former quarterback Albert, then coach Albert, watched from the sidelines, like a bird transfixed by a snake. He saw the game-winning pass travel an unlikely distance of 50 yards through the air, to the most perfectly defended, perfectly covered receiver the rules of the game would allow.

In those final seconds, the 49ers trailed 31–28. Tittle was unimpressed. "If the pass hadn't worked, Soltau would have kicked a field goal for the tie," he said.

"I would have?" Soltau asked.

Coach Albert was more to the point. "Winning games this way has got to end," he said flatly. "But my God, what a team!"

Tittle called it, "the greatest game of my life." Few would argue.

Owens said it was a basketball play that went back to his experience in that sport at the College of Idaho and with a team known as the Buchan Bakers of Seattle. "You learn when to fly up into the air," he explained.

Totally forgotten by now is the fact that on two occasions Soltau had to kick two extra points instead of one. Within the syndrome of it-could-only-happen-to-the-49ers, they twice were penalized on two conversion attempts because their guards and tackles were interlocking legs. This was — is — against the rules.

"It's a technicality," Albert explained afterwards. "The officials told me before the game that they were going to watch for it, but I didn't want to confuse the kids, so I didn't say anything

Lions   7 3 0 21 31
49ers   0 14 7 14 35

about it to them. We just took our chances."

Forgotten too is the fact that earlier in the game Owens had made another Alley-Oop catch in the endzone. But since he had been forced out of bounds on his way downfield, he became an ineligible receiver. All very San Francisco: guards and tackles who interlocked legs and an Alley-Oop pass to a man who arrived in the endzone by way of Parnassus Heights.

Better remembered by the Kezar crowd of 59,702 that day were three shining efforts by the defense, led by Matt Hazeltine and Marv Matuszak. On one occasion they stopped Detroit at the San Francisco 19; on another they forced the Lions to settle for a field goal after first and goal at the 49ers' 5-yard line. A third time they set up a San Francisco touchdown by creaming Detroit's Howard (Hopalong) Cassady for a one-yard loss on fourth and inches at midfield.

But the best memories must belong to the scoreboard operator, who must have thought at times he was operating in the fun house at the beach. First Detroit had a 10-point lead. Then San Francisco had a 28–10 lead with less than 14 minutes to play. Then Detroit scored three touchdowns, and led 31–28. With 1 minute and 28 seconds left, the 49ers were in possession on their own 22.

The man who would make the greatest contribution to the record book in the game was a substitute player on the losing team: Tobin Rote, newly acquired by Detroit in a trade with Green Bay. After relieving the established Bobby Layne, Rote completed 14 of 22 passes for 212 yards, 4 for touchdowns (one to Steve Junker and three to Jim Doran). There was jubilation on the Detroit side of the field when Doran caught Rote's pass for the final Lions' touchdown with less than two minutes left on the clock.

A different hero was honored just before the game, when Norm Standlee, one of the original 49ers, went to the stadium loudspeaker and asked for a minute of standing prayer to the memory of Tony Morabito, who had suffered his fatal heart attack during the previous Sunday's 49ers-Bears game at Kezar. No one expected that the incredible surge of emotion that had swept the 49ers to victory over the Bears could carry over to the Lions game, but the facts suggest it did. Detroit controlled the early going, first with a 34-yard Rote-Doran pass which gave the visitors a 7–0 first-quarter lead and then with a 9-yard Layne field goal that made it 10–0 early in the second period. Then Tittle took the 49ers 57 yards in 10 plays, finishing the drive with a 9-yard touchdown pass to Conner. Just before the half ended, he used 12 plays to move them 74 yards (30 of which resulted from two pass-interference calls against Detroit), and sneaked the final yard for the touchdown himself. The ever-helpful Soltau added extra points both times, and San Francisco left the field at halftime with a 14–10 advantage.

The 49ers added another touchdown in the third period, when the balding Tittle, retreating from midfield to his own 30-yard line in search of a forming screen-pass pattern, was forced to abandon the play. So he tucked the ball under his arm and started to run, leaving disbelieving Lions defenders strung out across the field like marbles on a Chinese Checkers board. Somebody finally jumped him at the Detroit 22. Tittle's run, which he later disclaimed as a form of madness, is recorded as covering a mere 26 yards, but that doesn't count his retreat before he made up his mind. Y. A. was nearly in his own endzone before he finally made his move.

Four plays later McElhenny took it over from the 6. "I need a block from somebody," he said in the huddle. "Who knows how to block?"

"Maybe I do," a voice said. The voice belonged to R. C. Owens, and, sprawled full-length,

he supplied the block that kept the lane open for the King.

Going into the fourth period the 49ers were in charge again, thanks to Larry Barnes's 64-yard quick kick. Tittle completed a 33-yard pass to Conner off a rollout, and Babb finished the 67-yard drive with a one-yard plunge. It was 28–10 San Francisco.

But Tobin Rote wouldn't quit. He hit Doran from 31 yards out for one touchdown. Then, following Detroit's lone interception of the game (an endzone grab by Jim David of a Tittle touchdown try); Rote took the Lions 80 yards, finishing the drive with a touchdown pass to Junker from 14 yards.

At this point, it was 28–24, San Francisco's favor. With only 3:10 to go, the 49ers had the ball. Not for long, though. On third down, McElhenny tried to spin free on a reverse (a play called from the bench). The ball was knocked from his hands, and 275 pounds of Lion named Ray Krouse fell on it. McElhenny was furious at Albert for calling the play and at himself for muffing it. "That's the second time this year I've fumbled on that damn reverse," he said later.

Two Rote passes later — with 1:25 left to play — and Doran had the ball in the endzone. Detroit led 31–28.

"What could the 49ers do," asked writer Brachman rhetorically, "against a snarling Lion line backed up by supposedly the best secondary in football?"

Starting at his own 28-yard line, Tittle passed to Wilson for 12. Then incomplete. Then he passed to McElhenny for 11; again to McElhenny for 8.

The 49ers had the ball now on the Lions' 41 with 11 — or was it 10? — seconds remaining. Maybe McElhenny could have broken either of his catches for more yardage, but he stepped out of bounds instead, to stop the clock.

Tittle knew there was only one thing to do.

"He knew it," reporter Brachman wrote the next morning. "Owens knew it. Everybody in the place knew it, and so the Lions set up a defense that blanketed R. C. all the way down the field, as if he were trying to make away with the family silverware.

"Tittle swung right. The protection was great. Owens made his way downfield with seven-league strides. Now there was the cluster in the endzone — Owens, David, and Christiansen."

What ought to be restressed here, perhaps, is that no one could fault the Lions' defenders. San Francisco coach Frankie Albert knew them simply as "the finest secondary in the league."

Brachman's account again: "R. C. had to make a little circle around Christiansen before zooming skyward between the two Lions. He was up there for what seemed an eternity before wrapping his huge hands around the ball and bringing it down into the crook of his elbow and firmly grasping it against his chest."

So San Francisco won it 35–31, and weeks later someone thought to ask Tittle exactly what he'd called in the huddle.

"I said Alley-Oop," he responded. "What else was I going to say?"

| Detroit | 7 | 3 | 0 | 21 | — | 31 |
| San Francisco | 0 | 14 | 7 | 14 | — | 35 |

Det — Doran 34 pass from Rote (Layne kick)
Det — FG Layne 9
SF — Conner 9 pass from Tittle (Soltau kick)
SF — Tittle 1 run (Soltau kick)
SF — McElhenny 6 run (Soltau kick)
SF — Babb 1 run (Soltau kick)
Det — Doran 31 pass from Rote (Layne kick)
Det — Junker 14 pass from Rote (Layne kick)
Det — Doran 8 pass from Rote (Layne kick)
SF — Owens 41 pass from Tittle (Soltau kick)

October 1, 1961

Lo again, the poor Lions. Not quite four years after a strong Detroit team lost in the final seconds to San Francisco's Alley-Oop, an equally strong Detroit team took the field against the 49ers' newest wonder, the Shotgun.

The Lions were unbeaten and they were playing before a home crowd in Detroit. As for San Francisco's Shotgun, Green Bay had plastered it 30–10 the week before. In fact, Vince Lombardi's Green Bay team had seen the Shotgun the season before, and had beaten it then too. The word was out: Red Hickey, the San Francisco coach, was running out of steam with his "new" formation and was about to abandon it.

Hickey had conceived the Shotgun formation on a Georgetown University practice field on November 22, 1960. Practicing there for the game the next Sunday at Baltimore, the 49ers seemed like a team going nowhere with excellent personnel. The San Francisco team had added hitherto undiscovered credentials, something called defense. That season the 49ers permitted fewer opponents' points than any other club in the NFL. Yet on that November practice day outside Washington, D. C., they had a 4–4 record, so coach Hickey thought something new was in order.

Actually, the Shotgun wasn't that new. Doubting 49ers found that what Hickey was teaching them was, basically, the ancient short-punt formation, not much different from what the Packers had used with quarterback Tobin Rote.

To quote from a contemporary account, the 49ers "found that the quarterback would be 5 to 7 yards directly behind the center, with the left end spread out 10 to 15 yards from the left tackle and the right end spread 3 to 5 yards from the right tackle. The tight backs (left half and fullback) were 1 yard out and 1 yard back of the left and right tackles, respectively. The right half was 10 yards out and 1 yard back of the right end."

"We're going to beat the Colts with this pattern," Hickey announced to his players.

They began to giggle, some out of nervousness, some out of disbelief.

"You won't be laughing by Friday," said Hickey, the laird of Hickeytown, Arkansas, an unmapped deadfall founded by his paternal grandfather. Then he plunged into a sales pitch for a formation that would undo what for some of his players was more than a decade of indoctrination in the intricacies of the T.

Strange to say, by Friday they *weren't* laughing. Hickey had supplied the something new. Until then, the short-punt ancestor of the Shotgun had been employed as an occasional formation, usually for the sake of a last-minute pass. Hickey intended to use it on *every* play. The quarterback could pass, run, pitch out, or hand off. And Hickey had more than one quarterback.

Unleashed against such perennial oppressors as Gino Marchetti and Art Donovan and Don Shinnick, the Shotgun effected the season's greatest coup. The 49ers beat Baltimore 30–22.

Word spread fast. A crowd of 77,254 descended on the Los Angeles Coliseum the following Sunday to see the Shotgun dismantle the Rams 23–7 with — of all people — fullback C. R. Roberts running wild. In the rain and mud at San Francisco the next Sunday, Green Bay ground out a 13–0 victory, but Hickey claimed that wasn't a fair test. Such a fair test would come, he said, the following and final Sunday of the year, when Baltimore, which had seen the Shotgun once, tried to solve it. The 49ers won 34–10.

In the 1961 season the 49ers had three quarterbacks — John Brodie, Billy Kilmer, and Bobby Waters — any one of whom could pass, pitch, hand off, or, (with varying frequencies) run off the Shotgun.

The 49ers beat Washington 35–3, but the next Sunday's game was against Green Bay,

49ers 14 7 21 7 49
Lions 0 0 0 0 0

and the Packers were veterans at stopping the Shotgun. They defeated the 49ers 30–10.

Would Hickey now give it up? He knew that the Chicago Bears, who would follow any plan George Halas gave them without even viewing films that might serve most to disconcert them, were lying in the weeds. He had convincing evidence that Vince Lombardi had solved the Shotgun too. On October 1, 1961, he would be going up against the Lions, a solid 10-point favorite. The Lions knew what the Packers had done to the Shotgun the week before.

"Ah," Hickey confessed privately, "what the Packers did to us wasn't the Shotgun's fault. It was my fault. I played it too conservatively."

To the astonishment of the football world, Hickey's solution for the Lions game would not be less Shotgun, but more. In an extraordinary departure from his — and the team's — traditional custom, he called the plays for the Lions game from the sideline. In so doing he had the aid of not only those in the spotters' booths but also two quarterbacks fresh from combat. His private plan included rotating all three men, sending each into the game for just one play at a time. To make it simple, Hickey even decided to abandon the presnap backfield shift that turned the T into the Shotgun. It would be Shotgun, period.

The game began with San Francisco safetyman Abe Woodson intercepting an Earl Morrall pass on Detroit's first offensive play of the game. In the next 22 minutes, the 49ers scored 21 points, and by the time Woodson ran back the second-half kickoff for 98 yards and a 49ers' touchdown, the Detroit crowd of 53,115 was actually cheering the 49ers. At 98 yards Woodson's was the second-longest kickoff return in 49ers history. The record-setter was one of 105 yards, against the Rams two seasons earlier. Woodson held that record, too.

Hickey had been thinking about turning the former Illinois halfback into an offensive force. He held off until the Lions' game, on the theory that San Francisco didn't need him on offense and it was always nice to have a fresh Woodson in the deep secondary on defense, just in case the ball came his way.

Woodson caught the second-half kickoff on his own 2, and Hickey was right: It *was* nice. He burst straight through the initial Detroit wave, spun away from the next, and found himself picking up blockers who thus far in the journey hadn't located anybody to block. The final move, at the Lions' 25, came when the blocking knocked down Detroit's Dale Messer and Woodson hurdled the group.

Detroit was no more successful defensing scrimmage plays. Every time the vaunted Lions' defense looked up, a new quarterback was bringing in something new from the bench. Quick kicks by Kilmer, for example. He had one for 57 yards, another for 64. He also threw three passes for 43 yards, and he carried the ball 16 times for a net of 103 yards and 2 touchdowns.

Waters, meanwhile, was averaging 5.4 yards on each of seven carries, and Brodie completed five passes for 108 yards, including a 45-yard beauty to Clyde Conner that set up San Francisco's second score. There were touchdowns by Waters and Cannonball Cooper, the latter on his first play as a professional, in addition to the two by Kilmer, the two by J. D. Smith, and the one by Woodson.

Twice before in NFL play, the 49ers had scored 48 points in a game — against the Dallas Texans in 1952 and again against Green Bay in 1953.

But never in NFL play had they scored as many as 49 points.

The game was unsullied even by the impurity of a field goal. If the thought of a field goal ever intruded, it was on the part of the Lions, whose one drive of the day got them to the San Fran-

The Shotgun formation devised by coach Red Hickey in San Francisco represented a radical departure from the T-formation used by every other team in professional football. In the Shotgun, the quarterback became a tailback, and stood five yards behind the center before the snap. At right, one of Hickey's three tailbacks, Bill Kilmer, is on the move from his position in the Shotgun. Hickey is shown below with all three of them: John Brodie, number 12, Bobby Waters, number 11, and Kilmer. Below is a page from Hickey's 1961 Shotgun playbook.

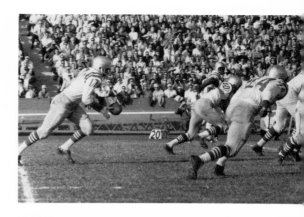

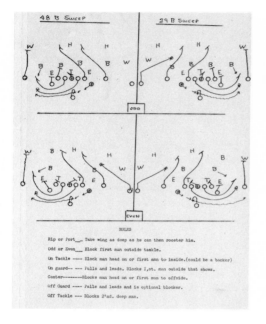

The Detroit Lions had been a casualty of the Alley-Oop pass just a few years earlier. Now they went down in defeat 49-0 at the hands of the Shotgun offense—and San Francisco's brilliant kick returner, Abe Woodson. He raced 98 yards to score with the second-half kickoff.

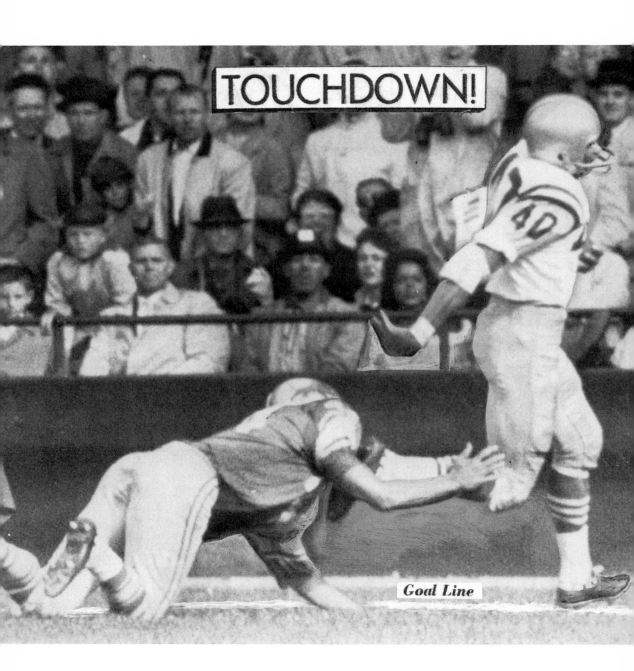

TOUCHDOWN!

Goal Line

cisco 9 just before the first half ended. Already three touchdowns behind at that point, the Lions understandably chose not to go for the three-point play, whereupon the gleeful San Francisco defense simply gang-tackled the drive to a stop.

Two Detroit fumbles, recovered by Monte Clark and Leo Nomellini, led directly to San Francisco scores. One of the fumbles was by Hopalong Cassady, the other by the Lions' fullback Nick Pietrosante on his own 2-yard line. Among other things, Detroit had four passes intercepted and run back for a total of 91 yards.

It was a complete defeat for Detroit. It was the first time in 115 games the Lions had been shut out (they'd lost 28–0 to the 49ers nine years earlier, in 1952). Even worse, the margin of defeat equaled the worst beating in the Lions' history.

After the game, somebody asked Hickey a funny question: "Who's your number one quarterback now?"

He shrugged. "The three of them."

"Was this the greatest game the 49ers ever played?"

"No," said Hickey. "I like that day in 1958 when we blanked the Rams 34–0."

At least he was quoted that way in the San Francisco press the following morning. He may have said "1959" instead of "1958," because the San Francisco papers were not above a typographical error here or there. The fact was, the 49ers scored that 34–0 win over Los Angeles not in 1958, Hickey's last year as assistant coach, but in 1959, his first year as head coach.

From the inception of the Shotgun through that spectacular 49–0 cuffing of the Lions, only one team — Green Bay — had beaten the 49ers, so the home papers were going slightly out of their minds. Said one writer:

"Red Hickey's use of three rotating quarterbacks drove the Detroit Lions daffy. When they looked for John Brodie they saw Billy Kilmer. When they looked for Kilmer they saw Bobby Waters. In their confusion, they got their hands on nobody.

"Many coaches employ linemen, mostly guards and ends, as messengers to bring the plays into the huddle. Hickey, we believe, is the first to do it exclusively with quarterbacks.

"It makes sense. Why tell a guard or end what play to tell the quarterback to call next when the information can be conveyed directly from the coach to the quarterback himself?

"Hickey's system eliminates intermediaries or go-betweens and hence minimizes the possibility of mistakes. Moreover, it prevents the defense from getting hep to the quarterback's moves.

"Every time Kilmer replaced Brodie, Brodie replaced Kilmer or Waters replaced either of them, the Lions had something a little different to cope with.

"As the scores will show, they didn't cope so well."

The scores indeed showed that, and they would continue to show it. The wonder is that the Shotgun didn't go on forever. "Since it worked, it was fine," Hickey said of that 49–0 high point the San Francisco team reached at Detroit. "If it hadn't worked, I'd be the one to take the rap."

| San Francisco | 14 | 7 | 21 | 7 — 49 |
| Detroit | 0 | 0 | 0 | 0 — 0 |

SF — Smith 5 run (Davis kick)
SF — Waters 10 run (Davis kick)
SF — Kilmer 2 run (Davis kick)
SF — Woodson 98 kickoff return (Davis kick)
SF — Kilmer 7 run (Davis kick)
SF — Smith 1 run (Davis kick)
SF — Cooper 1 run (Davis kick)

December 20, 1970

Lou Spadia, the president of the 49ers, called it "the greatest game in our history." Some folk looked at him as if he was nuts. He looked back as if he wasn't.

The difference in viewpoints may be appreciated on a strange plane if one considers that this was both the first and fifth game ever played between two teams whose home fields lie so close that, on a clear day, they are within view of each other.

Separating Candlestick Park, where the 49ers play, and the Oakland Coliseum, home of the Raiders, however, is a body of water. It is narrower than Hab el Mandeb, the Oresund, or the Strait of Le Pérouse, but to local football fans it possesses infinitely greater geopolitical significance. It is the southern extension of San Francisco Bay, and as far as the natives are concerned it splits two worlds.

Before the Raiders moved into the Coliseum and the 49ers into Candlestick, the same eternal waterway had separated Kezar Stadium and Frank Youell Field. The latter was a holdover from the Gay Nineties. Youngsters found their way into spidery bleachers for free because there was no practical way to keep them out.

In fairness, there were other reasons for the Raiders to let kids in for nothing, philanthropy and good sense. The Raiders, who came to the Bay area as an American Football League team in 1960 when the 49ers already were in their fifteenth season, had to find ways to win fans of their own.

"In those days no one took the Raiders seriously," says John McCasey. McCasey had grown up in Hayward, on Oakland's side of the Bay, but when he was young the 49ers were the only game in town. "I grew up as a 49ers' fan," he recalls, "but when the Raiders arrived, I got to see some of their games on the free-ticket basis." He did not become a convert. Indeed, in later life he went to work for the 49ers. "The

Raiders grew and they won," he remembers. "Coincidentally the 49ers had some dismal seasons and the Raiders became convenient to the East Bay residents. So the arguments started. But the proof lay in the Raiders' success. Or was it proof? After all, they still weren't in the NFL. The Raiders were in that inferior league."

Then came the two mergers: in 1966, when the Super Bowl was established, and in 1970 with the establishment of a single overall National Football League and interconference games. In between times, the 49ers and Raiders started to play each other. There were four preseason games: in 1967 (the 49ers won 13-10), in 1968 (Oakland 26–19), in 1969 (Oakland 42–28), and in 1970 (Oakland 31–17).

By that point the 49ers were acquiring an inferiority complex from problems with the Raiders. They had staked out the territory and introduced major league competition to the Bay area, only to find themselves being whammed yearly by the hated intruder that had set up shop across the Bay. It does not improve the ego when you've had four fights with the new kid in the neighborhood and lost the last three in full view of a capacity crowd each time.

Yet there was just as much of an inferiority complex on the Oakland side. By tribal instinct, East Bay residents dislike San Francisco. In return, the San Franciscans' tendency was to ignore them. For San Francisco already had a much more vibrant intercity rivalry with Los Angeles. In sports, it was Warriors-Lakers, Giants-Dodgers, 49ers-Rams. Like all natural rivalries, it relied on frequent battles to fuel it. Until December 20, 1970, by contrast, the Raiders and 49ers had never met in a league game.

This, then, was to be Oakland's first official opportunity to ruin the 49ers and, likely as not, to ruin their season as well. The Raiders already had clinched the AFC's Western Division title. The 49ers, on the other hand, went into that final

49ers	3	21	0	14	38
Raiders	7	0	0	0	7

Sunday of the regular schedule with a 9–3–1 record. They were one game ahead of the Rams, who, with an 8–4–1 record, would be playing the Giants in New York.

A Rams' loss at New York would enable the 49ers to back into the title in the NFC West, but few people were thinking of that. Their thoughts were diverted by a strange circumstance: This was not just the first official meeting between the 49ers and the Raiders. For the foreseeable future it was the official meeting, since long-range scheduling had ordained the teams would not meet again in league play in 1971, or in 1972, or in 1973.

This in itself gave the game something extra. The last game on both teams' schedules in 1970, this engagement represented the most vivid possible intra-area clash between the entire National and American Football Conferences. Even with a Rams' loss at New York, the prestige of two football conferences was at stake.

Surely league prestige had already been tested in the Super Bowl, but the Super Bowl lacks two ingredients: First, it is played in a setting that deprives the game of one of the great ingredients in football: the hysterical fan. The home city of any team may range from hundreds to thousands of miles away from the city where the game is being played. Second, the Super Bowl offers the loser a possibility of avenging defeat the next year. As noted above, the schedule provided no next year for the 49ers versus Raiders. The only thing comparable to the 49ers-Raiders game would have been a Giants-Jets matchup in New York for the 1970 climax to the regular season. And that wasn't scheduled.

The key game had three key elements:

1) It was San Francisco versus Oakland as cities, the 49ers versus the Raiders as teams, and the National versus the American as rival conferences.

2) If the Rams lost to the Giants at New York

— that score, because of the time difference, would be posted before the game at Oakland began — then the 49ers would become what the Raiders already were: Western Division champion of an NFL conference. Strangely, this would play a part in increasing the stakes simply by equalizing them. With both teams freed from playoff pressure, there would be no such excuse for losing. The 49ers were 9–3–1 going into the game against the Raiders; the Raiders were 8–3–2. It would become a matter not only of interconference prestige but of local king-of-the-mountain, and under such circumstances, it was supposed the Raiders would win the game and become known as the best team. Their motto was "Pride and Poise." They would be loose and confident; the 49ers would be going through the motions, out of sheer relief.

3) If the Rams beat the Giants at New York, the Raiders would be just as loose and confident as before. But the 49ers would have to contend with their lifetime reputation of never having won even a division title since they began in 1946. In a word, the 49ers didn't win the big ones, at season's end when everything was riding on one game. The Raiders, by contrast, did win when they had to. They'd been to the Super Bowl. For the 49ers, even a division crown was a wistful dream.

In an unguarded moment, Lou Spadia croaked, "I'd like to see the Rams win in New York, then have us win by thirty-three points." The figure was not idly come by. In the four preseason games between the 49ers and Raiders, Oakland had outscored San Francisco by a total of 32 points. All Spadia wanted in that one 1970 game was a 33-point margin. "Of course," he added, "we'll need a dry field."

He didn't get a dry field. It rained. And then it rained some more. To this day, John Brodie, the quarterback, remembers it as "the game in the rain." Charlie Krueger, the tackle, remembers it as "the game in the mud." So much for the differences in viewpoints between a quarterback and a member of the front four.

But one of Spadia's wishes did come true. The Rams did beat the Giants. So, as they took the field, the 49ers were fighting for their lives.

In Oakland, Ben Davidson, the merciless defender, waxed his mustache so thoroughly that its extremities became offensive weapons all their own. He was aware that the unsung 49ers' offensive line, including as it did the kind of "unknown" who starts 100 games in a row and yet goes unrecognized — Len Rohde for an example — had permitted quarterback John Brodie to be sacked only eight times all season. "This will change," Davidson predicted.

Despite the terrible weather, an extraordinary capacity crowd of 54,535 assembled at the Coliseum. Ordinarily, the rain would have kept them away. But they wanted to see that vaunted Oakland defense, and they wanted to see the miracle man — George Blanda — at work in a game that obviously had to be settled by field goals.

As the rain pelted down and the Rams' score came in, the question was not so much whether the Raiders would win, but how badly they would pour it on. Fans began exchanging informal little side bets: the Raiders would get more first downs than the 49ers; the Raiders would outgain the 49ers.

The side bets were well-placed. The Raiders did get more first downs, 17 to 16; and they did outgain the 49ers, 358 yards to 296.

And the only 49er who liked the rain was fullback Ken Willard. "I like a wet track," he said. "It makes everybody as slow as I am."

Things began with Brodie hitting the slow Willard, against even slower Oakland defenders, for an 18-yard pass. Then a field goal — by Bruce Gossett, from 42 yards — and San Francisco went ahead by an unsensational 3–0, midway through the first quarter.

Now it was the Raiders' turn. They reached the 49ers' 7, where a wet ball and a San Francisco rush caused a Hewritt Dixon fumble and a turnover. The Raiders were only momentarily stymied. Next time around, Daryle Lamonica passed to tight end Raymond Chester all alone for 29 yards and a Raiders' touchdown. It was 7–3 Oakland at the quarter.

(Somebody had brought a television set into the Rams' clubhouse at Yankee Stadium in New York, and in the afterglow of beating the Giants, some of the Rams began to giggle. Their last outing against San Francisco had been a 30–13 win, giving them the season's edge in points. To wind up tied in the standings against the 49ers now would mean a playoff spot for Los Angeles).

"Get towels," John Brodie said to the referee. He was going to throw the ball. He hit Gene Washington for 31 yards, then hit a leaping Ted Kwalick for 26 and a touchdown.

Lamonica, the Raiders' quarterback, was inspired. If Brodie would throw, he would throw. He did. Jimmy Johnson intercepted it and ran it back 36 yards for a 49ers' touchdown.

A mistake, reasoned Lamonica. He started throwing again. This time Bruce Taylor intercepted in a web of bodies. With Willard running, Brodie passing and Kwalick and Washington catching (the latter for a touchdown), the 49ers went to the dressing room at halftime with three second-period touchdowns and a 24–7 lead.

The crowd stayed on. The gathering did not favor the 49ers. The Coliseum was Oakland's home turf, and most of the crowd were Raiders fans. The 49ers had led by an identical score at halftime in that playoff game against Detroit in 1957. It is a well-known legend that the Lions, assembled in their clubhouse between halves of that 1957 game, could hear the 49ers laughing through the narrow partition that divided them. At the Oakland Coliseum in 1970 there was no

The 49ers met the Oakland Raiders for the first time ever in the regular season, and a possible division championship was at stake for San Francisco. Running back Ken Willard, never the fastest of 49ers, welcomed the rain that engulfed Oakland-Alameda County Coliseum. "It makes everybody as slow as I am," he said. At left, Willard powers through the ooze for eight yards. San Francisco scored three touchdowns in the second quarter, the last on a pass from John Brodie to Gene Washington, who made the catch between Kent McCloughan and Dave Grayson (below). Oakland recovered and drove into San Francisco territory, but Charlie Smith had the football torn from his grasp by Frank Nunley (pages 96-97) and San Francisco recovered.

Charlie Krueger had been superb all season in the middle of the 49ers' defensive line, and a measure of awe showed in the eyes of teammate Ken Willard as he shook hands with Krueger (left). San Francisco had manhandled its arch-rival, Oakland, by a 38-7 score. The San Francisco offensive line had allowed its quarterbacks to be tackled for losses only eight times all season. Oakland did not add to the total, and it remains an all-time record in professional football. Celebrating with offensive line coach Ernie Zwahlen after the game (right) were, front row, Forrest Blue, number 75, and Randy Beisler, and, back row, left to right, Len Rohde, Bob Hoskins, Cas Banaszek, Elmer Collett, and Woody Peoples.

partition (the dressing rooms are separated) and no laughter either.

The Raiders seized command in the third quarter and drove deep into San Francisco territory. Then Bruce Taylor fell on a kind of commune fumble by Charlie Smith; everybody had a chance to recover it.

Midway through the quarter, the Raiders drove again, this time 71 yards to the 49ers' 1-yard line. This called for a Pete Banaszak smash, but the play dissolved when he was hit so hard by Jim Sniadecki that he fumbled. Taylor recovered once again.

In the fourth period, Brodie passed 28 yards to Bill Tucker for a touchdown. It was 31–7, and time for an Oakland miracle. So Blanda became the Oakland quarterback.

The secret of Blanda's longevity was that nothing demoralized him, but he could not have remained unaware at this point that his dearest fans were by this time piling for the exits as if activated by a Civil Defense alert. Before half-empty stands — and the remaining half largely devoted to rooting the 49ers to even greater heights — Blanda took to the air. San Francisco's Mel Phillips intercepted. Seven plays later the ineffable Willard hauled the ball over from a yard out. It was 38–7, San Francisco.

That was the way it ended. There were some extraordinary statistics. The 49ers never fumbled that slippery ball. The Raiders fumbled it six times, and lost it four. Oakland had five passes intercepted, the 49ers none. Brodie wasn't sacked once, a tribute to the offensive line. Time and again the Raiders had penetrated to within yards of the endzone, only to be halted, a tribute to the defensive line.

The final call on turnovers was nine for Oakland, none for San Francisco. Other elements to one side, this was what made the game one of the most memorable ever played. Any division winner that turns over the ball nine times to

your none has got to be having an unusual day. More than that, you must have had something to do with it.

Spadia wanted to win by 33 points on a dry field. He won by 31 points on a wet field.

The 49ers had won their first division title ever in a game they knew they had to win.

Spadia's phone rang off the hook that night. Every team in the National Football Conference checked in. Even the Rams. "Damn it, Lou, we showed 'em," said the voice of a Rams' official over the phone.

It was a curious thing for the Los Angeles team to say. But then again, loyalties being what they were, maybe it wasn't.

San Francisco	3	21	0	14	—	38
Oakland	7	0	0	0	—	7

SF — FG Gossett 42
Oak — Chester 29 pass from Lamonica (Blanda kick)
SF — Kwalick 26 pass from Brodie (Gossett kick)
SF — Johnson 36 interception return (Gossett kick)
SF — Washington 34 pass from Brodie (Gossett kick)
SF — Tucker 28 pass from Brodie (Gossett kick)
SF — Willard 1 run (Gossett kick)

December 16, 1972

The effects of the 49ers' first division title, won in that 38–7 victory over Oakland in 1970, were to enhance the San Francisco performance for two more seasons.

One of the first teams to face the rejuvenated 49ers was the Minnesota Vikings, who had played the 49ers twice a season through 1966, and once a season thereafter. Beaten soundly the first four times (the closest they came was 10 points at 38–28 in 1961), the Vikings began rising in 1963 to Purple Gang prominence. They began striking the San Franciscans like a gong — winning eight, losing two and tying one — until they met in a divisional playoff the week following San Francisco's defeat of the Raiders. It happened on a slick, ice-covered field in Minnesota.

"We had to use our regular shoes because we didn't know what parts of the field were slippery," 49ers quarterback John Brodie recounted afterward. "But there were patches all over the place, and you never knew when you'd run into one. So I had to call straight stuff. If I'd called a play where a ball carrier had to cut, he'd wind up tackling himself."

That year, 1970, was the prime of John Brodie. United Press International named him player of the year in the National Football Conference, an award for which John thanked many people, starting with his offensive line. But none of the 49ers was picked for the Pro Bowl. By contrast, Kansas City, with an indifferent 7–5–2 record that year, had 10 men chosen for that postseason game.

"I don't know anything about the Chiefs," Brodie said. "But if they really had ten Pro Bowlers, how come they didn't do better?" He had the kind of praise for the offensive line — men such as Forrest Blue, Len Rohde, Randy Beisler — that could come only from a quarterback who had been sacked only eight times all year. He had praise for others, too: rookie Bruce Taylor and the magnificent other cornerback,

Jimmy Johnson; and other defenders, such as Mel Phillips, Frank Nunley, Tommy Hart, and Earl Edwards. Brodie also singled out two veteran defensemen: tackle Charlie Krueger and free safety Roosevelt Taylor. "They kept steadying the younger players," he said.

Interviewed by Darrell Wilson of the *San Francisco Chronicle*, Brodie had some other thoughts: "I was ready either to quit or be traded in 1967. Jack Christiansen (who was let go at the end of that year) and I are very good friends and we agreed on everything except one thing. He thought George Mira was a better quarterback than I was."

In fact, Brodie had been benched for the last few games of 1967. What would happen in 1968, now that Dick Nolan had become head coach? Brodie put the question directly to Nolan himself. Nolan gave him a straight answer: "I have you and Mira and Steve Spurrier. The best man will play."

It sounded evasive, but it was a judgment happily free of preconditions. "What he said was good enough for me," Brodie told Wilson.

Also in 1970 John Brodie became the third 49er, after Joe Perry in 1954 and Y. A. Tittle in 1957, to be named UPI's man of the year. The Brodie of 1970 won his first passing title in 14 years, finishing the season with 2,941 yards on 223 completions of 378 passes, 24 of them for touchdowns.

But that was only a part of it. Something new was happening, and the Minnesota Vikings began to find out what it was. In the mind of John Brodie, a clock was stopping.

In that playoff game against San Francisco in 1970, the Vikings, with their 12–2–0 league record and the home-field advantage, struck first when Lonnie Warwick forced a midair fumble from Ken Willard. Paul Krause grabbed the ball in midair and ran for an easy 22 yards and a touchdown. San Francisco tied the score when Brodie passed 24 yards to Dick Witcher. Then the 49ers moved ahead on Bruce Gossett's 40-yard field goal just before the half.

There was no scoring from then until only 1 minute and 20 seconds remained in the game. With the 49ers in possession of the ball on the Minnesota 1-yard line on third down, Brodie violated a personal rule. He began to ask for advice in the huddle.

He could indulge this luxury because again it was as though the clock had stopped. He heard Woody Peoples, the offensive guard, say, "I can move him out, John." "Him" was Minnesota lineman Gary Larsen.

"Then give the ball to me," said Brodie, who had a known distaste for carrying the ball himself. They gave it to him and he sneaked for the touchdown. That made it 17–7, and it didn't matter that the Vikings mounted a 71-yard drive and scored with only one second left on the clock. The 49ers had won 17–14 in one of the great physical conflicts of their history.

It was pure hitting that won that game. Temperatures were around eight degrees above zero and frozen-fingered receivers on both sides dropped passes — eight in all.

With the 49ers' common gift for understatement, Charlie Krueger would later call that 1970 game against the Vikings "memorable because of its consistency." The consistency was the fury with which the Krueger-led 49ers and the Alan Page-led Vikings hit each other.

The following year — 1971 — was another Brodie year. He had the best completion percentage, most yardage, and most touchdown passes of any NFL quarterback. In 1971 he became the first 49er in the team's history to play 16 seasons for San Francisco. At season's end he had an astonishing 55 percent completion mark for his career. In the final game of the regular-season schedule, needing a win to clinch another division title, Brodie passed for

three touchdowns and then — distasteful to him, but discombobulating to the Detroit defense — he ran 10 yards for a touchdown. Surely the myth should have been shattered by then, but the Lions behaved as though they had never heard of Brodie running. In the preceding game against Atlanta, Brodie had bootlegged for five yards and another touchdown.

Yet the key to that 1971 season lay in a midseason game at Minnesota, which was won 13–9 by the 49ers. Twice the 49ers stopped the Vikings inside their own 10, and Rosey Taylor intercepted a Norm Snead pass at the 3 with 1 minute remaining. Meanwhile, Brodie had found Gene Washington for a 6-yard scoring pass in the final period. That was the difference. Once again the clock stood still for John Brodie.

But never would the clock stop the way it did in 1972. In the last regularly-scheduled game of the year, it was San Francisco versus Minnesota once more. Once again it was a must game for the 49ers. They were 7–5–1. Atlanta, playing Kansas City in its final game, was 7–6–0. The week before, at Candlestick, the 49ers had routed the Falcons 20–0. Playing again at Candlestick, they needed a win against the Vikings to make sure of clinching the division.

What those Falcons and Vikings games had in common was the attendance figure at Candlestick Park: 61,214. Not 61,212 or 61,213, but 61,214 — the precise capacity of the enlarged Candlestick facility.

What they did not have in common was John Brodie. Sidelined by injury, Brodie didn't play in the Falcons game. As he had since Brodie's ankle was jammed in the fifth game of the season, Steve Spurrier was carrying the load and doing it well. Against the Bears he had passed for five touchdowns. Under his direction the 49ers had come to the final game of the season with their third straight division title in sight. All they had to do was win over Minnesota.

If they lost, the situation would turn into another one of those Manchurian fire drills that seem built-in to all 49ers schedules. Given San Francisco's 7–5–1 record to Atlanta's 7–6–0, some fans tended almost to overlook the Rams. Playing Detroit in *their* final game, the Rams had a 6–6–1 record. Los Angeles had brutalized the 49ers both times they had met during the 1972 campaign. These victories would give the Rams the playoff position if Atlanta lost and San Francisco and Los Angeles both wound up at 7–6–1.

So three of the four teams in the NFC West, each going into its final game against a different opponent, had a shot at the title.

It might have been nice for the 49ers to know in advance how the Falcons and Rams made out, as they had in the case of the Rams-Giants' game that day in 1970 at Oakland, but unless they hired Jeanne Dixon that was not going to be in the realm of the possible. The 49ers-Vikings game would be played on December 16, a Saturday. The Falcons and Rams would play on the following day. If San Francisco won — or even tied — the 49ers would be in, and the Rams and Falcons could play their final games in peace. If San Francisco lost . . .

Well San Francisco *was* losing, by a margin of 17–6, with slightly more than six minutes of playing time remaining. It would have been impossible for Minnesota *not* to be in front. So far the San Francisco team had lost the ball twice on fumbles and five more times on interceptions. Vikings quarterback Fran Tarkenton was even testing the area patrolled by the great 49ers' left cornerback, Jimmy Johnson, and getting away with it: 11 completions out of 18 passes, 2 of them for touchdowns.

The first of these, an 18-yard pass to Ed Marinaro, came after the Vikings' second recovery of a 49ers' fumble and just before the first quarter ended. Two Bruce Gossett field

goals helped San Francisco cut the margin to 7–6 by halftime. But in the third period — as if everything else weren't enough, it began raining — Fred Cox kicked a 43-yard field goal for Minnesota, and after the kickoff, Spurrier was intercepted by Jeff Siemon, the Vikings' rookie linebacker and number one draft choice from nearby Stanford. Siemon already had fallen on one of the 49ers' fumbles. He was on his way to a memorable day. It was the day's third interception against Spurrier, and on the sidelines the convalescent John Brodie started throwing the ball.

While Brodie warmed up, the Vikings moved 49 yards for another touchdown. The clincher was a 31-yard Fran Tarkenton-to-John Gilliam pass. Gilliam and Johnson were in the endzone together. They went around like dancing bears as they wrestled for possession, but Gilliam won the fall and it was 17–6 Minnesota.

Spurrier had not done badly, but the 49ers had been sputtering all during the game. Vic Washington's 56-yard kickoff return failed to produce a touchdown, so Gossett kicked another field goal. Washington and Larry Schreiber carried the ball 22 times for 110 yards. O. J. Simpson does that for breakfast, but by 49ers standards of the 1970s it was not to be sneered at.

Still, it was patently not enough. Something else was needed. The fans had an idea. "We want Brodie!" they chanted.

They got him. The Gilliam touchdown had come with less than two minutes left to play in the third quarter, and immediately after the kickoff the familiar number twelve came off the 49ers' bench.

Almost instantly, the 49ers picked up. Brodie led a spectacular march to the Vikings' 6-yard line. Then Vic Washington was dropped for a 5-yard loss and Paul Krause, the Minnesota safety, intercepted a Brodie pass on the 1.

When the 49ers got the ball again, in came

San Francisco was the site for a 1972 playoff battle between the 49ers and the Minnesota Vikings. When middle linebacker Jeff Siemon stepped in front of Gene Washington for an interception (far left) in the third quarter, it was the third of the day against Steve Spurrier (left). Then the Vikings took a 17-6 lead when Fran Tarkenton and John Gilliam (right) completed a 31-yard pass play for a touchdown.

Brodie. "You know," said Vikings linebacker Siemon, "it gave me a funny feeling. Having gone to Stanford, where Brodie played so long ago, I had always been a 49ers fan, and Brodie had always been my favorite player." Siemon managed to contain his admiration enough to intercept a Brodie pass at the Minnesota 22. The fans had an idea. "We want Spurrier!" they chanted.

The Vikings' Mike Eischeid boomed a punt that was downed by his teammates on the 49ers' 1-yard line. "We want anybody!" they chanted.

Midway through the final period, Brodie had to take his team 99 yards for a score. Coolly, he took up the task. A 12-yard pass play to John Isenberger, a 53-yard pass to Gene Washington, and a 24-yarder to Washington in the endzone did the work. The 49ers had moved 99 yards in 6 plays. With Gossett's conversion they now trailed by 4 points at 17–13. There were 6 minutes, 12 seconds still to play.

Still the fans needed convincing. For one thing, San Francisco was still behind, and a 49ers' loss would mean both Atlanta and Los Angeles would have to lose if the 49ers were to gain the playoff spot. For another, there was the haunting criticism: the 49ers couldn't win the big ones. Most persuasive of all, the crowd considered that 99-yard touchdown drive as a freak. On both of the key Brodie-Gene Washington passes, Washington had caught the ball in a crowd, surrounded by three Vikings.

What nobody knew — indeed, it was almost an occult private secret shared by Brodie and Washington alone — was that neither of those catches was very difficult. Washington may have *looked* surrounded, but in each instance, almost by some form of mysterious understanding, Brodie had thrown the ball to the one spot in the crowd where only his teammate could have caught it. It was a demonstration of sheer empathy — a kind of guru study — that both

were reluctant to discuss. "If you tell people about it, they don't believe you. So what's the use?" Washington said.

The crowd was aroused when Tommy Hart, the defensive end who led the NFL in sackings in 1972 and was known as Sackings, Inc., broke through to dump Tarkenton for 12 yards on third down. This forced a Minnesota punt from the Vikings' 11 with 4 minutes left to play.

Minnesota punted. The 49ers were called for defensive holding. Five yards and an automatic first down for Minnesota. The crowd's enthusiasm waned.

Marinaro shook loose for 18 yards. The crowd fell silent.

The Vikings controlled the ball and got it out nearly to midfield before they finally were forced to punt. Only 1:39 remained to play.

On the sidelines Brodie stayed aloof from a gaggle of advisers, huddling with clipboards and earphones as if bent on producing a new 49ers' first: a play worth exactly four points.

Eischeid punted to the San Francisco 21, but at this juncture Minnesota's John Ward was called for a personal foul and ejected from the game.

Brodie passed to Larry Schreiber, who ran out of bounds after a 9-yard gain. Then John pitched a lateral to Vic Washington for 8 more. The ball was on the 49ers' 44 with 1:22 left. Brodie passed incomplete to Ted Kwalick, but there was a whistle. The call was against the agitated Siemon for pass interference, and San Francisco had the ball on Minnesota's 26.

Clearly, it was time for a trick play: a lateral from Brodie to Isenbarger, who then threw a forward pass to Schreiber. The latter was alone in the endzone. Unfortunately, the Isenbarger pass behaved like a Frisbee, and by the time it reached its target, the target was no longer alone. Krause batted the wobbler down.

Schreiber went for 6. And then Brodie passed

to Vic Washington, who carried 18 yards to the Viking 2. There were 40 seconds left to play. The advisers on the 49ers' sideline had dispersed. There was no four-point play. They had checked every book on the subject.

Twice Brodie passed incomplete.

The football-wise Minnesotans knew what he was doing. He was setting them up for the short touchdown hit — the safe handoff on the power play.

They had one additional suspicion: though hardly known for his enthusiasm for such endeavors, Brodie might carry the ball himself. As they assessed the possibilities, the Vikings tended to eliminate the things that wouldn't happen. One of those things that wouldn't happen was that Brodie would roll out and run. And surely he wouldn't throw to the most obscure man in the 49ers' lineup: a one-time flanker turned substitute tight end, Dick Witcher. Witcher was not renowned for catching touchdown passes or any other for that matter. He'd caught exactly one pass all season long.

Thirty seconds left, said the clock. Then the clock stopped altogether. Oh, the second hand kept moving. But there was a suspension in time that Brodie would talk about later. Everybody on the field, not to mention the 61,214 in the stands and a strung-out national television audience in the millions, felt it.

The feeling was uncomfortable, almost like a chill. Maybe Rolfe Humphries, a Fellow of the Academy of American Poets, said it in his own way:

> Time is of the essence. The crowd
> and players
> Are the same age always, but the
> man in the crowd
> Is older every season.

Maybe they did not understand it, but they could feel it. Certainly no one knew to call this what it was in fact — the last great moment of

the playing career of quarterback John Brodie.

John Brodie took the snap from Forrest Blue and did the un-Brodie thing with it: He rolled out to his right. Recovering from its initial charge, the Minnesota defense squatted and stared.

Brodie wasn't going to run the ball in. Wasn't he? Time hung suspended. So did Brodie. He stopped and simply stood there. Suddenly he raised his left arm and began pointing with it.

Witcher, in the endzone, followed Brodie's directions. He cut between defenders and held up his arms as a target.

The ball was already in the air. It hit him clean, alone and undefended.

There is no describing that play unless you saw it. In football terms, Brodie had taken the most clever course of all. Given a choice between two things the opposition least expected (the rollout and the pass to Witcher), he had the ideal alternatives of selecting either one, a masterwork of play-calling.

But there was more to it than that. Why did time stand still — for Brodie, the 49ers and the Vikings, as well as the Candlestick crowd and a nation of television watchers? What element of *clarity* suddenly took hold in this game of fumbles, interceptions, penalties, and crowded plays that could have gone either way? Was it a throwback of nearly two generations, when Dutch Clark of the original Lions used to *run* audibles instead of calling them, pointing out targets to blockers as he proceeded with the ball? Or was it a matter of a Leo throwing to a Libra with Sirius under the sign of Mercury? Whatever it was, it transfixed the game. Of all people, Witcher won the game ball.

In the Minnesota dressing room there was a frosty difference of opinion between quarterback Tarkenton and coach Bud Grant. Behind 20–17, Grant had ordered a Cox field-goal attempt from 43 yards out with 5 seconds remain-

The game was building to a climax that would equal that of the 1957 Alley-Oop game. Veteran John Brodie was summoned from the bench to replace Spurrier. He marched his team to the goal line, but Paul Krause intercepted for Minnesota (left). Later, Brodie was intercepted a second time. Yet he drove San Francisco to two touchdowns in the fourth quarter to win the game. The decisive score came with just two seconds left to play, when Brodie (below) passed to little-known receiver Dick Witcher in the endzone in front of Bob Bryant (right).

ing. If it had worked, the 49ers would have won the NFC West anyway. Tarkenton wanted to try all-out to beat them instead, with a final pass play. The difference was that a field goal would have given the Vikings a winning season at 7–6–1 in their division. A loss would have put them at 7–7.

"I care only about us," Grant said. "In this business, we do the best we can for ourselves. It's not our business to knock anyone out of the running."

But Tarkenton had wanted to win, not tie. Then if either Atlanta or Los Angeles had won next day, San Francisco would have been out of it.

Maybe a Vikings win would have inspired the Falcons and Rams.

But both of them lost.

Minnesota	7	0	10	0	— 17
San Francisco	0	6	0	14	— 20

Minn — Marinaro 18 pass from Tarkenton (Cox kick)
SF — FG Gossett 14
SF — FG Gossett 37
Minn — FG Cox 43
Minn — Gilliam 31 pass from Tarkenton (Cox kick)
SF — G. Washington 24 pass from Brodie (Gossett kick)
SF — Witcher 2 pass from Brodie (Gossett kick)

The Men

Lou Spadia

Position: President, General Manager
Years: 1946-

Lou Spadia's memory is bright not only with rich detail from the uncertain infancy of the 49ers, but reminiscence of things that have happened since — some of them strange and wondrous indeed.

There was, for example, the locally celebrated feud between the Morabitos and the San Francisco press, stemming from the 49ers' refusal to renew a charity-game contract sponsored by one of the papers.

Directly after World War II, Spadia found himself stationed at the Treasure Island naval base in San Francisco, under an executive officer, John R. Blackinger, who was to become the first 49ers' general manager. This contact led Spadia to apply for a job with the new team.

"I didn't know what it would lead to," he said. "My navy salary, not even counting the benefits that went with it, was higher than I knew I could expect.

"But I was a sports fan."

When did you first sit down with Tony Morabito?

December of 1945. I'd read about the new team being definite, and Blackinger was going over there, and I met Tony. "Well," he said, "how much are you making now?" And I said, "I'm making three-hundred eighteen dollars or three-twelve a month, I forget which, and I'd like to start at three hundred." He said, "Gee, we've budgeted two-fifty."

For what job?

I don't think either of us really knew. But I would have taken the two-fifty — it was the best I'd heard. "Well," he said, "we'll go down the middle with you and start you at two-seventy-five, but we don't want you to come to work 'til the first of May."

That worked out well because my captain wanted me to stay in the navy. Being in personnel, we were releasing officers — there was a lot going on just after the war.

So I went to work for the 49ers on the first of May in 1946. I didn't have a car. We had a flat up on Sixteenth and Castro, in between Castro and Market, and I took the street car, and it was about a mile-and-a-half walk from there to their offices down on Evans Street. I was walking down there and I said to myself, this is going to be a hell of a way to go to work every day. Well, Buzz McGee, the publicity director, arranged to meet me, so that was no problem, but I remember being impressed by what the hell I was getting into because this was a lumber yard!

McGee was there, and Tony, and Blackinger, and that was our organization at that point. Unless you count a couple of players who were working there . . .

Doing what?

Unloading lumber. They worked in the yard. We used to eat lunch together.

Where?

We sat on a stack of lumber and brown-bagged it. But a real impressionable thing happened to me in those first few days. My wife was pregnant, and on the fourteenth of May Kathleen was born, and I'd been there thirteen days and had gotten to know guys who worked in the lumber end of it, and I brought in a box of cigars and handed them out. And that afternoon Tony called me in and said, "Mr. Blackinger says you're doing a fine job."

Well, I wasn't doing any fine job in only thirteen days. I remember, one of the first things I started to do was write sketches for our press booklet. Buzz had sent out questionnaires to all the players, and from those questionnaires I'd write sketches for our press booklet.

But Tony said, "You wanted to start at three-hundred dollars a month, so we'll make it three-hundred," and the next day, which was the fifteenth of May, I got paid on that basis. I don't think anyone ever got a raise in shorter order.

That's got to be a world record for fast raises.

But in getting to know the guy later on, I can imagine what went through his mind when I came in that morning with the cigars. I know he said to them, "Gee, that kid wanted three-hundred and now he's got another mouth to feed and I got him down to two-seventy-five — I'll get him back up to three-hundred." It was a great act of charity, and he was that kind of man.

How long did the operation stay at the lumber terminal?

Till about the first of July. Then we moved to our downtown offices. They had no concept of what the hell was needed in the way of a football office. I was the only employee, and thank God we lived at Sixteenth and Market and the new office was at Stockton and Geary, on Union Square, because now it only took me five minutes to get home.

Was that especially important?

Yes, in a way, because if it was five minutes to get home, that meant only five minutes to get back to the office. I was unable to do any work during the day because of the phone — I was the only guy in that office. Tony stayed at the lumber terminal, so there was Blackinger, who was in charge, and me. And John would call my home at night. What I'd do was, I'd go home at five or five-thirty, and then I'd go back downtown to do what dictation he'd given me — the typing that was necessary. And hell, I was doing that every night. And at the end I'd go home about ten o'clock, but then when I was at the office at night, he'd call me at home, and Maggie would say, "He's at the office," and after about four times he said to me, "Do you need some help?" I said, "Well, gee, we ought to get *somebody* in here, at least to answer the phone so I can get the typing done." I was preparing a season ticket brochure, and writing for the first program. Buzz was no writer at all. Buzz was a great p.r. man, but he was a *verbal*

guy. He went out and shook hands. But I can remember Buzz halfway through the season saying to me, "What's Beals's number?" You know, he didn't . . . details: they weren't for Buzz Mc-Gee, God bless him. So we hired Helen Dill, who was Blackinger's WAVE, who'd worked for him on Treasure Island. So that allowed me to work on the tickets.

We had a season ticket sale: I prepared an ad that appeared in the papers, you know, for season tickets — we actually advertised them — we thought we could sell season tickets. I learned very early that season tickets are not sold: season tickets are purchased.

Do you remember what your first season-ticket sale was?

Yes. It was one thousand eleven tickets.

And what was the figure for 1973?

Well, we shut it off at fifty-seven thousand four hundred some-odd . . .

A slight gain . . .

. . . So we could still have a couple of thousand left for individual game sale. We wanted some available for people who couldn't afford them or who for some reason or other didn't want season tickets.

But I think something else took place that first year that probably didn't take place anywhere else — maybe it did — and hasn't taken place since, but I prepared a mailing piece. In our attempt to sell season tickets we put an ad in the paper, and then we had an ad campaign that we handled ourselves right there. It was a two-fold piece that I prepared that had to be stuffed into envelopes, and we got mailing lists from various clubs in town — we had the Olympic Club list and the Family Club list and so forth. As I recall, we sent out ten thousand, and that meant that ten thousand envelopes had to be typed and stuffed. Helen and I handled the typing, but one night we did the stuffing, and boy, I'll never forget this, because we had the

pieces on this big table, and there was Buck Shaw, Jim Lawson, Al Ruffo, Blackinger, Helen and myself. And here was the head coach stuffing and sealing envelopes and throwing them in the pile, and we got them down to the post office, and, you know, at the time it didn't impress me; but thinking about it now, having your head coach participate in your first mail solicitation, here's a guy making his kind of money, stuffing and sealing envelopes, which was a little incongruous.

But effective?

No. Our return was pretty dismal. And I suddenly became ticket manager also.

Why?

Because we didn't have a ticket manager, and somebody had to keep track of the season ticket sale. It became obvious after a while we wouldn't be able to handle the Kezar Stadium sale. So we hired the Crane Box Office to handle our game sales. What we did was to close our season-ticket sale, with those one thousand eleven sold; then we turned the capacity over to Lou Samuels, who ran the Crane Box Office, and then he handled our sale. We used that method for several years — about ten years. I kept telling Tony, "You know, we should have our own ticket manager," and in 1956 we finally got one.

But we went ten years on a contract basis. I'm sorry I lost the records of it, because I have a reason for bringing it up. Our processing of tickets today is computerized. We're what you call "on line," with a terminal in our office, and if you write in and say, "I've moved," for example, "Mail my tickets to 123 instead of 456 Jones Street," our people take your code number and the computer down in Palo Alto acknowledges it. Okay, we say, change Mr. John Doe from so-and-so to so-and-so. That goes to the computer, the change is made, and the next time an envelope is prepared for you it's to this new address. And that applies to your seat location,

if we change your seat location, and the number of tickets. It even prepares the billing.

Why don't you have it print the tickets too?

It does. And all this gets me to my point — our first control system: my mother worked at the Home Laundry, and one of the benefits I had was getting free laundry — shirts especially, which my wife Maggie loved — and in those days the shirts used to come with a cardboard. And one side was almost like chrome-coat, and the other side was grayish. So I brought four of those into the office, because it became obvious to me that you needed some sort of control. You couldn't sell the same location twice. You'd better come up with something, to keep you informed as to just what you had. And I went to the stadium and charted the four center sections on the shirt cardboards — what I did was draw horizontal lines, which were the rows, and vertical lines, about, oh, a quarter-of-an-inch square, and I'd put a number in there. You see, over here would be rows one through thirty-four — section A in Kezar Stadium — that's indelible in my memory — and each row has twenty-six seats — so I went one-through-thirty-four here and one-through-twenty-six here, and if we sold four seats together in row so-and-so, section A, I'd just draw a line through them, so I couldn't sell them again.

And then you'd tell Crane.

No. They weren't interested. We'd hold out tickets, and they sold what was left. Now the season-ticket sale was closed, and instead of a sixty-thousand we had a capacity of fifty-nine thousand that Crane was responsible for.

And then came that Yankee game — was that the first year?

No, no. The big Yankee game — the Yankee game where I wound up selling tickets at the box office — was in 1948. By '48 we had a season-ticket sale of maybe fourteen hundred. Nothing really happened to our season-ticket

sale — we stayed around between one thousand and fifteen hundred until 1950 — so we had a season-ticket sale of around fourteen hundred and an advance sale for that Yankees game of maybe another thousand, and that day — it was our opening day at Kezar, a beautiful day — everybody that had ever thought of coming to a 49ers' game decided to come.

And you weren't prepared.

Prepared?! We were completely unprepared. And this part of it was nobody's fault, not ours, not Crane's, but we had to open box offices; Lou Samuels, I know, figured on having fourteen ticket sellers — we suddenly needed twenty-eight. I was one of them. I was down in the dressing room helping out, and Samuels handed me a roll of general admission tickets. See, we had very few reserved seats — only those center sections. Our prices were three dollars, sixty cents and two-forty for reserved seats and a dollar-twenty for general admission, so I'm out there selling general admission tickets, and it was then that we found a problem, and it was a result of a knock on the door of my booth.

I opened it and some guy handed me a bunch of tickets. He said, "These are from Gate Twelve," or something, I forget what the hell he said, and I didn't know what the hell was going on, but it didn't take me long to realize that somebody was double-selling general admission tickets, because they didn't have to be torn.

As a result of that, Blackinger hired Pinkerton people, and we started putting spotters around. You see, there were no turnstiles, so there was no way you could get a count, and I know that in that Yankees game we had a paid attendance of fifty-six or some-odd thousand. The stadium held sixty thousand. And there were people sitting on the track.

So God knows how many people got into that game on streetcar transfers, snuff-box tops.

When we did put in that new surveillance starting in '47 and attempting to get some sort of control, we actually got reports from plain-clothes spotters of checks being passed. The fans weren't even dealing in cash! They were writing checks and handing them to the men at the gates. We didn't press any charges, but we made a lot of changes, and the operation greatly improved.

Speaking of problems — what about the 49ers' feud with the press?

Well, I was involved in the day-to-day stuff — handling the mail, etcetera — so I really would only hear about that. I knew that there was a feud — that was obvious — between Curley Grieve, sports editor at the *Examiner,* God rest his soul, and Tony, God rest his. One of the gratifying things that took place after I became president is that just before Curley Grieve died, he made a road trip with us, and I think it was a matter of two men — you see, Tony loved the 49ers as you love your children, as I love my children. He simply couldn't accept criticism of the 49ers.

The feud started, I guess — there was a game played each year from '46 through '49, a charity game for the San Francisco *Examiner.* And this put Tony in a bad position with the other morning San Francisco paper, the *Chronicle,* because the sports editor there, Bill Leiser, with some justification, felt he was responsible for Tony getting the franchise and introducing him to Arch Ward. And one of the things that used to bother Tony is that the *Examiner* would promote this game — would promote the 49ers — as the *Examiner* did in those days of promoting things, and then in his opinion at least, and Buzz McGee's, they'd kind of forget us for the rest of the year, and I think Leiser probably called that to Tony's attention.

But I wasn't in on those discussions. I'm sorry that I wasn't, but I wasn't that high up in

the organization. But I know that it got bad. And I think the result of it was Tony's refusal to renew that contract, because when the game was first announced, I know that Bill Leiser was very upset, and I'm sure that Tony said, "Bill, when the contract expires — I know I've made a mistake — but if I have, I'll give you my word I'll not get involved again."

And, you know, I learned something from that: you can't align yourself with one entity that way when there's another one competing with it. And down through the years, when I've had the Heart Fund come to us and the Cancer Fund and all types of people wanting a charity game . . . when we started making the move to Candlestick, I felt we should get involved, so now we have this Mayor's Youth Bowl game, which I feel is the perfect way.

This way we're dealing with our city. The mayor has these revenues that come to him each year for distribution to the youth of San Francisco, and he doesn't have to go to the Board of Supervisors.

The thing that kind of focused it in my mind — the need for something like this — was the year they tried to raise I think twenty-five thousand dollars for a swimming pool at Hunter's Point, and they must have spent thirty thousand trying to raise the twenty-five. And now . . . well, in 1972, for example, as a result of their sharing in one of our preseason games, we gave the Mayor's Youth Bowl Fund a check for one-hundred four thousand dollars, and I was told that forty different organizations, ranging from the CYO to the Hunter's Point Boys Club benefited from this thing. And I think that Tony, and Vic, would be damned proud of it.

This gets back to that feud. I think that Tony was trying to do something good, but in doing something good, it created a monster. And when Tony refused to renew that contract, the *Examiner* really started taking some shots. And that

really started things between the two of them.

But I wasn't really in the trenches — Tony and Vic were, and Buzz McGee. I know that at one stage there, in those early fifties, I became involved as sort of the road secretary. I'd make arrangements and I'd go on the trips, and we would travel by train, once we got east. We'd come east for three games, and we'd fly a DC-4 to Chicago, for example, to play the Bears, and then the next week we might be scheduled in Detroit, and in going to Detroit or in going to Pittsburgh — wherever we were going — we'd take a parlor car and a dining car. And they'd be ours — only our people could be in those two sections.

Well, Bob Brachman was covering us for the *Examiner* in those days, and my orders from Tony were that no one from the *Examiner* be allowed in any part of anything controlled by the 49ers. That included our dressing room, our meeting rooms, our train, our plane.

But Brachman was trying to do a job as a reporter, and it was my job to keep him out of there, and he's a tenacious reporter and Grieve had told him to cover the 49ers. Well, I'd see him in the parlor car talking to one of the players, and I'd go up and say, "Brachman, you're not allowed in here," and we'd go back and forth. I don't like to argue, but I'd have to almost physically throw him out of the damn car.

Another time, over at St. Mary's College, the feud was still on, and he was trying to get into the dressing room. And it really got ludicrous. It got down to this: the hallway to the dressing room, he said, legally is not 49ers' property. He said, "I can stand here. I've checked it with Brother Albert. You're leasing specific rooms that are outlined in your contract." So all right: "You can stay in the hallway but don't step in the dressing room." And thank God the day of the feud is over. It was wearing on everybody.

But it lasted a long time.

‛Oh, boy, did it ever last for a long time.

And you finally put an end to it?

Yes. There were still things smoldering. Curley and I talked about it, and I was glad that he finally felt that he could take a trip with us.

And you were in charge in 1966 when the thing with quarterback John Brodie happened.

Yes. John and I had had some discussions — Tony signed John to his first contract in 1957, and Tony died shortly thereafter, then I signed John to several contracts after that. We never had any problem. He was the easiest; a level-headed man. And we'd had a couple of discussions about the '66 contract and we were close. I think we were down to where we had the figures — we were at that stage where we were trying to decide whether it would be a one-or-two-year, or two-or-three-year thing, and I said, "Well, I've got to go to Portland. My son's graduating from Portland University. We'll get together when I come back. You tell me how you want it."

So I'm up at Portland on a Saturday for commencement exercises that were to take place at three-thirty, and at two-thirty — Maggie and I were just getting ready to leave the Benson Hotel — I answered the phone, and he said, "Hi, Lou, this is John." I knew it was Brodie, and I said, "What the hell are you doing in Portland?" He said, "I'm not in Portland, I'm in Houston." I said, "Houston? What are you doing there?" He said, "Well, I'm down here with the local football people. They asked me to come down and they've offered me a contract, Lou, that I just can't — you know — well, I haven't *signed* it." And I don't know why he didn't, but he's that kind of a guy.

He said, "You know I want to play for the 49ers, but I've got to think of myself and think of my family," and he told me what the figure was. And crying out loud, you know, I should have said, "Is that just for preseason — what are

they offering you for regular season?" It would have been a funny line, but I was in no mood for funny lines.

Well, I remember saying this to him: I said, "Look, don't sign anything — let me get back to you. I've got to go out to this graduation of my son's, but I'll get back to you. You'll hear from me before the day is out."

Now I've got to get Maggie out to this commencement, and there was some guy up there making a speech — I don't know what he was saying — and I finally said to Maggie, "Look, I gotta get out of here. I've got to go and do something." I went back and found a phone and called Jack White, our vice-president, and told him what had happened and told him, you know, get the hell down to Houston and see what we can do and call me when you get down there.

Well, he called from down there and he told me that John by then had a written memorandum of agreement from them. And the next guy I called was Marshall Leahy, our lawyer, because John was legally under contract to us, since we had exercised our option on his services, and from then on it really left my hands. Eventually, an arrangement was made with John's lawyer, and John signed a contract with the 49ers.

The problem has never affected John's relationship toward me personally, or toward his organization.

What was your title before Vic died? In effect, you were signing players and acting more or less as general manager, weren't you?

Yes, but only up to a point. I didn't establish policy. I implemented — did what Vic wanted me to do. And Vic was tremendous. If I felt something should be done a certain way, he'd allow me to argue the point. But I used to have a line that I used with him, after I'd exhausted my arguments. I'd say, "Damn it, if you think for one minute we're gonna do it your way,

Tony Morabito and fellow NFL owner Edwin Anderson of the Detroit Lions (center) listened patiently to the question of interviewer Tom Harmon during halftime of a 1952 game. At right, Vic Morabito signs Hugh McElhenny, rookie of the year in 1952, to a 1953 contract.

you're right." Of course, if he wanted it done his way, even though I disagreed with it, that's the way we'd do it. I never second-guessed him.

And we do that now. We have a lot of arguments — Jack White and I, and Dick Nolan and I — no, *discussions* is a better word — but my only responsibility now — my role now — is to *maintain an environment*. By "environment" I mean physical and psychological — under which these people — the coaches, the rest of the people, and the players — can function comfortably. I think, really, that's management's basic role. That's about all you can do. I think if you have a bad physical set-up, the environment is affected. We do things first class. Tony always wanted that. That's the physical aspect of it. The psychological aspect of it: I think that you've got to eliminate problems, because when there are problems, then the environment is affected. If you have a feud, for example, like the one with the press — there was an environment there that had some effect on people in our organization.

Did you ever attend an All-America Football Conference meeting, or were you one of the lucky ones?

I was one of the lucky ones. They never took me to one of those. The first National Football League meetings I attended were draft meetings, and then the first *league* meetings I attended were in about 1954 or 1955 . . . maybe earlier, because Tony had a heart attack in 1952, and he stopped going to meetings. Then Vic and I would be the only ones there.

There again, Vic would allow me a lot more freedom than I see others allow the man that's with them. And he never once said anything about it. I look back on it now, and I'd be allowed to make a statement in the meeting not knowing whether Vic agreed with it or not, which is allowing your guy a lot of freedom. I really admire the guy, because I'm not that way

with my people. I want to know what we are doing before we say something . . . let's make sure we agree on what our position is. Because I can remember a couple of times, Vic contradicting me in the meeting room, and of course I knew whose position was going to be maintained: his.

But he never once said to me, "Look, next time we're in that meeting room, before you pop off, let me know what you're going to say."

One of the 49ers' most memorable games was their first league game against Oakland in 1970.

Yes, and I couldn't go to the game! My wife had just had surgery and was just getting back on her feet. The game was blacked out locally, but Lou Simon of KPIX allowed me to use his office to watch it on closed circuit. Maggie and I were there alone. God, what an eerie feeling. I'll never do that again. I'd rather not see it than to see a game that critical on television where you don't see everything as you would by being at the game.

Isn't it true that, during your years with the team, you have done almost every job in the organization, including manage the equipment?

Listen, I think I'm the only president of a National Football League team that can speak to an equipment manager in his own language, because I served as one. It was kind of a surprise to me, certainly because I thought I was going to be an office worker, and the first game ever played by the San Francisco 49ers was against the Los Angeles Dons in San Diego, in August of 1946. And I remember John Blackinger saying to me early in that week, "Spadia, we want you to come to San Diego, make the trip." And my reaction was, gee, that's awfully nice, they're going to be taking me on these trips. There was glamour to it. I'd played baseball, and I was a sports fan, and there was no television in those days, and it was great to be

going down there to see a football game.

Well, they had been operating on the theory that the trainer could be the equipment man, too. Well, poor Bob Kleckner, our trainer — it had worked out all right at camp, but when it came time for a game, he said, "I'm going to need some help," and hell, there was no help around.

And I remember, we were getting ready to get off the plane at San Diego, and Kleckner, who was a great guy but a tough son of a bleep — oh, boy — he was an abrupt fellow, you know — well, with him there were no social amenities. There are none. It's just that he's basically a hell of a guy, and he said, "Hey, kid, you stay with me," and he's six-foot-three, and when he said it like that I stayed with him, and we wound up under the plane loading these duffel bags on the damn truck and going out to Balboa Stadium, and then I helped him lay the stuff out, but it became obvious that they were going to need an equipment manager, and it's kind of funny how they wound up with one. A halfback, a young halfback by the name of Ziggy Zamlynsky, from Villanova, strained a knee — you know, it wasn't a serious strain, but they had to strap it. So he worked with Bob as the equipment man, and when his knee got well, the squad had been cut and, you know, there was no place for him to play — we were down to our limit. But he stayed on as the equipment man, and Ziggy Zamlynsky stayed with us until his wife probably said to him, "Look, you're a college graduate and knock this off — you should be something more than an equipment man." And Ziggy is doing very well with the Pillsbury company, but he stayed with us for about three years. He just liked being around the guys.

And you did too.

Well, yeah, I enjoyed it. I really did. Hell, as late as — you know, when I was sort of the road secretary — I remember handling the equipment if we went over in a hurry to make a plane someplace, or a train. I remember, whenever we went to Cambridge Springs, everybody had to help with the equipment. It's just outside of Erie, and we'd go there by train, and we'd have all these duffel bags and trunks . . . it was kind of our focal point to play Cleveland or Pittsburgh or Buffalo, and we'd take that Erie Railroad, but whenever we got there from wherever we were coming from, the conductor would say, "We're here for three minutes and if bleep isn't off the train . . ." And it wouldn't be in the baggage car; we'd put it all in the vestibule.

The first instance of letting it all hang out?

Well, I remember an All-America, Len Eshmont, helping us unload. We had to get that stuff off the train, and whether you were a halfback or a coach, you helped.

You'd do your train traveling in the east, but you flew the long leg from the Coast?

From the start. Oh, gee, that's another thing that used to bother me. We would take a DC-4 east, and then we'd either take the train or DC-3s. The DC-3 carried twenty-one passengers, and Buck would have to split the squad. And it was an ominous thing, because he'd give me the names, and he'd put Albert on one plane and Freitas on the other — he'd never put both quarterbacks on the same plane, and he'd put Standlee on one plane and another fullback on the other one, and so forth. And I'd always say to myself, I hope I'm on the one that stays up. The whole thing was planned like one of the planes wasn't going to get there.

But I enjoyed it. Traveling by train, you know — the dining room service in those days was really great. When we used to go from Chicago to Minneapolis on that Hiawatha — lord almighty, what food and service! I learned later it was because there were three railroads competing, trying to out-do each other on that route. What steaks you got! What living!

A little different from the airlines.

Oh, God. Although I'll tell you, I've seen great improvement in that. In those early days, that airline food — you couldn't eat it. And I remember flying into Denver on those DC-4s. They were non-pressurized, and you weren't much higher than the mountains. And you'd get in there in the middle of the day with those thermal drafts, and by the time you landed everybody was green. John Mellus — we traded him after that first year. Do you remember him? The tackle. He just wouldn't fly any more. He'd been a pretty good tackle with the New York Giants, and then during the war he played in the service and in '46 he played with us. And we hit Denver about three times that year, and he said "No more." I think he went to Pittsburgh or someplace, where he didn't have to fly into Denver or come out of there. He just wouldn't fly in an airplane, and I'll tell you, I wasn't too hot for it either.

But speaking of flying out of Denver, let me get back to that first exhibition game we ever played, against the L.A. Dons in San Diego. You know who missed that game?

Who?

Tony and Vic Morabito.

They both missed it. Tony and Vic had gone to the All-Star game in Chicago, and they had worked this thing out so that — the All-Star game was played on Friday night, and our game was played in San Diego on Saturday night, and they had it worked out so they were catching some kind of a flight to San Francisco or L.A. — I think it was L.A. — so they go from Chicago, and the plane lands in Denver.

Now because of either mechanical trouble or weather, I've forgotten which, they're stuck in Denver. So there's only one thing to do. They go down and they charter a small airplane. I wish Vic was here to tell this story. They get into this small airplane — it only took two or three passengers — and Tony says, "Can you get

us to San Diego by six o'clock tonight?" The guy says, "Yeah, sure, get in."

Now they get up in this small plane in these thermal-draft things and they both get sick — heaving all over everything — and they get to Albuquerque, and now because of something or other . . . weather, I think . . . the guy says, "I can't take you any further."

They're in Albuquerque and it's Saturday afternoon and there's no — finally, they get a flight, you know, and travel was restricted then. It was just after the war and you still needed priorities to travel. And they get to L.A., I think about one o'clock Sunday morning, and they call the L.A. *Times* or somebody to find out how the game came out, and they can't get the score. So they hire a limousine in L.A., and they get to San Diego at three o'clock in the morning, to find out we had beaten the Dons 21–9 or something like that.

But can you imagine that? Here this guy had waited all his life to have a team and he doesn't see them play their first game. He has to look at the film.

Well, in a way you could make a comparison between . . .

Oh — and Tony never paid the guy, because the guy had guaranteed him San Diego, and instead gave him Albuquerque and said, "I can't take you any further, that'll be eighty bucks." And Tony said, "You told me San Diego and here I am in Albuquerque. And you didn't fly over the Rockies. You flew through them."

The Morabitos missed the first game the 49ers ever played, and a quarter of a century later you missed the greatest game they ever played. That is a strange kind of progress.

Well — but I was watching over television and they were throwing up over New Mexico. So you'd have to say we did come a long way.

John Brodie

Position: Quarterback
Years: 1957-73
Height: 6-1
Weight: 200
College: Stanford

Having been a unanimous All-America in college and having broken all passing records held by another Stanford/49ers player (Frankie Albert), John Brodie was quite logically the San Francisco team's first draft choice for the 1957 season. He broke into the NFL by coming in to win a crucial game in the final seconds. From then through the 1973 season, in which he announced in midcampaign it would be his final year, he completed 2,469 passes for 31,548 yards.

Successor to Y.A. Tittle, Brodie owns or shares 17 of the 49ers' 22 listed passing records. He was all-pro twice and in 1970 won the Jim Thorpe trophy as the National Football League's most valuable player.

But such records are largely peripheral to the essential John Riley Brodie. It should be noted, for example, that the following interview with Brodie took place before the 1973 season and before he announced his retirement.

The timing of Brodie's official announcement struck many 49ers fans as curious. Though coach Dick Nolan insisted that he and Brodie had discussed it earlier, the fact is that Brodie, replacing backup quarterback Steve Spurrier, animated a 40–0 49ers' victory over New Orleans, only to have Nolan announce that Spurrier would start against Atlanta the following week. The next day, being very nice about it and saying the 49ers were in good hands, the 38-year-old Brodie announced he was quitting. At that point the 49ers had an unexpectedly mediocre 3–3 won-lost record for 1973. It became 3–4 with a loss to Atlanta the next Sunday.

He was well-fixed financially and the career he would leave behind was one of the most illustrious in professional football — more so for the fact that over all 17 years, he played for just one team.

He had other interests. He was an expert tennis player and had played in professional golf

tournaments. But most notable was his participation in drug-control programs. Not that this took away from his concentration on football. Brodie thinks today's players put out just as much as those of yesteryear. Almost poignantly, he stresses the *fun* of professional football.

Yet all of this does not reflect the complete John Riley Brodie. When he announced his retirement, he said he wanted to devote more attention to scientology.

Scientology?

The January, 1973, issue of *Intellectual Digest* contains a dialogue between Brodie and Michael Murphy, president of the Esalen Institute. They are talking football, and yet they are talking something else too. It is a something else perhaps not fully perceived in the sports pages or even, perhaps, by the participants in the dialogue itself.

When the sports pages talk about the "timing" of something, such as Brodie's retirement announcement, then timing is a reflection of time. And what is time?

"Often in the heat and excitement of a game," said Brodie to Murphy, "a player's perception and coordination will improve dramatically. At times, and with increasing frequency now, I experience a kind of clarity that I've never seen adequately described in a football story. Sometimes, for example, time seems to slow way down in an uncanny way, as if everyone were moving in slow motion. It seems as if I have all the time in the world to watch the receivers run their patterns, and yet I know the defensive line is coming at me just as fast as ever. I know perfectly well how hard and fast those guys are coming, and yet the whole thing seems like a movie or a dance in slow motion. It's really a beautiful thing."

It was fascinating to read an account of how you perceived situations and gained a sensation of the slow motion of things.

As one is keyed in, time has no presence.

Of course, because of what you do, your thoughts on this have been expressed in terms of football. But does this kind of thinking apply to any field of specialization?

It applies to anything where your abilities are channeled in one specific direction, to where you're able to get them all focused. If you have one hundred attention units, and to the degree you can get all one hundred of them applied to the project you're involved with at a specific time, obviously you feel no time consideration. If time is only a consideration, it doesn't really have any hold on you at that particular moment. Things seem to slow down occasionally. I can remember vividly everything that happens in certain instances. It's not transcendental. It's just something that happens.

We're told we have complete dreams in the period of ten seconds.

Sure.

But does the way you're expressing it here presuppose that you'd be pretty good at what you're doing?

Well, let me put it this way. I don't know if it is presupposed. I think everyone who has the ability to put himself totally into a situation has a better chance of being good at what he's doing. And I think it's a prerequisite to being able to play well.

Play anything.

Yes. Play well — or do well.

What relationship does this have — in football, of course, but not only in football — to the qualities either of fear or apprehension?

Well, obviously if all your attention units are applied to what you're doing, fear and apprehension are a consideration *about* what you're doing, so there would be no fear or apprehension. The whole attention is geared on the doing.

In other words, in your case, the fear of a blind-side sack or tackle . . .

Let me put it like this: Everyone has a different viewpoint of that. And, as I said a minute ago, if you have one hundred attention units, and three or four of them are being applied to the fear of the situation, maybe six or seven are being applied to the apprehension, maybe five of them are being applied to "What happens if I do well?" or "What are the fans thinking?" — maybe they could be applied to the importance of the event itself. And to the degree that you take attention units from what you're actually doing, you're not as able to do what you're in the act of doing.

In your case, how much of a problem does that prove to be? Do you find that you are taking the attention from what you're doing?

Oh, I just feel that to the degree I have to think about it, I'm not doing what I want to be doing. This is just theoretically having taken the situation apart, and in effect, that's what happens . . .

In effect, you're looking back on it now . . .

Yes, and — have you ever heard a guy say to himself *"Concentrate!"*? Well, that's an admission he can't, or he's not. I don't sit around and say, "How'm I doing at this now, let's see, I'll put myself outside my body here and check it out; I'll see how well I'm concentrating." I just go do it. All your practice and all your preparation is geared to getting you to the point where you can just go do it.

You expressed some feelings along these lines in connection with the chess match of Bobby Fischer and Boris Spassky in the summer of 1972. Perhaps those two men had a great sense of the same thing you're discussing.

Probably. Both their awareness levels are very high.

Yes, but all the commotion Fischer was making on the outside was one thing . . .

Sure. The gamesmanship that took place before those matches could possibly have been to

San Francisco rookies Jim Ridlon, a safetyman from Syracuse, and John Brodie, arrived at training camp in July, 1957, with their wives and youngsters (left). The baby in Brodie's arms is his daughter, Kelly. An All-America quarterback at Stanford University, Brodie was named most valuable player in the East-West Game (below) and was, also, a star player on the Stanford golf team (right).

get his opponent's attention units in other directions, and to the degree that he was successful in doing that, he had an edge, or felt he did. It does apply to that situation.

Yes. But you also got the feeling that Fischer himself wasn't having to say to himself, "Concentrate!"

No. He had it all there.

How *frequent* a phenomenon is this? Obviously, it's there all the time, but how frequently does it have meaning for you? You say that things, for instance, can play themselves in slow motion. How frequently does . . .

Oh, I don't say it happens all the time. This is strictly a philosophical discussion.

In the *Intellectual Digest* article you said that you had it in that pass that won the game for the division title in 1972.

Yes, but I don't relate to it in that way. I don't say, "I had it there — oh, good, I had it there." I was just talking theoretically.

But you did talk specifically afterwards.

No, because I had spoken about it before that. I'm just saying the whole purpose is to get where you are right now and be doing the thing you're doing with all your attention on it.

Do you think this has some function in controlling physical condition or physical injury?

I really don't know. I hadn't given it a whole bunch of thought. You know, there's no reason for anyone to have his attention on anything other than what he's doing right then and that's as sane as you can be.

There are always ways to improve the areas where you're having trouble, if you're letting things affect you that you should be having no concern with. You can improve that. There's no reason to worry about how we do, or the importance of an event, or what have you. You're supposed to just go out and do it.

That's really, I think, the responsibility of the coaching staff. That's what they mean when

Three of the four men who coached the 49ers during John Brodie's career were Frankie Albert (left, walking past rookie quarterback Brodie on the sideline in 1957); Jack Christiansen (right, with Brodie and Bill Kilmer); and Dick Nolan (far right, with Brodie). The fourth coach during Brodie's career was Red Hickey, who is not shown.

they say "Get them ready to play," "Get them up," right? In essence what you're really saying is you're getting them all heading in one specific direction so each individual will be able to go do his thing on that given day, as well as he can.

How do you relate this to bad moments — to things that don't go well? What happens when you are intercepted four times in a game, or something?

Well, to the degree that you postulate, bad moments happen. There are certain amounts of risk involved in whatever decision you make to go ahead and do something. Hell, it's not something I pay a whole lot of attention to. After it's over, I'll look specifically at why something happened that I hadn't planned, and I generally find the reason. But if I went off half-cocked and threw everything into one category as to how these things "always" happen, I'd *compound* the problem. I wouldn't be attacking it at its real source. So I just let those things take their due course, and I look at each specific situation as a single situation. If something went wrong, I correct it. That's my way.

You've also mentioned the degree of unspoken communication with certain teammates. You talked, for example, about Gene Washington as a receiver.

You see, that doesn't come into the area of being far out, or . . .

It seems that way.

. . . or difficult to understand. I'll tell you how it happens: two people sit down and discuss situations, and to the degree they both understand each other's thinking about these situations as they develop on a football field, you can almost predict the reactions of the other fellow. To a degree that seems almost totally predictable, you can do things that appear psychic to an observer.

If, say, I know the position of two defensive backs in a particular game, if I'm prepared to

see that picture, and if when I do I know what reaction the receiver will take, then I don't have to wait until he reacts to throw the ball. I anticipate his reaction. To the degree that receivers and quarterbacks do this, discuss it, and are aware of the different possibilities of defensive structure, they can take advantage of it when it comes up. They don't have to regroup after they've seen this new picture and try to figure out a way to handle it. They've already seen what happens.

And when you talk about the possibilities of defensive structure, you are including the personnel on the defense.

Sure. Every aspect of them.

The habits, and . . .

Habits and tendencies, as far as the defense it concerned. Just being there, just being able to play that game at that given time, takes into consideration a lot of abilities, confidence, and freedom for the receiver to do what he sees he should do, so he can do it without a real conscious thought. He sees a picture and he moves. I see the picture and I react to it the same way he does. David Parks and I had a very good understanding in that area, and every receiver that I've ever really been effective with, has had that same communication. That is what I mean by "non-verbal." We might call a pattern, but the way we both react to the picture we see is the measure of whether we will be successful or not.

And this understanding doesn't come about in a far out way either.

Of course not. It comes from looking at defenses together, from my understanding of his viewpoint of the best way to beat the particular picture he sees. It all boils down to your knowledge of your subject.

On to your knowledge of another subject; What is your account of the time you called Lou Spadia from Houston, and the situation as it was and as it finally panned out.

Okay. What happened was I was contacted by Don Klosterman of Houston, who said, "Come on down here. We're passing out dough pretty freely, and we'd like to have you play in the American Football League."

My contract had ended at that stage. And I'd just had my best year, in 1965. So I told Bill Johnson, our line coach at the time – I just wanted to make sure that he knew; he was in charge of the offense – that I was going down there. Then I told Jack Christiansen, the head coach, and Lou Spadia. I said, "I'll get back to you, but I'm going down."

When I got down there, there was a lot of discussion. A contract was offered for something like two-hundred-and-fifty thousand per year for three years, and that was more money than I could realistically dream of making, so I told the Houston people, "It sounds fine, but I want you to know that no matter what figure you state, I'm going to call Lou and give him an opportunity to match it. If he matches it, I'll stay home. And I'll give him x amount of time to do so. And at the end of that time, I'll consider myself, however it stands, their property."

So that's how it worked out. They offered me x amount; I phoned Lou and told him about the deal; then whatever happened was like, you know, history.

Now, the merger; somehow the leagues got together quickly, and the next day the AFL was trying to get out of what they'd already promised me. Hell, I'd considered it a contract – whichever team worked it out. I'd already put myself in the position of making a decision as to how it would work. I had accepted the Houston offer tentatively, dependent on the reaction of the 49ers. Then the 49ers tried to say there was no contract, which to me didn't make sense. So I just left it, and it just came to be that the 49ers finally signed me. When I first went to camp, nobody took it very seriously. I didn't

– I knew that I had already put myself in a position of accepting something that they had offered, and there was no more negotiation as far as I was concerned. That was the whole consideration as far as my holding out, because I wasn't holding out.

I just said, "Well, wait a minute – I already have a contract. Where I play, that's your problem. But I definitely would *like* to play in San Francisco, and you guys see what you want to do about it." The rest of the information will have to come from the other side, because I don't know what transpired there. But I do know I finally played.

And when you finally got to training camp . . .

I got fined. That was really the only part I couldn't understand. But it never became a very serious thing from my viewpoint. It was simply a matter of that was the way it was.

And all this happened just when the leagues decided to merge.

Yes. It was misinterpreted a lot because some people had answers to subject matter that didn't even apply. I just left. I never did make a statement concerning it, and it worked out. I had nothing to hide, so there was no problem as far as I saw it.

Well, there are people who point to you and say you were one of the comparatively few who went through a question of which league it would be, without any real effect on you as a result.

I don't see where there should have been. I'm a professional football player, and although I've lived in San Francisco or the Bay area all my life, I had made a decision. Obviously, I preferred to play in San Francisco, but the fee was just too big. I didn't see any way I could justify my not earning what had been offered.

And really, the game is something that has nothing to do with how much you make. Sometimes people have said, "Hey, you make x

Severe stress is inherent to the business of playing quarterback in the National Football League. Two of the best pass rushers to charge Brodie during his NFL career were Carl Eller of the Minnesota Vikings (left) and Gino Marchetti of the Baltimore Colts.

amount of dollars, and therefore you should give us *x* amount of product." Well, that might be true in some areas, where your product depends on your time invested, but when it depends on your ability to perform in a certain time period, any time they say you should be playing commensurate with your pay, hell, they're saying that you're not putting out one hundred percent all the time. All a football player can do is play as well as he can play and prepare himself to play that way. Whether you make ten dollars a game or ten thousand should have very little to do with your preparation.

Of course, that's true of most professions. You hear people ask, "Why does so-and-so get three million dollars to make one movie?"

Simply because people will pay. The supply and demand theory works out that way.

Criticism of that kind has never particularly affected you.

It never has. I don't find it to be sane or logical, so I cannot really involve myself in it. That's the only final reward you have — the degree to which you're not affected by things that really don't have to affect you unless you let them. If you know where *you* are, then you've got nothing to hide, nothing to be affected by.

How much abuse from the stands can you hear in football?

You can hear it on occasion, depending on how close they are and how dedicated they are to making sure you hear them. If you're not playing, you hear it, like when I've been injured. You can hear certain abuses, but you should be able to laugh at that. They're there — they're an effect of what you're doing. To the extent you do something well, they're going to applaud; and to the degree you don't, they're certainly entitled to do all the yelling and booing they like.

But how about the abusive fan — and there is such a breed — the kind of people who show up

and get on you for the wrong reason, or for no reason?

That's okay. It would be sad if all people thought the same way. There are going to be people who dislike me for whatever reason, and they're free to do so, as long as they do it in a stadium. There are personal areas where it's not acceptable, but in a football stadium, I think a guy is entitled to say whatever he wants. You're never going to change the way he feels.

Talking about the concentration factor, and how you "come down" from a game after it's finished; people get "up" for games too. What would happen if you were preparing for a game that meant a lot, and for some reason it rained so hard or snowed so badly that it was put off one day.

It's never happened to me. But I don't look at it that way, because I don't consciously gear myself to peak on game day. My system takes care of that. I don't sit and second-guess whether or not I'm ready, I don't have a checklist on which I say, "Okay: I went to the bathroom . . . I can tell I'm nervous, so I'm ready . . . I'm talking faster . . . I know all my plays." I just go and prepare to play.

Before a game, I may find myself going over situations that I expect might develop, but it's all geared to the actual performance itself. It's not "Am I ready?" or "I am ready." I just assume it will take care of itself. I feel good, usually right before, and I expect to, that's all. I don't try to program myself into some unreal condition. I don't want to get into some unreal state. There are times when I actually feel like going to sleep.

Then possibly your pregame state of mind might change from game to game.

I really don't think much about it. I've seen guys sit there and try to make judgment on whether we're up or whether we're not up for a game. I've seen guys walk in looking like

they're crippled and play good football, and I've seen guys jumping and ready and then play horrible football. I've seen too many different things happen on a football field, and it all relates to how well you play when you're out there, not how you feel before. It only relates to what's going on.

What you've just said goes against an awful lot of sports literature.

I agree. It goes against a great deal of what's been stated, like — if you ever took it apart, a lot of that "getting up" — ooh! You just get ready. If that's what they mean by that, fine.

I'm talking about the position I play too. Situations fluctuate so swiftly you have to be there all the time. You must be ready.

The more you know, the more able you'll be, and the better you'll feel about your preparation. I don't see any reason to feel uptight.

Then what about this business of momentum?
Ol' Mo?

Ol' Mo.

Well, success breeds success. That's worth stating. To the degree a team is winning, you find an awful lot of positive viewpoints. The feeling of confidence in one another and in yourself increases to where you're much less susceptible to allowing something detrimental to impair it. One or two bad breaks or incidents does not affect a team that's winning.

And that's what momentum is. You don't overcome bad breaks. You just ignore them. It's just "Next play, folks, let's go."

And they know, if they have confidence in themselves, it's like throwing crap at the wall — some of it's going to stick.

So momentum is not being affected by what the other team does, or what some outside agent, like a referee, might call; or by a ball hitting a goal post. There are a lot of things that can happen in a football game, and to the degree that you don't allow them to take you off your own course, then, that's what momentum is.

But here, when you talk momentum, you're talking about the action on the field, not the state of mind of the players in the clubhouse before the game.

Right. Right.

In terms of momentum, how would you define what happened when Franco Harris caught that pass off the guy's helmet in the Oakland-Pittsburgh game.

I'd call that damned luck; what would you call it? There's nothing to do when that happens. School's out. The game's over. All you can say is, it shouldn't affect the Raiders the next season, and it didn't. They're a mature group.

And of course, that doesn't happen very often.

If it does, you send for the witch doctor.

On the subject of what games mean to Oakland, Lou Spadia was talking about that 38–7 game in 1970, and how some people claimed that game didn't mean very much to the Raiders, since they'd already clinched their division.

I don't buy that. When we've played Oakland, we've played very competitive ball games. We've had great football games with Oakland — look at the scores. All our games have been active, and I don't buy the fact that they didn't care that much.

Once the game is over it's a pretty philosophical statement to make that it didn't mean anything to them. Well, if a team isn't concerned about how important it is for them to win before they decide how important it is for them to play hard, you've got a team that isn't any good to start with. They'll seldom get into a position where they *have* an important game, because they don't understand what the game is about in the first place. Oakland definitely is not that way.

They do understand . . .

You bet your life. They're out there to play their best, and I know for a fact that John Madden was very concerned *after* the game, because

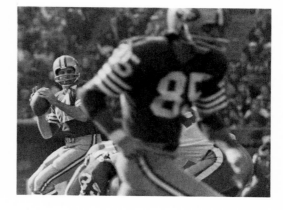

San Francisco's string of three years in a row in the playoffs began with a 1970 postseason game at Minnesota. Brodie sneaked one yard for the winning touchdown (left) in a 17-14 victory. The streak ended in 1972, when the 49ers were defeated 30-28 by Dallas. After a remarkable comeback by Dallas, Brodie's own comeback failed (right, he sets to pass as number 85, Preston Riley, starts his route).

of his team's performance. Whether it was our outstanding performance or their under-par performance, it certainly didn't roll off their backs like, "Well, next week it'll be different." No team ever wants to be beat. If they do, their team isn't good enough to win consistently.

To the extent that you can pick one game over another, was that 49ers-Raiders game among the most memorable? You had a good game in the rain that day.

We won thirty-eight to seven. Yes. I remember that one vividly. I'd played fourteen years and we hadn't won a championship, and it got down to where we had to beat Oakland in order to win it.

Now, you can't tell me that Oakland didn't want to beat us. And I think the conditions that existed could be stated to have had more effect on our players than theirs.

But your stake was . . .

That's exactly my point. Who's to say how you should do it? They should be free and loose and have a go at it. Generally, when a team is that way, they're playing better football.

But for some reason, *we* seemed to play that way that day. And it was terrific. It was fun.

But the stake: It was a game you had to win, because you already knew the Rams had won.

All right. That spells out what I am already saying. But that same thing happened three years in a row: 1970, '71, '72. When we played Detroit the last game in '71 — I think *that* was the most memorable for me.

Why?

Because we came back. Everyone had counted us out. We'd lost to L.A. We'd lost to them, our prime division opponent, six times out of six, or five out of six, in those three years, and we still won our division every year. To do it, we had to win the last game every year.

And when we played Detroit, they were a tough football team, and they were really play-

ing well. So were we. And that was as good a game as we could have played. We'd fallen a game and a half back with two to play. Then L.A. lost two and we won two. Or maybe we were half a game back with two to play, but they had a cinch game, and they lost it.

What about the games you didn't win? The games where you got in front, like the playoff with Dallas in '72?

That was a bad situation. There's no way you're supposed to lose a game when it's twenty-eight to sixteen with two minutes to play.

Do you incline to play those back in your mind?

No, I really don't too much. I've heard several times . . . well, here's a typical example of fan reaction: People would say you played too conservatively in the last few minutes. It's a half-true statement. We did play conservatively. But play *too* conservatively? There's a difference between conservative and *too* conservative.

That has to do with your thought process, like what play are you going to use. You're going to use a play that has a very low margin of error involved in it, so your chance of having the ball turned over is very small. The best teams in the National Football League over the years have had conservative offenses — look at Washington and Green Bay.

However, they were *aggressive,* and we might not have been as aggressive as we might have been. But it didn't have to do with being too conservative.

If someone was out there throwing the ball all over when it's twenty-eight to sixteen, with two-and-a-half minutes to play, I would have him examined.

When I look back on it, I don't say, "Yeah, I should have done it this other way." We did it exactly the way I saw fit, and I think the rest of our staff was in agreement. We didn't play conservatively throughout the game, but we did in

the last six or seven minutes. And I don't sit and second-guess that.

There's another favorite fan word: "complacency." And not just a fan word. Players, like Joe Perry, have something to say about it.

No quarrel there. Complacency is something that's not good in any area. But it has nothing to do with conservatism. A conservative tone in a person is not a bad quality. Maybe it states that you're trying to preserve something that you have. But "complacent" is, like, unconcerned.

Well, would you charge complacency to what happened to you in the Dallas game?

Oh, no. Not at all. People who said that would have to give a definition of complacent — they'll find one right in the dictionary. I disagree heartily with anyone who said we felt complacent. If they would check our systems at that time I think they would have found to the contrary.

This can contrast with some things Perry said, but there's agreement on one point: The other team has a little bit to do with it.

It's a funny game. That's what makes it wonderful. There are two sides to these games, and both sides are very competitive. The game has a very high action level, because both teams are composed of very up-tone people, and are high directed. And I wouldn't attach a low tone to the team that got beat. I'd just give the other team credit.

Does that lead to a focus from the broad outlook? Have you ever given serious thought to saying, "This is my last season?"

At the end of every year I think I've had enough. For a while. But I think the action of the game itself — I'm doing something I really enjoy — and know — and I just haven't found any alternative that can measure up to the satisfaction a guy can gain from football. I mean, it's really a *fun — fun* — game, for the participants. And so the thought never lingers long. Everyone has to decide how long he can play, but I

just get in there and play. I hope that I'll be prepared to do something of my choice when I quit.

I'm not dependent on this game, at this stage, for my standard of living. But I like it, and I'm glad they pay us.

And when you've been injured, have you wondered . . .

How long I'd be able to go? No. I never had any doubts about that, because I was never injured to the degree where I thought, "Wow, no way." I was a little concerned when I got hurt in 1972, because of the severity of the injury — a broken ankle. Obviously it would have impaired me. At thirty-seven or thirty-eight it might have been a little tougher. But it feels like it's okay now, so I really don't dwell on things like that very often.

Do you dwell on other things, such as your own specific ability? Have you ever been told that you have extra-peripheral vision?

I've got good peripheral vision. I know about what's going on most of the time. But it has to do with awareness rather than actual physical seeing ability.

It does?

Oh, sure. People will relate peripheral vision to someone who throws the ball over here having been looking over there, and actually, the reason he's throwing it over here is he sees a picture one place which dictates his throwing the ball another place. Well, once you see this picture and get yourself properly disciplined, you know that when something happens here, you go there. You don't sit and say, "Wait a minute, what do I do?"

You've seen quarterbacks freeze with the ball, and people say they just don't have the peripheral vision. Most of it has to do with the way they discipline themselves before the situation develops, so that when it does develop, they can react. You often see basketball players the same way. I don't think it has to do much with the

physical ability to *see* as it does with the ability to *see something* and have it tell you something, and be able to react to it favorably.

Otto Graham was quite a basketball player in college, but there are very few sports fans who remember him as such.

Sure. Or look at Cousy, or Walt Frazier — all these great guards related to the same quality. They know enough about what's going on to know what has to be somewhere else. I guess people relate this to "peripheral vision."

But isn't it a fact that physically there are some people who actually have such vision, more than others?

Oh, sure. But I'm curious as to the relationship between the ability to see and the awareness of the situation at the same time. I've seen some guys who can't see a wall in front of them — Tittle couldn't see *at all,* but he seemed to know where the hell the ball was going.

Would you say the worst combination is no peripheral vision and no awareness?

Well, I grant you don't have much going for you.

Excluding Tittle and those you have played with, what quarterbacks do you rate most highly?

It's hard. You know so many qualities are involved in what you see as the product of a quarterback. The structure of the offense, the teammates around him, his ability to do what he sees fit to do.

Some guys are bound by the structure of their offense. You'll assume a guy doesn't have an ability that he actually has, because of a predetermined decision, about how he is to operate. Norm Snead's a perfect example: He has outstanding ability, but until he went to New York he never had the offense, the whole structure that would implement his ability. Because of that, and some discipline that he had not had before, his ability level seemed to rise consid-

erably in 1972. He was still the same guy — it was just that they were starting to use his abilities.

You take the guys who have done well, consistently, over a long period of time, and all those guys are really outstanding quarterbacks. But I wouldn't pick a "best," because they're all so different. Oftentimes, you hear that, to be a good quarterback, you have to be over six-two, or weigh so much, but I don't think physical limitations are very severe at all for a guy playing quarterback.

The guys I think are the best — like Unitas, Starr, Namath, Hadl, Gabriel, Tarkenton . . . and others — are all different physically, and they all approach the game a little differently. But the best ones are the guys that use their abilities to the fullest. They find out what they can do best, and they get their offense tuned to that. They find out what other players can do best, and they get a lot of production out of them.

Do you have any moments you recall in particular?

Well, the first game that I played. That was my most exciting moment. It was against Baltimore in 1957. I hadn't played a play all year and with about thirteen seconds left . . . or about thirty-five seconds left . . . Tittle came off hurt. And all I could think to do was laugh.

Laugh?

Just looking at the situation I was in. We were behind thirteen to ten and a field goal does not help us. We have to win the game to tie Detroit. I was thinking, "How in the hell could I be put in this position?"

We were on their fifteen-yard line. I threw one pass, and the defensive back almost choked Billy Wilson. So that went incomplete. The next pass was to McElhenny, and I didn't even see it. He told me where he'd be, and I saw a little something going out there, so I just put it there. He caught it, and everything went nuts. So I

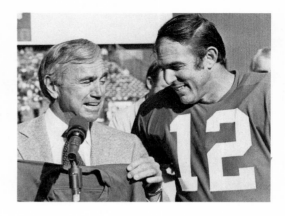

knew then that something big had happened.

That was pretty exciting, because we'd never done that much. It was a pretty emotional year. Tony Morabito had died in the stands during a game, and . . . well, it was . . . I can remember a whole series of incidents that led up to my playing. I remember walking into the huddle and saying, "Well, has anybody got anything?"

Did anybody?

McElhenny.

What'd he say?

"Just throw me the ball." That's the way it worked. Very complex.

Didn't "game plan" used to mean what the players were going to do after the game, and "loss of communication" meant somebody dropped the ball?

Right. It still is a loss of communication, from what I see. Where there has to be so much duplication of statement in order to get a very simple point across, oftentimes it's because the guy doesn't understand the whole situation himself. He has to use a lot of confusion to try to illustrate a point.

Depending on how well you know the subject, there are things that happen, but when you stay on top of them they come up automatically. The techniques and what have you are just evolved improvements in the game.

There's a lot more attention in that direction than there used to be. There used to be certain givens, that you just assumed were true. The coach says we'll do it, so we'll do it. But this has been taken apart. I think the guys who play the game are asking "Why" more than they used to.

I don't think the game itself has changed. They still have eleven people; the sidelines are the same width; the length of the field is the same; I think the makeup of the players is pretty much the same. They may be a little more worldly because of acceptance outside of the game itself. They may be more involved in their own community because of the exposure. But the makeup of the players is still pretty similar.

What about the idea that the greatest change in the game has come about because of the amount of playing you can do now with two minutes left?

That's funny, because we used to do that in 1957. Tittle was the master.

Oftentimes, a team will get into a situation where maybe five or six games are determined by what happens in the last two minutes. And when that happens, the outcome of that game is going to dictate what people think of that guy's ability to move the ball.

And Tittle — well, in '57 we won five games in the last minute. They can say he was a master at using the clock. But what he really did was throw the s.o.b. fifty yards in the air, way down in the endzone. Then R. C. Owens jumped up and grabbed the thing.

Well, that can be related to theory. It can be related to anything you want. Or just plain super-execution by two people, right? And even though Tittle was good at doing this, he was always good at thorough preparation — at trying to figure out what's going to happen before the game starts.

And anybody who can move the ball in the last two minutes has to do that. This whole deal, where you throw the ball to the sideline, or where there are certain ways you *have* to do it is nonsense. The people who do that go broke because they're the guys that read the books and say, "Yeah, I guess that's what I'm supposed to do."

Well, what you do is, you take apart a team's defenses and the variations they use in the last two minutes. You try to apply one simple, good thought to each defense, where you can be right and they can't be.

That seems very complicated, because you may hit one of four or five receivers on each

Brodie called it a career December 15, 1973, as the 49ers played the Pittsburgh Steelers at Candlestick Park. Former 49ers quarterback and coach Frankie Albert emceed a ceremony honoring Brodie (left). Later, he left the field for the last time after 17 years in the uniform of the San Francisco 49ers (below).

play, and they all might be different. But the pattern's probably the same. If you have one good solid pattern, that's all you need. As long as they're playing that defense, you're going to use that pattern. So it looks complex. But what happens is a guy runs out, and just before the ball's snapped, he says, "I got it — watch me." You take a look at what their defense is and apply a simple little offense to it.

You can take care of all those situations. It's just the quarterbacks using a little good sense in what they're calling, using their time outs properly and not making a big, confused deal of it.

It's important to keep everybody relaxed, too, to get them back and tell them what to do before the ball's snapped. I think we use the ball well in the last couple of minutes. We do so because the guys who can run formations get in it.

I'll call whatever I see fit at the time. It might be at the line of scrimmage. It might be in the huddle. But don't worry about it. I'll take care of it. I don't want any sage advice in the last two minutes from a guy who says, "I think if I go down here and run about six extra yards . . ."

No. Just do what we're accustomed to doing — and do it the right way.

I'm paid for this, and if I don't do it the right way, I can tell. When I walk off the field, I can hear it. But this is the 49ers we're talking about. I've only played here, and I can't think of a place where I'd have been as happy. I can't think of a better situation for a guy than to be playing in San Francisco.

Charlie Krueger

Position: Defensive Tackle
Years: 1959-
Height: 6-4
Weight: 268
College: Texas A&M

Even with the recognition to "the men in the trenches" that has come in professional football's maturity, there remains the element of some being better than others. The typical fan is likely to cite the position of defensive left tackle as most important — and not without reason. Since football players, like other people, are essentially a right-handed breed, the right side of an offensive formation has come to be known as the "strong side." The power goes in that direction, and it is the task of the defense to meet that irresistible force with an immovable object.

Such objects have been celebrated: Alex Karras, Merlin Olsen, Alan Page, and, without much question, the "pro's pro" — Charlie Krueger of the San Francisco 49ers.

"Krueger is exceptionally solid, exceptionally strong," wrote Jerry Kramer, who had to play against him. "When he was drafted by the 49ers ten years ago someone predicted he'd outlast three or four coaches, and he's outlasted three already... (He) beats on you unmercifully... gives you headaches and neck pains. Charlie's especially tough on running plays. It's almost impossible to move him, and he almost always gets a piece of the ball carrier."

Krueger was an All-America lineman at Texas A&M. So was his "baby brother," Rolf Krueger, who came to the 49ers in 1972 after playing out his option with the St. Louis Cardinals, an event which led to amusing charges of collusion.

For a teammate, you have a "baby brother" who weighs more than two-hundred fifty pounds . . .

This is Rolf's fifth year and my sixteenth year. So we're ten, eleven years apart. When I left high school he was in first grade. 'Course, when I saw him drafted out of college by St. Louis — the first couple of years were happy years for him. He played and did well. Their

situation wasn't really that settled. He developed contract problems, and that perhaps led to other problems. Now he's here.

There's a story around that there was tampering involved, but it turned out you did the tampering, so there wasn't very much anybody could do about it.

Let's get that straight. I mentioned it. I knew that he was playing out his option. I thought about the possible places that he might go. There were a number of clubs that he talked to. But the way Dick Nolan does business here, it makes for a good environment in which to work.

So I went to Nolan or Jack White, I can't remember which, the last part of the season, and I said the guy was going to be looking for a place to work. And nothing was said. Months went by, and it approached the first of May — I believe the first of May is the date on which they can remove — and as it got to the first of May, with never any move on the part of the 49ers, I said, well, I'm going to give it one more shot. I can't know what they're thinking, or planning. They may or may not be interested.

So I went by — this was after the first of May — and I mentioned it to Jack White again, and mentioned the fact that Rolf had been talking to Washington and Detroit and New Orleans and Houston. So Jack said, "Have him come out," which he did, and they signed him. It was perfectly legitimate.

One columnist popped me on this particular thing a year ago — this brother move — and the truth simply is, there was no tampering.

The point is made because people can remember when there was nothing of the kind of fan attention, if that's the word for it, for the lineman that you find today. You saw this change take place.

I got here just as television was making its move. It was about to take off. It was about 1960 that things really began to happen. 'Course, in

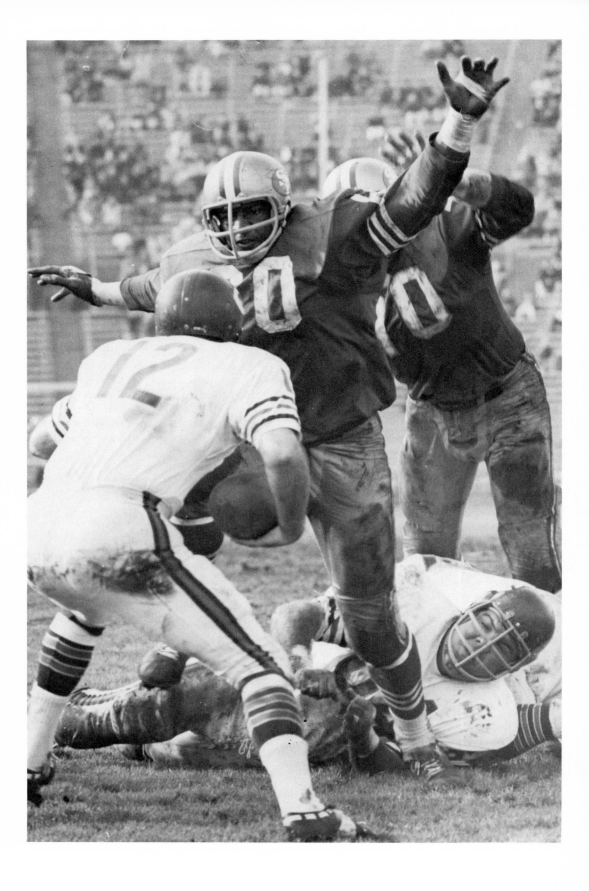

Tackle Roland Lakes (left) and linebacker Matt Hazeltine (right, pulling Detroit quarterback Milt Plum to the ground) were durable teammates of Charlie Krueger on the San Francisco defense during the 1960s.

those days, the coaching staffs were smaller, the scouting staffs were smaller, and the tickets cost much less. The total budget, I imagine, for a club was nothing like what it is today, nor the total income. There's a lot more involved. They're a lot more businesslike, rather than sportslike, about it today, which is certainly reasonable to me. And I was here to see the change from one to the other. The fan today is exposed to the Saturday afternoon commentaries, NFL what-do-you-call it . . .

Previews?

The previews, the countdowns, the inform-the-wives, educate-the-public, the great exposure. This created stimuli and caused a reaction in the fans. So there's been learning.

You're talking about exterior elements. In the game itself, a lineman then had basically the same job he has today.

Yes, the lineman has basically the same job. It's a game of territory control, or territory achievement, or you can go to the anthropologists and use the old terms, but they're a hell of a lot more complicated. They do a lot of stuff today that they didn't do then. I'd need a blackboard and about three days. No, really, I can't answer that question, except to say that there are more and more refined techniques. But it's the same game. There are people who played then who could play today and any time, ever.

But there's a greater body of acquired knowledge now.

And a larger number of able, capable people.

Then for you, it's actually been a learning process too.

Continuous.

In your judgment, how many seasons would it take for a lineman with some talent to bring that talent to its maximum output?

Well, there are exceptions . . . I'm looking for examples . . . Carl Eller is one, and Alan Page —

they came on fast and did well, with their exceptional ability. For the lineman with average ability, it takes you — if you've got a decent system — say, two or three years in a good situation.

When you say territory control . . .

That's a defensive term.

It *is* a defensive term, and . . .

I also said territory *achievement*. Does that communicate?

It does, but to narrow it down: Does it mean just where the ball is on the field, or does it also mean what charge you take of your own territory?

Well, the ball is simply an object, just a point. You play with a bunch of rules. If you'd all agree on a magic spot, you wouldn't need to have a ball.

All right. The ball is snapped at the line of scrimmage, and you're in action on the play. Do you relate to the ball or to your territory?

First to my territory. Then the ball.

And you relate also to your teammates on either side of you.

Sure. You're coordinated.

Then how much of a plus is it to be playing alongside men you've been playing with for some time, so you're used to them?

Large. But a good coach is the first thing. He can make the communication good among the players, as well as the communication between you and *him*. So it's a plus to be playing with people you can communicate with easily, or to a higher degree of proficiency.

In the defensive huddle, do you . . .

Our middlebacker calls 'em.

Just signals, or is there conversation?

There's very little communication that doesn't relate to business. Be direct with it and be quick, and let him get down to calling it. If it's relevant, well . . . but if it ain't pertinent to the situation, just forget it. Shut up. You may be discussing

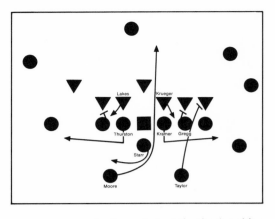

some crap you don't need. And they're breaking their huddle and coming out and you're waiting for a call, you're in trouble. Just get your business done and get out.

But if you notice something, you want to bring it up.

Oh, yeah. You want to notice. Everything they do — adjust, cheat, whatever. They've got a reason for everything they do — either that, or they're poorly coached. If they're poorly coached, you're in pretty good shape. And if you can see what they're doing and know what it means, you're in pretty good shape, too.

Can you give an example of a situation where you found somebody on the other side doing something wrong?

Well, usually it's not when they're doing something *wrong*. Instead, it's when they're doing something deliberately to help cause a play to be more effective.

They can adjust or split, or the back can cheat up. Or maybe it's the way they come up to the line of scrimmage and get set. It might indicate a first count. If it does, then it gives you a slight edge.

The guy that's doing something wrong isn't the general situation, because you don't have too many guys who do a lot wrong. Usually, it's by design and coaching that they have all these arrangements and rearrangements, and it takes a little time to know that these things mean something — even to *see* 'em.

Like, there are certain teams, and certain situations . . . they can line up on the ball, and I can tell if the snap is on the first sound. I just know. It takes a while to be able to know. There are certain times during a game, if they have a particular play that they've run against you, when you get a feeling that they're going to run it. You don't do this a hell of a lot of the time, but you do it enough for there to be something to it.

This has to go for individuals as well as teams, doesn't it? Over all the years you've been playing, you must have a certain "feel" for players you're up against.

Oh, yes.

Who are some of them?

Unfortunately, most of them are gone. John Gordy . . . Jerry Kramer . . . Joe Scibelli . . . Jim Cadile. I knew them, knew them personally, knew their style of play. So on a given day you could tell pretty much. And they in turn would know you.

Well, that's what Karras always said — learning from each other . . .

Karras was a fine, fine rusher. They talk about a lot of other people, but maybe it's our age group and we tend to remember them best. But Karras was just a hell of a pass rusher.

Among the defensive linemen . . .

Well, there you go right back to . . . Deacon Jones. There are a lot of good ones. We've had fine ones here: Hart and Hardman and Edwards. But you go Alan Page and Carl Eller and those guys; Merlin Olsen and Deacon Jones. Oakland's defensive line, *collectively,* has been great. I think they sacked the quarterback sixty-seven times last year. Bob Lilly is a fine *football* player. Not just pass rush, but everything.

By the time you came into the league it was completely specialized, wasn't it?

It was specialized. You played one way.

Do you pick up much value in watching the films before a game?

Sure.

The films of the other team?

They're necessary. Very necessary.

What about the films of yourself?

Well, you want to see certain situations. Sometimes you don't understand exactly what happened in a particular instance, or in several. Sometimes you start developing habits, little things that grow. And if you don't pay atten-

tion to them from week to week, all of a sudden you can see yourself getting into bad habits. It's a form of discipline.

Can you recollect one such habit of your own?

Well, mine are more individual instances. Usually I understand what's happening, but sometimes I don't understand why things didn't work on a certain play. I want to see the film for that reason.

Can you think of an instance?

I can give you a good one. Green Bay ran a double iso on us one time . . .

Double iso?

Double isolation. The guard pulls in front of you to the outside and you react to the play. The isolation is the influence of one guard. Usually they pull the guard behind the center, and the tackle who's a keying tackle — a reading tackle — will follow the influence and be playing across the center's head in pursuit. Then they run the back through the area you've just vacated, virtually untouched, and if the middle backer isn't reacting right, he's good for about from eight to forty or fifty yards or whatever.

We were playing Green Bay a tight ball game —third quarter, the score was like ten-oh or ten-three — and my guard pulled to the outside and I took the key. We were playing a hard-keying defense at that time under a different coach. I got a slight tap from the tackle, as though he were trying to give me the E-G-O picture — that's the Green Bay sweep picture. I really flipped the tackle, I thought, and was on my way out in pursuit.

Then I glanced over my shoulder and saw the ball carrier coming up the middle. He ran thirty-one yards.

How do you remember the exact distance?

Because it was the exact distance to the goal line. It put them out in front seventeen-three or something like that, and the game wound up

seventeen-ten, and that play was the difference in the ball game. It was the turnaround. It was a big play.

When we came off the field the coach asked me what my guard did and I said he pulled outside. Then he asked Roland Lakes and Roland said *his* guard pulled to the outside. The coach looked at both of us and said, "One of you is lying."

And that was the double isolation. Both offensive guards pulled out in opposite directions?

Well, it was the first time, I guess, that that play had ever been run. I don't know — maybe it's been run before, but I'd never seen or heard of it. So we didn't know what had happened.

I went over to Forrest Gregg on our way off the field after the game and said, "Forrest, what was the play?" and he denied any knowledge. He said it was a busted play. So I said, "Don't lie to me, you s.o.b., I'll see it on the film."

We ran the film, and it was a double iso. They simply ran the center at the middle backer and let the fullback break off the side. The backer has to take a side, so they had the fullback take the side opposite the side the backer chose. And he's open and away.

What would happen if you had to play a team tomorrow and they were playing the single wing — they weren't playing the T at all?

Well, we'd probably just line up in a four-three outside and play that for a while. Then we'd look over at the bench, and the coach would decide what to play and we'd just play it. He's probably thought about that.

Actually, San Francisco did a variation of that with the Shotgun. A novel formation.

It *was* a novel formation. And it was wonderful for a while. Then the Bears shot us down.

What thoughts do you have about memorable games over the years?

Well, there are different kinds of memorable games. There are some that are memorable

because you simply lived through them. You
might have been getting your brains kicked out.
There was an exhibition game down in L.A. we
lost forty-five to thirteen. I was in my second
or third year, and I damn near died. That was
a memorable game.

Memorable games. . . . my rookie year, I got a
game ball. We were playing Cleveland, and beat
them twenty-one-twenty in something like zero
or three degrees, and deep snow. *That* was a
memorable game. Beating Washington in the
playoff in 1971. Getting beat by Chicago sixty-
one-twenty in 1965 was a memorable game.

Why that one?

Two reasons: (A) Gale Sayers scored six
touchdowns. (B) I survived. I remember, I
looked up and Matt Hazeltine was saying, "Gee,
it's a good thing we've got them defensed."

There I was talking to Hazeltine. He's dirty
and tired and disgusted, and I was the same. It
was the fourth quarter with about three or four
minutes to go and I was dying . . . humiliated.
Over Hazeltine's shoulder the scoreboard says
they've got sixty-one points. And that's something just as memorable as the best day you
ever had.

One day at Detroit, we beat them forty-nine
to nothing. It was an absolute shutout — they
did nothing right; we did everything right — but
as memorable as that game is, that Bears game
is just as memorable.

**You grew up in a small town with one high
school. What was your motivation then?**

Well, it was in the surroundings and what there
was to do. You either played in the band, or you
went out for football.

Players come from different situations, of
course, but twenty years ago a greater number
had the same common denominator. They came
from the same sort of background, more than
they do today. Probably there's more variety in
the personalities and in the backgrounds of

players in the game of pro football today.

I know that fifteen years ago, Texas produced a great number of professional football players. That state has all but one school of the Southwest Conference in it, so that — like Indiana in basketball or swimming — it was something that people did in that part of the country. Or you can take a state like Arkansas, with the University of Arkansas the only school of note in that entire state. High school and college football are something of great importance down there, simply because there's nothing else to challenge them.

I suppose it is more meaningful for a boy to be accomplished in high school or university sport — especially football — in a state like that. The University of Alabama is another example. So is Louisiana State University.

And in a small high school, in certain areas it's common for the options to be limited, as basketball is in certain parts of the United States. If a fellow with some ability doesn't play basketball in Indiana, I guess he catches a little bit of hell. Same way with football in the southeast and southwest.

It's just simply that you're pushed toward it.

A form of social pressure?

We've been avoiding the phrase "peer group pressure," but that's what we're talking about.

Now, in college, motivation has to do with how well your coach can screw you down psychologically. Let's clarify that: What I meant is how well the coach can adjust your reasoning so that he could put you in a workable, accomplishing, winning program . . . and keep you there and motivate you, by whatever means — by pride, sense of duty, fear, or whatever combination instills in you the idea that you need a college degree, and must further yourself.

And he keeps you there. He is motivating. To me, in college, the main motivator was the coach. 'Course, when you get out of college you're given

some alternatives, and if you're drafted high — probably the best alternative is to play football, if you're thinking strictly of short-term money, and you probably can't think ahead more than five, six, seven years, reasonably.

So you accept football, and you go off on a tangent. And once you're into it, there comes a time when there has to be a motivation other than money, and usually that's pride. Later on, when age begins to be a factor, good coaching and motivation *again* are important. Motivation created by your player-coach relationship. It's necessary, along with pride, to maintaining a workable situation for yourself.

What about the factor — team loyalty is probably the wrong thing to call it — of enjoying the team you're with?

That could be answered in two parts. It's been a long and good association with the 49ers and I appreciate and feel good about my long association with Lou Spadia, Dick Nolan, and the 49ers. I've known a lot of players in the league who didn't have as good a break. That comes down to plain good fortune.

The second thing is: peer pressure again. You do your job as well as you can, for your own self respect and for the respect of the people you work with. You sort of enjoy the camaraderie, the schedule and the situation. But it's a personal thing and certainly not the great motivator.

But is the fact that you are at home with one team — you have a fairly good idea you're not going to be changing teams — a factor in keeping you going from year to year?

Certainly. I have an idea that I'd be here if I was anywhere at all. I don't really care to play anywhere else. I'd damn well like to do as good a job as I can. But this is the only obligation I have. To myself and Mr. Nolan, and Mr. Spadia.

You were talking — before this discussion started — about one player with the Bears. He'd

come to camp year after year, and finally he . . .

Doug Atkins. He'd played for eighteen years, and he finally said it was just the monotony, the repetition, the sheer drudgery of the situation, that drove him away. He is the great exception there. Usually age and other limitations cause you to find your way out or push you out of the game. I'm not at that eighteen-year point yet, but I can understand what he's talking about.

The Bears had the players run a mile the first day in camp.

George Halas used to have them come in and run a mile without a time. You had to run a mile. They'd struggle with it, and we heard about it, and thought it was grossly inhumane.

But today, as you can see in many camps, there are a variety of different requirements — a number of conditions under which they'll have you report in order to be acceptable to their camp — training conditions that are to be met — tests to be met when you report.

In our case, it's a mile and three-quarters against a clock. It varies with other teams. I understand Houston does a variety of different sprints with different times, one back of the other, closely spaced . . .

What is it with the 49ers? A mile and three-quarters in thirteen minutes for a lineman?

Yes, thirteen minutes for a lineman. And there are variations of this physical testing. I don't know how in the hell to discuss it intelligently, but there's a lot of thought put into what they ask of you. It accelerates the program in training camp. There are a lot of other things built into camp that are new. Camps are run a lot more efficiently now than they used to be. Not that camps were wrong then and right now; it's simply a matter of evolution.

But in that evolution, the mile that once seemed inhumane became a mile and three-quarters for you.

That's right, but don't limit it. There was a time when you'd go to camp and wear pads for four or five weeks, then you'd put 'em up. You may have worn them during the week every now and then, then again you might not have had them on for the rest of the season — in practice, that is. Most of the teams didn't wear their pads for practice sessions, unless there was something special they wanted to solve. Now we wear pads everywhere, all the time. It's an understood thing. When you go over to the fieldhouse, it's pads.

Like dressing for an actual game.

We tape and dress just like for a game every day, except for Tuesday, when we go out without pads. But then, the schedules used to be a lot different. There were only twelve games and one playoff game, and so — well, that's a day gone by.

Is it true that in your first game with the 49ers you broke your wrist on the kickoff?

This is the one-thousand thirty-ninth time I've been over that. It's how myths grow. It was the *fourth* exhibition game of my rookie season. I saw my old coach, Frankie Albert, not too long ago, and I stood while he told the story of how it happened in my first game.

But it was my fourth game. We'd played the Browns and the Cardinals and I forget who else . . . the Giants . . . well, it was in the Browns game that I broke it. But I missed my rookie year with a broken arm from that kickoff. Fellow named Billy Reynolds.

He was the man with the ball?

Yes. I haven't been on a kickoff team since. Billy Wilson separated his shoulder in the same game. At that time Billy Wilson had been in the league about eight years and had been all-pro about six years. He laid out for a ball and came down on his shoulder with the back on top of him. So he and I were waiting at the hospital for the doctor to come from the game when Frankie came in and said, "Hi, Billy, how you

feeling, what does it look like?" And they exchanged some conversation. Then he turned around to me and said, "You dumb rookie."

One of Frankie's things was to try to crack people. I came from Bear Bryant's school of life where it was strictly "Yes, sir, no, sir" and — I've told Frank this several times since — if I'd had any more sense my rookie year, he probably would have been able to crack me.

But I didn't know anything but "Yes, sir, no, sir." So actually that was the beginning of my rookie year. I stayed there during the course of the year. I carried towels and oranges at orange breaks. I'd help carry them out and gather up the peelings, and with one arm push Frankie's towel around — with him in it.

But in effect that was his way of being good to me. He kept me alive through the "injured player" phenomenon. A week goes by; two weeks, three weeks. A month goes by, five weeks, and pretty soon you feel that nobody on the club knows you, because they're caught up and involved in something happening on the field and in the meeting rooms.

They might walk by and give you a casual "Hi," but pretty soon it's just "hi" — "Hi" here and a "Hi" there with a lot of misses. And pretty soon you begin wondering, you know, damn . . .

But Frankie kept me alive because never a day went by without me getting a gig, once, twice, or half a dozen times, from Frankie. We've remained friends over the years, and I really appreciate his friendship.

What is it like for you before a game is played? How do you "get up?"

Well, I've always been a nervous-energy type, with energy wasted in anxiety, nervousness or anticipation. It's not good. But there are certain things you can change and certain things you can't, and this is one of them I can't.

Over the years, it's toned down a little bit, but when I wake up the day of a game, it's the first thing I think of. For years, I didn't eat before a game. The last five or six years, I've been able to. I go down and eat at six-thirty or seven in the morning rather than wait until nine o'clock. Maybe bacon and eggs. Steak and potatoes. But just let me eat at six-thirty or seven. Nine o'clock — forget it. I'm not going to be eating.

At eight or eight-thirty I catch a cab and go to the stadium at home or on the road. Chico Norton, our equipment manager, is there, and I get my ankles taped, put on my stockings, pants and T-shirt, and tape my hands; then light a cigarette and sit there and think for a while.

For a long time we had an early group, and after a while we'd start bitching at each other or joking with each other. Then it'd become all bitching and then it would taper off to silence, the closer it got to eleven-fifteen or eleven-thirty.

The alternative wasn't good. It became routine that I would go crazy sitting in a hotel room, waiting for a bus at eleven o'clock to go to the stadium. I'd hurry to get dressed and hurry to get on the field. The hell with that.

Mr. Nolan lets us go to the stadium by cab early. He's never had anyone abuse this privilege, and it is a privilege — because it's a variation from our regular schedule.

Most of the team goes on the bus. There are five or six or seven that go early. And it's worked out so far because no one has gone off to pick up the laundry or anything like that. So I go out there and get ready that way, and usually the nearer you get to kickoff time, it gets you there; You're ready.

How long does it take you to wind back down afterward?

I have a night occasionally where I can be home in bed by eight or nine o'clock. That's only been in the last two or three years. Generally it's twelve or one o'clock. If things are bad — not happening right — I might stay awake all

A gnarled relic of another time, Krueger stood framed in sunlight, watching the Los Angeles Rams break their offensive huddle during a 1973 game. It was his fifteenth NFL season.

night long. I don't like that sort of situation. I really don't enjoy it at all.

What was this about not eating as late as nine o'clock in the morning? Trouble keeping food in the stomach?

It was just that I couldn't eat. I had no appetite, and I was afraid that if I did eat it would bother me. I used to take honey to the game, or dextrose — it's a form of sugar but is much more digestible.

Actually, it's best for you to eat a baked potato — a single baked potato — the morning of a game. The carbohydrate's a hell of a lot better for you than a steak. A steak will make you feel full, happy and satisfied, but a baked potato will give you something you can use.

What about the Raiders game in 1970? Your first division title.

In the mud? Well, there was always something of a rivalry there. They resented us, because in the beginning they had a tough time. Then they became a very good football club, and for awhile they liked to look over their shoulder at us because we weren't doing too well. But above all, it is generally a desired thing to be professional and maybe they weren't always professional.

But they were good. They were a good football team, year in and year out. That game was memorable in that we won it decisively, and it was very critical for us. They had a lot of turnovers that day — six or seven where they lost the ball to us. And you might say that affected the score.

The Minnesota playoff game in 1971 was memorable because we played *consistently*.

It's obvious that you place a great deal of stock in the importance of coaching.

It's the name of the game. You can just look, and you'll see. If you've got it, you've got it.

Gordy Soltau

Position: End, Kicker
Years: 1950-58
Height: 6-2
Weight: 195
College: Minnesota

Gordy Soltau was known flatly as "the best trade the 49ers ever made." In his first year with the 49ers he played two positions not mentioned above, as defensive end and part of the kickoff unit. Working from those two unfamiliar positions, neither of them calculated to put points on the board, he still led the 49ers in scoring that year. In one astonishing 44–17 win over the conference-champion Rams the following season, Soltau — now permanently installed as a pass-catching end — scored 26 points on three touchdown receptions, a field goal, and five extra points. When he retired after only nine years of play, he had scored 644 points and was the third leading scorer in National Football League history in an era when the field goal on fourth down with short yardage was seldom invoked.

Upon his retirement, he became one of the earliest — and most articulate — "color/analysis" broadcasters for television and radio, a position he still fulfills as partner with the 49ers' superb play-by-play sportscaster, Lon Simmons. And Gordon Leroy Soltau remains the club's most sought-after banquet speaker.

He played for Bernie Bierman at Minnesota in the immediate postwar era when the Gophers had the two best ends in the Big Ten. Both won repeated all-conference recognition. "The main difference between them," Bierman told a friend, "is that one of them will never become a coach." He was referring not to Soltau, but to his other end — Bud Grant.

Soltau's college career was delayed by World War II. Enlisting in the Navy in 1942, he became one of the original "frogmen," then worked for the highly-secret OSS for undercover (and underwater) operations that included swims of up to five miles. He was a top baseball pitcher, and one of the few collegians who could play basketball and ice hockey during the same winter season. He did and won varsity letters in both.

But for Soltau, seasons never have been in conflict. Among other things, he serves today as a top executive of Diamond International, the match company, which took over the functions of San Francisco's leading office-supply firm, where Soltau started as a salesman.

The message is unmistakable: He was — is — football's man for all seasons, and his recollections reflect it.

If somebody started you off with one of those who-was-the-greatest questions, what would . . .

Hugh McElhenny.

Well, what was it that *made* him? His talent? His love for the game?

Both and neither. His enthusiasm — his love for the game — was obvious. And his talent was obvious, too.

What other qualities come to mind when you discuss McElhenny?

Well, the first would be Hugh's great self-confidence. The first time he got his hands on a football in a professional game, he ran it in sixty yards for a touchdown. I don't know who that surprised, but I know it didn't surprise him.

What was the other quality?

His refusal to complain.

Complain about what?

What the other team was doing to him. Don't you think he was a marked man?

But there are marked men today — O.J. Simpson . . . Larry Brown . . . Mercury Morris . . .

Yes. And all of them benefiting from McElhenny. Because when he came on the scene, you could still get up and run with the ball after you were down. They changed the rule because of him. In his case, there'd have to be nine guys on top of him, and no motion left, before they'd blow the whistle. You can't imagine how many cheap shots they took at him. Sometimes it was like he'd have to stop breathing before they'd blow a whistle. So he was fair game in a way you don't see in professional football today.

Then the hard hats came in, and then the masks, and they can rip you pretty good. You don't see blockers using the shoulder the way they used to. Instead, they snap their necks and bring up that helmet.

But Mac never complained.

Do you think the fans appreciated that?

I wouldn't be surprised, by and large. But fans don't wear striped shirts with whistles around their necks.

Well, supposedly, fans are more knowledgeable today because of the presence of the television camera at football games.

Not the camera — the *cameras,* plural. They can give you instant replays from three different angles. No one set of eyes can follow a football game that way, and I include the coach and any spotter upstairs.

But television, too, had to make progress. Do you know we lost a game when I was in college — the 1947 Minnesota-Illinois game — because of television?

Television in 1947?

It was just starting. The camera work was experimental, the sets were so small you could hardly see anything anyway. The reception was lousy, and the broadcasters weren't sports people at all. They were announcers from the local television station. You'd get a play where the official would call pass interference, and the announcer, not knowing what was going on, would say, "Hey, did you see that?" That's *all* he'd say. Meanwhile, the cameraman had followed the fullback into the line on the fake hand-off, so the pass wasn't on the screen anyway. It was wild.

But it seems unlikely what they did with television could affect what you did on the field. How did you *lose* because of television?

Well, we were supposed to play Illinois at Champaign, and the Saturday before, we sent a scout down there from Minneapolis to watch them play and give us a report. He had to overnight in Chicago before taking the train from there to Champaign Saturday morning, and he got drunk and missed the train. So on Saturday afternoon he wound up standing outside an appliance store on Madison Street, watching the Illinois game through the store window, on a display set.

Then he sent in his report of what he'd seen. The part about Perry Moss, the Illinois quarterback, said "Play him for the short pass, because he can't get the ball more than twenty yards."

Well, maybe the *television* couldn't get the ball more than twenty yards, but when we got down there to play them, the first two times Moss got his hands on the ball, he sent out deep receivers and we let them go. He threw two forty-yard bombs and we were behind fourteen-oh before we even got our pants on. And we never did catch up.

In a funny way, that story could make a case that television is overcomplicating football. You hear that said.

Football is overcomplicating football . . . the tendency toward specialization. Who were the best teams, year in and year out? The ones that played simple, yet purposeful football — Lombardi's Green Bay teams.

You know one reason Michigan and Minnesota were the winning teams in the Big Ten in my years, just after the war? Because they stayed with the single-wing when everybody else went to the T.

But they wound up going to the T, too. Do you remember the argument about who really invented the T, Halas or Clark Shaughnessy? Halas was bitter about it. He always said he had the basic idea for the T, and he put it in for one reason: It made a blocker out of the center. He'd be looking forward, not backward through his legs.

Halas also had Sid Luckman for a quarterback. My point is, you go to the T when you have personnel trained to handle it better than any other formation. For some clubs to go back to the single-wing today would require training — or retraining — the center all over again. He'd not only have to center the ball: He'd have to "lead" the ball carrier with it. It wasn't all that easy.

But Michigan and Minnesota had the personnel at that time to execute the single-wing, so they weren't that fast to convert to the new formation. Under Bierman we had the horses for the buck-lateral series, so that's what we did. You could have put our "playbook" inside a match folder, so I don't think we ever mystified the other side. But it's one thing to analyze an offense and another thing to stop it. And when you had people like Bud Grant, Clayton Tonnemaker, Leo Nomellini, you were going to do a little damage.

Then theoretically, do you think some pro teams today might benefit — because of their personnel — by going back to the single-wing?

I don't know. Sometimes I wonder, for instance, what the Bears, with that big quarterback of theirs, would be like if they suddenly came out running off the single-wing.

What's more basic is how many plays today are basically single-wing plays anyway: The pitch-out sweep following the interference, the quarterback roll-out, the reverse. Even the Shotgun that the 49ers used — with the long snap back from the center.

I remember what might have been the first or second game the 49ers tried the Shotgun. It was against Baltimore, and Baltimore had the strangest defense you ever saw. They decided they'd put three guys in the line and have Big Daddy Lipscomb as a roving linebacker behind them.

At that point the 49ers had three quarterbacks — John Brodie, Billy Kilmer, and Bobby Waters

— and you knew Brodie wasn't going to do much running, but you couldn't tell about the other two.

So Big Daddy, all three hundred pounds of him, had the job of running to either side, depending on which way the 49ers' quarterback ran. Here's this huge man, twenty-five yards away from the ball carrier, running his tail off from side to side. It was a strange sight.

Is this part of the "overcomplication"?

It might have been for Big Daddy. Halas and, I believe, Shaughnessy finally figured out the way to shoot down the Shotgun. I can remember Halas drawing the defense for me on a tablecloth during a postseason league meeting in San Francisco. "Just you watch," he said, and he was right.

But if the Shotgun was essentially single-wing, why did you call it a tendency toward specialization?

I didn't. The specialization is something else. For one thing, I feel sorry for the quarterback. He's got more to do than he used to, in the sense that other players have less to do. He's in there for the same number of plays he always was, while other players who used to have to do more than one thing now do only one thing.

But the "two-quarterback" vogue is there now, and . . .

Does that help? I don't know.

Well, you hear television commentary that two quarterbacks with different habits make a team doubly hard to defense.

Maybe. I wasn't thinking of that part of it. I was thinking that there's one man in that huddle who's in charge: The quarterback. He's the leader. He's the leader by definition, regardless of how good he is. Now if you've got two leaders and one's better than the other, you pick up a pretty good set of problems right there. It can bring on divided loyalties and all kinds of things.

Well, isn't it the coach's job to take care of

those problems when he encounters them?

He can send in plays. But does he always have a play to send in? I know it looks impressive, in those time outs on television, where the quarterback comes off the field and the coach, with a headset running up to the spotter's booth, talks so earnestly to him.

But do you know what gets said? In the first place, the headset is a prop, because at that point the spotter doesn't want to say anything. So the quarterback says to the coach, "What do you want?" The coach says, "First I'll tell you what I want, then I'll tell you what I don't want. What I want is a first down. What I don't want is a fumble or an interception."

I'll never forget one conference at the sidelines against the Rams, in Los Angeles in 1953. We were in the final minutes, and they were ahead twenty-seven — twenty-four and we were on our own fifteen-yard line.

Tittle hit Billy Wilson with a pass; then me. Then a screen to McElhenny, and he took off, and the next thing you know, we were on their seventeen-yard line with a minute left to play.

Now we got into the huddle, and Tittle called a pass to me. We broke from the huddle and lined up, and all of a sudden the Rams called time out!

Now we were all on the sideline talking to Buck Shaw. He was the finest gentleman I ever played football for. The thing that made him a great coach was his way of getting something extra out of players who didn't know they had it — in fact, they *didn't* have it.

But the major problem at that moment was, why would the defense be stopping the clock at that point? The best guess was that they knew what we were going to do and wanted time to talk it over and change their defense. The play we had called took me out against Night Train Lane, their deep man on my side, and Tittle had a notion it was going to work.

But nothing really made sense. Maybe they suddenly thought it was a good time to take a breather, but that hardly justified giving us the benefit of a stopped clock.

So I don't know what they were talking about on the other side of the field, but it was just a plain mystery session on our side. Nobody came up with anything.

Then the whistle blew. Time in again. We got in the huddle and Tittle called the same play. What else was he going to call?

We broke from the huddle, and there were the Rams in the identical defense they had before the time out. Tittle hit me with the ball for the winning touchdown.

Did you ever learn about the Rams' reaction?

Only what everybody else learned: They had fired Night Train Lane.

As a result of *their* calling time out!

Well . . . look, he went on to a great career in the league. This is a problem I have here and now as we talk. I know you want me to talk about the great players I faced, but there's a complicating factor: Some of the greatest were the ones we had good days against.

Is there a reason for that?

Because they were like Mount Everest — they were *there!* The 49ers were just one hell of a football team. Everybody in the league feared them — *feared* us! You whispered "McElhenny" or "Hardy Brown" to them, and they began to shiver at the sound.

But the blessing was also the curse. Frankie Albert's greatness lay in the fact that he was such a little guy. Being physically small himself, he was an inspiration to everybody else, because of the things he could do.

You weighed what?

The program said one ninety-five.

But if you could . . .

Look, you can't keep throwing a line that averages two-hundred twelve pounds against a

line that averages two-hundred fifty-five pounds. Hardy Brown wasn't a big man for a linebacker, but ball carriers avoided him like the plague. He was something else.

I remember once I was on the kickoff team, and we were playing Detroit. Wild Horse Mains was lined up against me but I didn't even know it was him. We just counted off, and I was lined up against him. So I blindsided him, and it made him mad. They were kicking off and he was my guy to block.

Well, the next year Wild Horse ran into Hardy on a kickoff return, and Wild Horse was passionate. Hardy was in the wedge and Wild Horse threw himself into the wedge, by accident, not by design. The result was that it tore open the inside of Hardy's thigh. I mean, tore it open. So they took him to the dressing room and put thirty-seven stitches in his leg, and then there he was back again, playing the whole second half.

Ball carriers hated the thought of coming into contact with him.

They hated it? *He* hated it! He couldn't watch the postgame movies on Tuesday. He would have racked somebody up, but when it was ready to come on the screen, he'd cover his eyes. "My God, I can't stand to watch this!" he'd say.

I think Hardy may be the only man who ever played in the old All-America Conference, National Football League, the American Football League, and the Canadian League. He started out with the Chicago Hornets. Nobody ever *heard* of the Chicago Hornets. I think he wound up with Denver in the AFL.

But they used to call him "pound-for-pound, the greatest linebacker in the game," which was a polite way of saying he didn't weigh enough. He was under two hundred, and you just couldn't play linebacker in the National Football League at that weight. Even if Hardy could.

This doesn't take us back to the question of specialization.

Not in the way I had in mind, no. The thing with specialization is in a direction every fan can see for himself — penalties.

Penalties?

Putting it another way, who commits them? What's the penalty that stands out? It's the penalty committed by the special team, like clipping on punt and kickoff runbacks. Why? Because these are the rookies, the youngsters who do their learning on the special teams.

If you were coaching, would you do it any differently?

I never gave it that much thought. Obviously you don't play without developing theories of your own. But I . . .

Did you ever get a coaching offer?

Yes. When I retired in 1958 . . .

You quit early.

I was thirty-four. You'd have to know my father to appreciate this, but he's the one who understood my retirement the least. He was active in hockey and baseball until he was fifty, and he hasn't forgiven me yet.

Then what was the story?

Well, 1958 was a pretty trying year. We played the Rams, our arch rivals, twice in our first three games and we lost to them both times, fifty-six to seven in one game and thirty-three to three in the other. Two games and they outscored us by seventy-nine points! That was an indication we weren't going to ring any bells that season. And Albert decided that would be his last year as coach, and it was pretty obvious Red Hickey was going to succeed him.

I was reduced to placekicking in 1958, and I'd made a good business connection in San Francisco, one with a permanent future. I didn't think I figured in Hickey's plans for the 49ers.

He wanted me to come to camp in '59 on what amounted to a "tryout" basis, but that would have made it embarrassing whether I "made" the club or not.

CBS was picking up television interest and asked me if I wanted to do color. That was another factor in my decision to retire.

To this day, I can kick as well as ever, and — look at Blanda — I could have caught on with somebody. Age doesn't make that much difference in that situation.

And, looking back on it, I have to say I regret not playing one more season, because 1959 became the cut-in year for the player pension plan.

Now, you asked about coaching: Vince Lombardi wanted to take me to Green Bay with him to be one of his coaches, and who knows where that might have led if I'd done it.

I even got an offer for a front-office job from the Atlanta club when they were forming.

But overall, I thought it was the thing to do at the time, and things have been good since then. If I was confronted with the same details of the same situation tomorrow, I suppose I'd do what I did all over again.

Meanwhile, Bud Grant, the other end at the University of Minnesota when you played there, went into coaching.

Yes, and he took a lesson out of college with him. In 1949 we were undefeated when we went into Ann Arbor to play Michigan. We got there two-and-a-half hours early, and they were all charged up. The papers were after the scalp of their coach, Fritz Crisler, and there must have been a hundred thousand people at the game. We fumbled the opening kickoff and they scored and held on to beat us.

And to this day, Grant's Vikings teams get to the stadium at the last minute and come out on the field at the last minute. He doesn't want any more of those long waits.

Did you take any lasting lessons out of college football?

Well, I don't . . . I remember one thing, that same Illinois game, at Champaign, the one I was telling about. We had a first down on their

five-yard line, and I was lined up against Alex Agase, their All-America lineman. All he would do was talk: "Gonna double-team me this time? Which two of you?" That sort of thing. Talk, talk, talk.

The next thing I knew he talked me into jumping offside, so we were back to the ten-yard line, and Bierman sent in a substitute for me, and when I got to the sideline he said, "Why don't you just tell that Armenian to shut up?"

It's a funny thing the way talk can get to you. Take Nomellini, a big guy, but so nice, so docile. He wanted to be friends with everybody. Of course, you couldn't make certain remarks about him or his family or whatever, but the other teams in the NFL knew that. Instead, it was always, "Hi, Leo, put it there". . ."How *are* you, Leo?". . ."Gee, Leo, it's good to see you."

And he'd just beam. It drove our coaches nuts. Same as Bierman: "Leo stop *listening* to them!"

But he had some big games for the 49ers.

You'd better believe it. I remember him in a couple of Rams games . . .

Maybe your own biggest game was against the Rams.

I know the one you're talking about. The one in 1953. Not the one at L.A. where I caught the last-minute pass and we won thirty-one to twenty-seven, but the one at San Francisco before that. They were ahead twenty-nothing in the second quarter, and we wound up winning it thirty-one thirty.

And you kicked the winning field goal with five seconds left.

Yes, and the Rams raised hell. Some of them are still talking about it to this day. The ball was kicked at an angle, and they swore it didn't go through.

They said Tittle, who was doing the holding, faked out the officials.

What really happened?

Well, there was an official standing right be-

The Cleveland Browns had Mac Speedie (far left) and Dante Lavelli to play end, so they were free to trade Soltau to the 49ers in 1950. Frankie Albert, Soltau's first holder for placekicks, occasionally crossed him up by running with the football (right) rather than placing it down on the ground to be kicked.

hind me, and the minute I kicked the ball, Tittle jumped up right in front of him, holding up his arms, signaling a score. I'm not sure the official even saw it, with Tittle blocking his view.

Well, you *saw* it, didn't you?

Nope.

I know you keep your head down when you're kicking, but you bring it up on the follow-through, don't you?

Ordinarily, yes. But like I say, this one was from an angle — we were down at the west end of the field — and as I brought my head up I found myself staring into the setting sun. I was blinded.

You hear of funny things happening on field goals. Like an official calling defensive holding on a missed field-goal attempt. How can you have defensive holding on a field goal?

Oh, you can have it. Don't kid yourself. One of the pet stunts is to grab an offensive lineman and pull him at an angle, so somebody else on your team can shoot the gap.

But tricking the referee . . .

I don't know that he *did* trick the referee. At least, he wasn't tricking *me*. Frankie Albert used to do that when he was holding the ball for me on points after touchdown.

He tricked *you?*

Well, you know Albert. He'd get the snap, and the next thing, he'd be rolling out. If he could take it in himself, he would. If not, he'd throw a little tip pass to somebody in the flat. Meanwhile I'm kicking air.

I finally took him over to the side and said, "Look, I would like to go through one season with my leg attached to my body."

Maybe he didn't tell you because he wanted to make it look realistic.

He told the end to look out for a pass from him.

But the end was on a need-to-know basis. You weren't.

Could be. Those were different times. The Browns, with Groza, were the ones that first started making the field goal an "automatic" play. But even then, and for years after, most teams wouldn't settle for the field goal with fourth down and short yardage inside the twenty, the way they do today.

Cleveland had you and Groza at the same time.

Yeah. The Packers drafted me and swapped me to the Browns. Groza's probably the reason why I came to the 49ers. I was in two preseason games for the Browns as an end, but they already had two ends named Mac Speedie and Dante Lavelli. I could placekick, but they already had Groza.

So Paul Brown called me in and said, "Look, I think you can make this team, but I'm damned if I know how much playing you'll do. We can deal you to San Francisco, and I have an idea you'll do a lot of playing there." So I went out to San Francisco, talked with Buck Shaw, and made the move. It's something I've never been sorry for.

That was in 1950, and you led the team in scoring. As you say, the field goal wasn't all that popular then — especially with the hashmarks out so wide that you'd be kicking from the difficult angle.

I wish I knew what the difficult angle was. That business about the angle is one of the great sports-page myths. The distance between the goal posts doesn't change.

But you stressed the angle in that Rams game . . .

Because it meant I was looking into the sun. It didn't have anything to do with the kick. The only adjustment we'd make for the angle would be to put an extra lineman up front on the wide side, so the defense wouldn't pour in on the short side of the triangle. And the holder would adjust for the angle. But a kick is still a kick.

Then what is all this business over the years of getting the ball in front of the goal posts, centered for a field goal?

Maybe it helps some kickers, and maybe coaches have that in their mind. But I can tell you, if I missed one from easy range, it didn't make any difference whether it was from an angle or not. The coach yelled just as hard. I missed one from an angle in a preseason game once, and the coach charged on the field yelling at me.

What did you say?

I didn't say anything. While he was yelling, they were dropping a flag and calling the defense for offside or something. So the next thing I knew, I was trying it again, only this time the ball was five yards closer to the goal line, so the angle was even worse.

Was the kick good?

Yes. Can you imagine if I'd missed it twice in a row?

In a way, your condition was unique — as a placekicker you knew linemen and linebackers. As a pass-catching end, you knew cornerman and safeties.

Yes. And they were all named Don Paul.

He was a linebacker with the Rams.

He was also a deep back with the Browns ... two guys with the same name, like the two Gene Washingtons. I'd rate the linebacker Paul along with George Connor of the Bears as the best two defensive front men I ever saw. And there was Will Sherman, the Rams' safetyman, and a defensive back with the Colts, Don Shula, and four Lions who were amazing as a defensive secondary *in combination* — Lary, Christiansen, Smith and David. No one you'd single out, but the way they worked together!

The Don Paul who played for the Rams. He loved to just sit there and wait for me, and I used to lie awake nights thinking what I could do to him in return. I knew one thing: He hated

to be hit low. Block him below the knees and he hated it.

The one with Cleveland knew how to hold you up when you were going down for a pass. Today they have a phrase for it — "bump and run" — but that Paul was doing it years before they had a phrase for it.

I remember one game against the Browns, when he'd been playing in close all game, and I told Tittle in the huddle, "I'm going to get behind him and cut. Throw me the ball."

Then we lined up and the play started. Paul wasn't playing close. Not that it made any difference, because Tommy Thompson, their linebacker, put out his foot and tripped me.

So the officials . . .

The officials never saw it. Officiating goes in waves. In those days, they weren't looking at linebackers as much as they should have. Today they're looking at linebackers but not looking so much at the deep men.

But Tittle didn't see it either. All he knew was that's the kind of pass you throw not to where the end is but to where you know he's going to be. The pass went to the only man still standing up — Don Paul — and he took off down the sideline, and the only thing left between him and the goal line was Tittle. So he went over and belted him out of bounds, and everybody lay there for a long time.

Finally, Tittle got up and looked at me and said, "Do me a favor: next time you get an idea, keep it to yourself."

Speaking of things going in waves, "spiking" the ball after scoring a touchdown seems to be a fad.

One trouble with "spiking" is those two or three times, like that Pittsburgh fellow, where the guy threw the ball away before he reached the goal line. I remember the way McElhenny acted when he'd score standing up. He'd cradle the ball 'way up here, on his palm, like a waiter

bringing in a Long Island duck, and then he'd just let it spill back onto the ground behind him. But you'd better believe he made sure he scored first.

But all that spiking had its influence — television again — on college, high school, and even Pop Warner. Everybody else was imitating the pros.

Mm-hmmh. More than you might suspect. You know all the speaking appearances I make: Do you know the one question I hear most often?

What?

Why aren't the professionals as enthusiastic as the colleges and high schools.

What do you tell them?

I tell them the truth: The professionals are *more* enthusiastic. They may not always show it. A fellow-professional doesn't have to hug you in public to let you know you did something right. You even hear about prayer sessions, and about the teams that *don't* hold them. Well, this is something intensely private, a matter for the individual himself. But most of all, there's the hidden element.

The hidden element?

Surprise.

Surprise?

Yeah. At the college and younger levels, there's surprise when somebody does something unusually well, so everybody jumps up and down congratulating him.

But at the professional level, there isn't anything surprising about doing something right. It's expected of you. It's what you get paid for.

Joe Perry

Position: Running Back
Years: 1948-60, 1963
Height: 6-0
Weight: 207
College: Compton Jr. College

Like Lou Spadia, Joe Perry is active today (as a scout) in the 49ers' management, and he goes back into the team's history almost as far as Spadia.

The major difference is that Perry carried a football with him most of the places he went. In his first nine seasons with the National Football League, he had already eclipsed Steve Van Buren's mark as the NFL's all-time leading ground-gainer, and was the first man in the league's history to gain more than 1,000 yards two seasons in a row. He owns 14 different ball-carrying and scoring records for the San Francisco team.

Born in Stevens, Arkansas, and reared in Los Angeles, Perry was the first — and for a time, the only — black player in the 49ers' lineup. Times were tough in many ways then, including "slow whistles" by some officials while "the Jet," as Perry was called, absorbed extra punishment. But feelings can change, like those of Hugh McElhenny.

"Joe confers a distinction by letting you line up with him," the King said.

The coin Perry wears, suspended from a gold chain around his neck, has two faces in bas-relief: His mother on one side, Tony Morabito on the other.

Do you remember playing the old Chicago Rockets at Soldier Field in Chicago? They were sort of the symbol of that old All-America Football Conference.

Oh, that goes way back. The lighting was bad enough, and then they became the Hornets with those yellow shirts and the yellow ball. You couldn't see the ball, and you could hardly see the players either, especially down at the south end of the field. No matter how many people they got into the stadium it always looked like a handful.

Did you play any in 1947?

No. I was signed in '47, but I started playing the next season. I can remember it vividly. John Woudenberg was a tackle with the 49ers. I was back from overseas and stationed at Alameda Naval Air Station. John came over — he was helping our coach at that particular time — and he went back and told Buck Shaw and Tony Morabito about my playing over there. For about three or four weeks Buck and Tony were out to our games. From then on Tony and I became very close, more or less like a father-and-son relationship in reality, because when I did finally decide to go pro, I never even signed a contract.

Never in all the years?

Never in all the years that Tony was living. Of course, I had a *contract* — what I mean was, there was never any negotiating between us, never any arguing. He'd call me, or my wife if I wasn't home, and say, "Okay, I'm sending your contract," and that was it. It was a trust that you couldn't believe between two people.

And all those years actually brought you from the old era into the new.

Right. I had a total of seventeen years — fifteen with the 49ers and two with the Colts. So I guess you can say I saw all the transitions. Unless you go back to the thirties.

At what point in a seventeen-year career — say, like yours — are you at your best? In the beginning you have the sheer youth. At the end you have a lot of wisdom. Where do the two lines cross on the graph?

I think it's different for each individual. For instance, I stay in shape even *now*. There are a lot of kids out there I could outrun, although I'm twice their age. Look at your European runners. They don't mature until their late thirties, and they run like hell. I know the game of football is a young man's game. Sometimes a coach looks at a player and says, "His body can't take it any more." But I don't think you can always say that. It's up to the individual:

how he takes care of his body, what he does at night — how he takes care of him*self*. It's the same as buying a 1938 car — if you keep it up, it's just as good as a 1972 car.

Would you apply this to the time it takes you to recover from injuries?

I assume so. Again, I have to refer back to myself. I tore the medial-lateral ligament in half when I was playing in a preseason game for Baltimore against the Washington Redskins in 1962. It was about August eighteenth or something like that and I opened against the Los Angeles Rams on opening day, September fifteenth.

Miami was in the old AAFC when you first started playing?

Miami Seahawks, right.

And in those days, a black football player would have separate housing in Miami?

Yes. Also in Baltimore. And I can remember an incident in Cambridge Springs, Pennsylvania, against me.

What was the incident?

They didn't want me to stay at the country club.

How'd it work out?

Well, it worked out all right, since Tony and I had a great relationship and we understood each other. I was a hot-headed kid right out of the navy, and I just didn't go for it. I'd always said, if there's going to be any discrimination or segregation, tell me beforehand and then I'll be prepared. This time I wasn't told beforehand and there was a big uproar. The same thing happened in Baltimore, Maryland, and . . .

Both times, you didn't find out until the event?

Until I was there, and . . . it worked out.

Well, how was the Cambridge Springs thing worked out?

It was a big ruckus, but it finally terminated.

You got to stay at the country club?

No.

You moved?

No, no.

Then what?

The team moved.

Were there any special problems connected with your being the *only* black on the team?

Well, I was the only one for a long time, and then we acquired Bob Mike from UCLA. Then a couple of years after, we got a kid out of San Diego High School, Charley Powell. But San Francisco — the 49ers — I shouldn't say San Francisco since I think the nucleus of our team in the forties was southern boys, and we got along fabulously. We were like one big, happy family. If one guy got angry, it didn't do any good. He couldn't fight, because he'd have to fight all of us. And hell, I was part of the family. This team has always been like that. In fact, it has tried to run it that way, although I guess the big business factor has entered into football and most of the young players don't think like the older players. They didn't go through the same things we did. Consequently I don't think they're as close-knit as the clubs were back in those days, when you only had thirty-three ball players.

What are some of the signs of it, as you saw them come along? Was it mainly rising costs, or what?

Well, I think there were several things. First of all, the American Football League brought about a war of salaries with the bidding for players. Teams hid guys and tried to keep the other league from getting them. Pretty soon this brought on the agents, and the guys who build big businesses for the players. Then came the union, and a multiple of things. Football to me has really become America's number one sport. It's taken over everything. It's big business, and looked upon as big business it would be the right thing to cut a guy who can't do you any

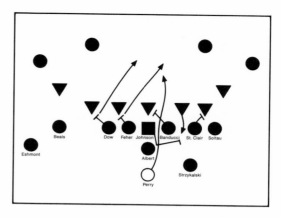

Joe Perry had broken the color line on the 49ers during the team's first season, 1946. Bob Mike (far left) joined the team in 1948 and Charley Powell (number 87, tackling Ron Waller of Los Angeles) became a 49er in 1952. Verl Lillywhite (left), was Perry's first roommate The "Eagle defense" that was used widely in professional football during the 1950s lacked a middle linebacker, so it was easy pickings for the trap plays run by Joe Perry (right).

more good, but I can't ever remember the 49ers being that way.

You were talking about how the big men hit so hard today, but wasn't it just as physical when you broke in?

Sure it was. But in my day, a big man was six-three, six-four, two-hundred-fifty pounds. Those men are midgets now. I'd be a midget as a fullback because I'm six-foot, a hundred and ninety-something pounds. They're looking for the gigantic fullbacks, six-two, six-three, two-thirty-five, forty, run a forty in four-six. We had some that large and some that fast. But today they're that large and that fast all rolled into the same guy. I don't know what they feed them. Actually, the size accounts for some of the injuries today. You get a guy six-five, two-sixty, runs a forty in four-six . . . with that size and velocity hitting another guy, someone's got to hurt something.

And over all the years, you never won a title.

No, we never won it. Not in the NFL or the old AAFC. One year we were in the title playoff with Cleveland at Cleveland. But they beat us. In my time, we had a lot of offensively-skilled people, but we never had a defense that let us win. One year, for twelve games we averaged something like thirty-six points a game, so you have to say we lost it defensively. Any time you average five or six touchdowns a game, you should win.

When did coaches begin to go defensive in their thinking?

Well, I remember that we had a trap called thirty-one and thirty-one-F when Greasy Neale first installed the Eagle defense. We'd love to see it, because we'd go flying up the middle. All of a sudden they went to the four-three and four-four, and I think that was in the fifties, and the coaches were getting defensive minded. Now they're trying to do something about it by moving in the hashmarks, but I think for awhile now

it's going to be a defensive-oriented game, unless you get the horses, as they say, to blow 'em out.

The fans are a lot more defense-conscious themselves. Is this a result of watching the games on television?

Possibly so, but as you well know, good or great defensive ball players demand as much as good offensive ball players, so consequently the salaries are at a par. Now there are good players on both sides, where previously all the good ball players went to the glamour and the gold of offense.

When you broke in weren't there players in both leagues playing offense and defense?

I was one of them. The kids today don't know. They say: "Oh, that old fogey, he doesn't know what he's talking about." But when we played both ways it was always the best eleven men on the field. We couldn't afford luxuries, such as a placekicker. Every man had to do at least two things, not just one.

So today's game could be expected to add to the lifetime of a player because he's not giving it sixty minutes a game.

Most definitely so. He not only gets a breather, but he has only one thing to concentrate on. He can put all his energies into that one assignment. So his career could last longer, unless there's some injury, or he's made enough money. The salaries are astronomical today, and the guys are more business-minded than in my time. I can't say they're not dedicated, because it means money in their pockets and bread on their tables, but I think some of them have too many outside concerns during the football season. This can hurt their performances.

How much of the game was sheer enjoyment for you?

Let's say one hundred percent of one hundred percent. Now I go back to the old 49ers' teams — 1948, 1949 — I'd say from ninety to ninety-six

159

percent of those fellows didn't even know what the hell a paycheck was. I don't mean they didn't expect to get paid, but they didn't care for the check — hell, it was *football*. I think the team still gives off this sense, otherwise they wouldn't have won those divisional titles in the seventies. But you could see it everywhere in the old days. The most complete ball player I ever saw was Marion Motley. He was two-hundred-fifty pounds and could run like a deer once he got under way. It took ten people to haul him down. He could back up the line as well if not better than Dick Butkus or any of your linebackers. And no two men could run around him to get to Otto Graham. People forget, he blocked for Otto.

Then you're saying that there are players in the game today — not so much because of their own individual makeup, but because of all the outside conditions we've talked about — with enormous skills who might be saying to themselves, "Oh, God, I've got to play a football game."

Right. And they say — oh, tomorrow in my business I've got to do this or I've got to do that and that's where they fall down. Ninety-eight percent of the football teams today are equal in talent. A team wins because of its mental attitude. If a team is not ready mentally, it's going to go out there and get the hell kicked out of it.

What happens if you *are* mentally prepared, but freak things start happening, and you wind up behind?

I can relate a little story to you. We were playing the Chicago Cardinals at Chicago, and we were leading twenty-one to seven with three minutes to play. They beat us twenty-eight twenty-one.

Was that their doing or your lack of doing?

It could have been complacency on our part. Or that, combined with more desire on their part. As Y. A. Tittle used to say, never criticize

the trapper with the skin on the wall. Same thing in our Dallas playoff game in 1972. We were leading by ten or thirteen points with a couple of minutes to play. But Dallas won.

So you can be "up" for a game in every respect and just run into somebody who's a little more up than you are.

That's correct. Also, you can be so keyed up that you become tight and tense and make more mistakes than you would if you were relaxed and loose.

What are the things you remember most about your own career?

I remember the mistakes. Any athlete hates to make a mistake, especially if he's in front of fifty or sixty thousand fans. After fumbling in the open, I've seen grown men — myself included — sit down and cry because they hurt the team. You don't see as much of this sort of thing these days.

The game that stands out most in my memory is there because it haunts me: the loss of the 1957 playoff to Detroit. Talk about complacency. We were ahead twenty-four to ten in the third quarter when McElhenny returned a kickoff and got us down to their three-yard line. We couldn't get it in and we wound up with a field goal so it was twenty-seven to ten in the third quarter. We didn't score another damn point and they beat us thirty-one twenty-seven. If you'd walked into our dressing room after that game, you would have seen thirty-five grown men crying.

But if you separated the personal side from the team side . . .

It wouldn't make any difference. That game was the closest in all the years I'd been to the NFL championship. I think we would have slaughtered Cleveland in the title game — Detroit beat them fifty-nine to fourteen. One personal memory does stand out. I cracked my zygoma in that Lions game. I remember distinctly, I came

The 1963 NFL Record Manual (left) was the last to list Joe Perry as the leading ground-gainer in the history of professional football. A year later, Jim Brown of the Cleveland Browns (below) had passed Perry, and eventually, Jim Taylor of the Green Bay Packers (right) did, too. The rushing totals of Perry (pages 164-165) would have been greater if statistics of the All-American Football Conference had been accepted for the record book when the league dissolved in 1950.

back to the huddle and Tittle looked over at me and said, "Hey, what's wrong with your face?" I said, "What the hell are you talking about?" He said, "Your *face*." I stuck my hand up and it just kept going all the way over to the left side of my face. When you crack the zygoma bone your whole face caves in — it collapses — there's nothing to hold it up.

Was that the end of your football for the afternoon?

No. It happened in the fourth quarter and I played till the game was over. I have a high pain threshold. It felt like I'd been hit on the side of the head, and that was it. It happened on a screen pass to McElhenny. I'd swung out of the backfield and peeled back on the middle line-backer, Joe Schmidt. I blindsided him, and I think his mask went through my mask and caught me on the zygoma. It was just a little twinge.

So I don't think I ever got great gratification out of my most *personal* moment because we never won the damn thing. But I'll tell you a secret: the *greatest* moment that *any* running back can have is when he does something right when he doesn't have the ball, which means the fan isn't likely to notice it. But you make a block that springs your running mate, or you make a block, then get up and make another block. Maybe the fan doesn't see it, but your team-mates know.

Of course, that can work the other way, too. You could make a mistake that nobody sees.

Not quite. It isn't missed in the movies. That's the time when the guys slink down in the seats — not because they're trying to hide but because they feel so bad about what they did.

Of all the coaches you've played for . . .

I didn't play for too many — Shaw, Strader, Albert, Hickey at San Francisco and Weeb Ewbank at Baltimore. That was it in professional football. Buck Shaw was one of the greatest

offensive minds going. He helped me tremendously. Football players must have faith in their coach and trust him. Those are the main ingredients: faith, trust and respect. The coach has to stay aloof of everyone. He cannot chum around with one guy or prefer one over another. I have the greatest amount of respect and admiration for Buck Shaw.

But the game has become more complicated since those times.

Yes and no. Let's take this tape recorder for example. How complicated is it? I'll just ask you that question. You've never seen it before. But is it complicated?

It's more complicated than it might have been ten years ago.

Yes. But there's only three or four buttons to push and it took five minutes for you to figure it out, right? That's as complicated as football is. To score, you have to be able to block. To keep the other team from scoring, you have to be able to tackle. So there's only two things you can do: block and tackle. *How* you go about doing it is a different situation. If you want to make it complicated, you can.

There used to be times when it was standard to punt on third down. They don't do that any more.

And there's the difference between "sophisticated" — my word — and "complicated" — your word. It's like when they introduced the forward pass. It was still the same game. More complicated — no. More sophisticated — yes. You can afford specialists in the game today. But that's not a complication; like I've said, it's a luxury.

That's why I prefer the word "sophisticated." You can't take the kids today and go back to the thirties when they called them big dumb oafs. They'd point a guy and say, "Run through the wall," and he'd run through the wall. Not so now. You have to have a sophisticated mind. You have to absorb and retain what's given to you. The off-tackle play can be run twenty-five or thirty different ways these days. The game is more *cerebral* now. Now you need mental as well as physical ability.

The'n maybe the players don't get as tired *mentally* either, because of today's total platooning. That has to be important in prolonging a career. What was your thinking in your last season in the game?

I never in my mind figured that I couldn't do it physically. My thinking was that I had played for seventeen years. I'd become vested in the pension plan. I wanted to get out when I was up there, before I went down to the bottom of the barrel. Prior to his death, Tony Morabito had told me, "I'll tell you when you're going to quit," because I was thinking of quitting before he died. But when you've been a running back for seventeen years, the coaches kind of frown upon you. So I figured it was time for me to get out before they said don't come back to camp.

What about home crowd versus road crowd?

Again, it didn't make much difference to me. Remember, I broke into pro football when there were very few blacks, and that's been the story most of my life. I've always been the one fly in the buttermilk wherever I was. It never bothered me *per se,* because this is the way I was reared and taught by my mother. My mother and Tony are the two people who had the greatest influence on my life — in tutoring and bringing me up to be a man. It never bothered me one way or the other. Hell, I've been called everything but a child of God, but words don't hurt me unless you put your hands on me. You put your hands on me, you've got a different situation. Call me anything, but don't hit me and call me that.

But there are so many people who say "Home crowd means so much to me on the plus side."

Well, it could motivate the nucleus of your ball club. But speaking for myself, if you are an athlete and you want to win, you don't give a

damn where you are. Let's take a track man — why is it when American track men go to Germany or Switzerland, they run and win? They're not in front of an American crowd. If they win, it's because they *want* to win. They don't care who, where or what.

How good were the 49ers when they first went into the National Football League?

We were on a par offensively, but not defensively, as I've said. We were three and nine in our first year, 1950, so we built up the defense because we knew we already had the horses on offense. If we'd had the defense then that the 49ers have now, nobody in the National League would have touched us. As far as whether the All-America Conference was ready to merge, at least with its top teams, Cleveland proved it. They won the whole damn thing that first year.

How much confidence did you have that you could make it in pro football?

Well, in order to be any kind of an athlete, you have to have a great degree of self-pride, maybe even an air of cockiness, though not to the point where you make an ass out of yourself. I knew that I could play football, and I never had been in awe of anyone on a football field, from childhood on up. I started playing varsity football in junior high school at thirteen.

As for confidence coming into pro football, there were actually two teams after me in 1947. Tony came down to my house in Los Angeles, but the Rams had already sent someone over to offer me ninety-five hundred dollars. Tony came down and he offered me forty-five hundred. There was never a lie between Tony Morabito and myself. I told him, "They're offering me five thousand more than you are." He said, "Yeah, well, I know." But he went on, and he said, "We've been looking for a black player in San Francisco. I've checked you out on all facets of life and everything, and you're the guy we want. I can't afford to pay you the amount of money

the Rams have offered you, but if you go with me, you will never regret it." So I mulled it over for a while, because five thousand dollars was a lot of money in 1947.

In fact, I was digging up my front yard for planting, with blisters all over my hands — I'll never forget it — so I offered Tony some lemonade. It was hot as hell, about a hundred and six or seven degrees, so I said, "Come on in." He says, "No, I'll sit out here and we'll drink lemonade." So we sat out there and drank lemonade, and finally I said, "Okay, we've got a deal." No contract, no nothing — we've got a deal. He took me on my word and I took him on his word.

What was there about the Rams you didn't like — aside from what you liked about Tony?

It wasn't so much against the Rams. It was that Tony sold me. It's an old adage I was told as a child — whenever two people meet, there's a sale going on. Either I sell you or you sell me. And Tony sold me. He was like a father to me.

But if you'd gone to the Rams, it would have meant playing for Los Angeles, your home.

That didn't even enter my mind. It was the man. I had been offered a scholarship to Columbia University. I would have made more money if I'd gone there. But I felt I would have done myself and the school an injustice because I couldn't sit in a classroom right after getting out of the navy. I had majored in mathematics and wanted to be an engineer, but I just didn't figure I could do it.

At the end you made it to the Hall of Fame. And your mother wasn't there and Tony wasn't there.

Neither one. I lost my mother in 1968, just prior to the announcement that I would be inducted into the Hall of Fame. I'll never forget when we went back to Canton, Elroy Hirsch — who was a great friend of mine and one heck of a man — told me, "It won't strike you until you get up on the podium." I'd been trying to prepare

some kind of speech for eight months and finally I just got disgusted and threw it out of my mind.

So the day arrived and I was up on the podium before I knew it. I got up and just said what I felt. I told the audience that at this particular time, at this moment in my life, what came out came from the heart. And I elaborated for maybe a full minute and a half. Then it came to me that the two people that meant the most in my life, the two who had made me the type of person that I was and gotten me where I was weren't there to share this event with me. That's where the speech ended. I couldn't talk any more. I started crying. I don't care how harsh, callous or hard you are — the emotions get involved. It all ties in. You asked me earlier about my most gratifying time. When I first came with the 49ers, Tony explained to me that I was the only black and to hold my temper and this or that. I did have a very bad temper at the time. I would never start anything, but I wouldn't take anything off anyone. I was reared that way.

But the most gratifying thing was when I knew I'd garnered the respect not only of my teammates but of everyone else throughout the league, including the officials. They accepted me as a man. Not as a black man or white man, but as a man.

Maybe there was some common sense involved here or there. At the beginning, we used to train at Menlo College and stayed in a two-story building there. I was a rookie and got all dressed to go into town. And here came a bucket of dirty water down on me. I didn't say anything. I turned around and went back in and got dressed. The same thing happened again but it didn't do me any good to get mad, because all thirty-two other guys would throw me in the pool if I did.

But a year or so later — I can remember very vividly — we were riding the train from Cleveland to New York. We'd just beaten Cleveland

in an exhibition game and were going up to New York or Syracuse or somewhere to play someone else. I was the only black on the team, and of course the porters and the waiters on the train were black. I just happened to be walking through this car and a friend of mine who had had several beers, said something about "that goddam nigger." Then he looked up and saw me and said, "Oh, Joe, I didn't mean you," and he started crying. He started *crying*.

I told him, "I don't care what you say; you don't bother me unless you put your hands on me." He was telling me in essence that every other black guy out there was a nigger, but not me.

Now take it up to today. The name "black" has alleviated a lot of problems.

So it was a question of continuing progress, not just one given moment in time?

We all know the progress. More and more, a man came to be respected for what he could do, instead of for what he was. But you ask me to clock that progress, I truthfully can't do it.

I remember when the Sayers-Piccolo book came out, it said they were the first black and white players to room together. They forgot the late forties. Who in hell roomed with me?

Who did?

Verl Lillywhite! We were opponents in college — he played at Modesto and I played at Compton Junior College — and we were very great friends.

So like I say, all the books that have come out today may be telling it like it is, but they're not telling it like it was.

The Other
Years

One midweek morning in 1964, announcer Jim Lange was doing a commercial for a savings and loan company over San Francisco radio station KSFO. "Big, safe, friendly," he said, intoning the slogan of the firm. Then, helplessly, he added: "Like the 49ers' line."

There were times like that. 49ers lineman Charlie Krueger has referred to Green Bay's "double isolation" play, but San Francisco had a version of the same play.

In the Packers' version, which one of their players told Krueger was an accident, the left guard pulled to the left, the right guard pulled to the right, the defenders followed them, and the middle was left wide open.

In the 49ers' version, which was also an accident, the left guard pulled to his right and the right guard pulled to his left. The result was that they smashed head-on into each other, sometimes (if the execution was swift enough) making a sandwich out of a screaming 49ers' quarterback.

Such collisions were the exception rather than the rule. So, too, in the case of the San Francisco team, was abrasive human contact at almost any level. The single-family control of the club throughout its lifetime, and the intense loyalties this bred, minimized the intramural feuds that seem built into some other football clubs.

For example, when the National Football League players formed their association in 1956, Tony Morabito, like most club owners, could have been expected to fight the move. Instead, he helped his players. In the words of Gordy Soltau, "If we thought we could better ourselves by forming the association, he'd stand behind us. He even paid our player representative's expenses to go to the first association meeting in Philadelphia."

There was something, of course, of the father whose affection for his long-haired son outweighs his affection for haircuts, but that was

Morabito. "His word was his bond," Y. A. Tittle said. "Any player with financial or other worries could always go to Tony."

"Many people don't know the nice things he did," says Joe Perry. "He didn't want them told."

To a great degree, he got his wish. In many respects, Morabito's love of his team was balanced by his suspicion of outsiders, and he never really understood the press. Morabito expected "fair coverage" from newsmen. He didn't get it. He failed to understand that news itself is unfair. No columnist or commentator is about to "balance" the news of a plane crash by giving equal space or time to a plane that didn't crash.

In fairness to Tony, the reporters covering his team committed excesses that left only the bottom-line argument that the one thing worse than a free press is the absence of one. For example:

• Morabito was accused of being cheap when it came to salaries. Actually, the 49ers' pay scale was above the median line for its time. The charge was misleading since salaries in those days didn't differ that much.

• Morabito was accused of putting the Catholic colleges in the San Francisco area out of the football business. Three such schools — St. Mary's, the University of San Francisco, and Santa Clara, Tony's own alma mater — played Sunday football at Kezar Stadium because they could not buck the competition of Stanford and the University of California on Saturdays. The 49ers pre-empted the Sunday dates.

The real facts were that Sunday attendances for the college games had begun to slip before the 49ers came on the scene. The fate of those games was sealed by a Pacific Coast Conference decision of 1935. This decision, known as the "freeze-out," required that PCC teams — not only Stanford and California, but UCLA and Southern California, Oregon and Oregon State, and Washington and Washington State — not schedule any key games with the independent

college teams of the San Francisco area.

• Morabito was accused of being one of a breed of NFL clubowners "interested only in blood and shoulder separations."

• Morabito was accused, at least by inference, of bringing on the fatal heart attack of Norman (Red) Strader by firing him after just one season as the 49ers' head coach.

That last accusation appeared in the *San Francisco Examiner,* whose contract for the annual preseason charity game between the 49ers and Redskins was not renewed by the Morabitos. The charge might help explain the estrangement between Tony and Vic on the one hand and the *Examiner* on the other.

But Tony was getting criticism from other San Francisco papers, too. Part of this might have been caused by his signing an exclusive game contract with the *Examiner.* Another version, offered by Dan McGuire in his history of the 49ers' early seasons, was perhaps ingenious. "Tony," McGuire wrote, "was to find that among writers on other papers the merits of his case were lost in the general journalistic tradition of sticking together."

That does not explain why Tony tried to get the football writer for one of the other papers taken off the 49ers' beat because he didn't like what the reporter wrote. (Nor does it explain why the Morabito demand was successful.)

The dimensions of the problem can be illustrated by Morabito's decision in January, 1947, to go after the two most glamorous college stars in the country. According to reports, they were offered what was then a fabulous salary — $35,000 apiece. Stung by the way the Chicago Cardinals of the then-rival National Football League had "snookered" Charley Trippi away from the New York Yankees of the All-America Football Conference, Morabito arranged draft rights within his own league so that he had a clear track to both players. Pittsburgh was trying the same in the National Football League.

Both players had gone to the same school, and the great coup would be to land them together. There was only one difficulty: Glenn (Mr. Outside) Davis and Felix (Mr. Inside) Blanchard had played for West Point. The taxpayers had paid their way through college, and the public morality demanded that they serve their country, not a professional football team.

As the outcry increased, Pittsburgh beat a strategic retreat, letting it be known that San Francisco had the inside track.

So San Francisco caught the heat.

"It's my understanding," Morabito said, "that Davis and Blanchard will receive a routine ninety-day furlough when they get their commissions in June. They think it would be possible to delay the furloughs until later. Thus, with army permission, they could play for us during the regular season in September, October, and November."

Now even members of Congress were in the act, bellowing at this "unmitigated gall . . . unadulterated crust." The War Department put an end to it with a formal statement:

"The requirements of military training and service for young officers are such that the War Department cannot favorably consider granting extended leave of absence for engaging in private enterprise."

A few seasons later, along came Tony ("You Gotta Be Hard") Morabito.

This was the creation, in a sense, of Prescott Sullivan of the *Examiner,* probably the least vindictive sports columnist in the Bay area.

The 49ers had a $20,000 guarantee to play an exhibition game at Baltimore. In those days, if the gate looked unpromising, a preseason game could be, and occasionally was, canceled. Things looked bad for Baltimore, and so Baltimore sought to call off the game. Tony Morabito said no. He wanted his $20,000. The Baltimore

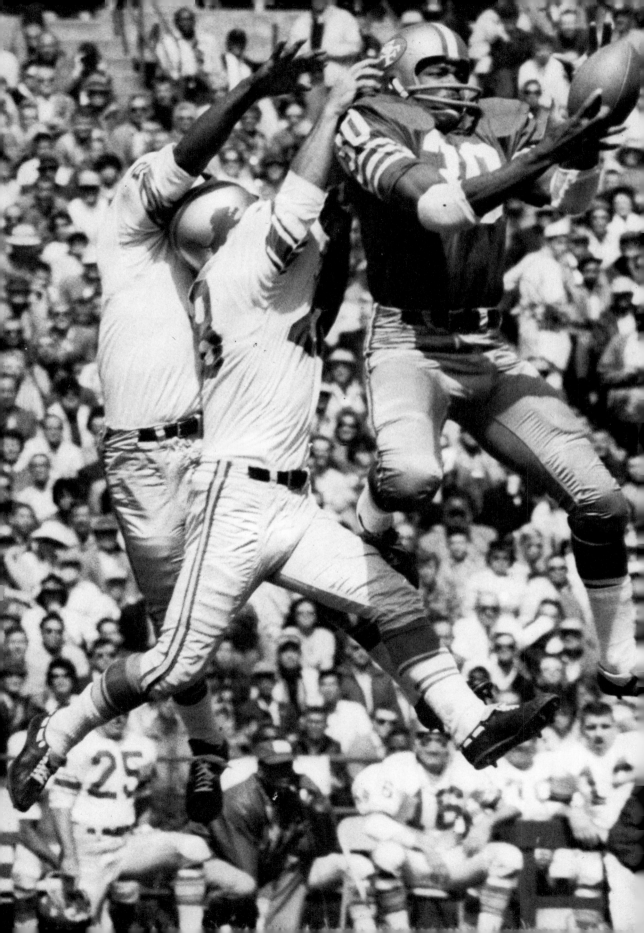

Far-ranging targets for John Brodie passes in the mid-1960s were Bernie Casey (left), who caught 50 or more passes in four out of five seasons between 1962 and 1966, and Monty Stickles (right), rugged tight end for the 49ers.

people sought to appease him. They offered him $10,000 not to show up. Tony Morabito said no, he wanted $20,000. "You gotta be hard," he kept telling the Baltimore folks. "You gotta be hard."

There was an element here of returning the cold welcome Morabito first received when he sought a football franchise for San Francisco. Those were the days when *he* was being told "you gotta be hard." Now it was his turn. He insisted the game be played, and the 49ers showed up to play it.

Sullivan, traveling with the team, was searching for a Sunday morning column, and the search brought him to a Baltimore official who told him the story of Morabito's intransigence. "He kept saying, 'You gotta be hard. You gotta be hard,'" the Baltimore man told Sullivan, and so Sullivan wrote it for his paper.

After the game, Sullivan accompanied the 49ers to Chicago, where they were to play the Cardinals in an exhibition the following week.

"We got to the hotel at Chicago," Sullivan said, "and I got a phone call asking me to come to Tony's suite. They said they were all sitting around up there, so I supposed it was going to be a nice social gathering. I went up. There they all were, with my column spread out in front of them. They accused me of being a spy. That was for openers. They said the *Examiner* had sent me on the trip with orders to find something nasty about the 49ers.

"Did Tony ever deny the story? No. Did he ever argue that it wasn't a proper story to print? No. The story was both newsworthy and true, and Tony conceded that. Yet in a way he didn't concede it. It was both newsworthy and true but to his mind it still didn't excuse my getting it or my paper's printing it. To him the press was vindictive and I was disloyal."

Morabito never explained the "disloyal" part, nor did his brother Vic in the years following

Tony's death. The younger Morabito proved in some respects even quicker than Tony to react to newspaper slurs, real or imagined, and to cut the offenders "off the list."

To the Morabitos, the press often became part of the hostile outside world.

Candlestick Park is an excellent example of the Morabitos versus the outside world. Candlestick was built by the city to house the baseball Giants when they came west. It was renovated a decade later, at enormous additional cost, to accommodate the 49ers as well. The process of renovation not only increased the seating capacity but, with its completed double-decking, provided an effective baffle against the winds that had frozen fans for 10 years and reduced the quality of competition at times to the level of a bad joke.

Why wasn't Candlestick built for football as well as baseball to begin with? Why didn't the 49ers, destined to play there anyway, move in with the Giants in 1960?

The city fathers were all for it, not only for the increased revenues from extra customers and extra dates, but because big crowds at Kezar Stadium were a constant headache. The lack of parking there caused game traffic to block private driveways (or pay rip-off prices to homeowners who allowed drivers to park in them), and would addle the police every Sunday.

The Giants were all for it too. It would have given them a bigger and better ball park. But the 49ers weren't interested.

"We asked the 49ers to give us a reason," said Tom Gray, a civic leader who played an active role in bringing the Giants to San Francisco. "They said they didn't have to give us a reason. They implied they were happy where they were."

Were the 49ers happy at Kezar? There is evidence to the contrary. Franklin Mieuli remembers a time, some years before the Giants came

Dave Parks (left), playing only his second season in professional football, caught 80 passes for 1,344 yards for San Francisco in 1965. Below, Parks is wrestled to the ground by Irv Cross after making a catch against the Los Angeles Rams. The 1965 totals of Parks were best in the NFL and set 49ers club records for receptions and passing yardage.

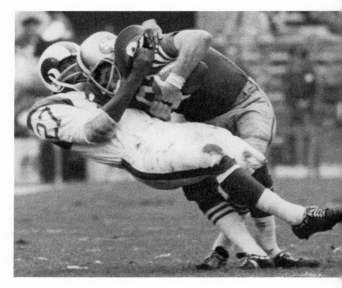

to town, when he and Tony Morabito stood
outside Seals Stadium, the old Pacific Coast
League ball park where the Giants were to play
their first two seasons in San Francisco while
Candlestick was being built. Seals Stadium held
fewer than half the people that Kezar could
hold, and its parking and customer-service facilities were, if anything, even worse.

"But Tony had an idea Seals Stadium could
be rebuilt with more than one deck," Mieuli has
said. "The parking didn't worry him; surface
transportation could take care of the fans. And
that would be a perfect new home for the 49ers."

The arguments and counter arguments as to
the feasibility of such a plan could be repro-
duced here, but the unspoken point of the whole
thing was not that Morabito could be satisfied
at Seals Stadium, but that he was not satisfied
to remain at Kezar. Yet the 49ers were to stay
at Kezar 11 seasons longer than they had to
before finally moving to Candlestick.

A few reasonable explanations: The 49ers
may have had their doubts about Candlestick's
location, just inside the southernmost city line;
they may have wanted certain facilities, such as
escalators and an elevator to the football pressbox installed at the outset. Such facilities were
not on anyone's drawing board at the time.
They may indeed have felt that San Francisco
tradition, so much a part of themselves, so little
a part of the Giants from New York, required
an existing playing field, not a new one. Seating
capacities at Kezar and at today's Candlestick
were virtually equal.

A powerful issue in favor of the 49ers was
the matter of access versus parking. Candlestick
had more of the latter, less of the former.
Candlestick debouches in a single direction onto
the heavily traveled BayShore freeway. Kezar,
for all its faults, could be reached via city streets
from all directions.

It was not until the seventies that the highway

department completed direct southbound access
to, or egress from, Candlestick on the one hand
and the freeway on the other.

Add to this the ultimate facts that the 49ers
played only seven home league games per year,
perhaps nine dates in all, and that their foot-
dragging could force the city to install additional amenities, the 49ers may have decided
simply to sit back and adopt a wait-and-see
attitude before finally making the move.

But the most valid explanation is one nobody
on the outside can remember being given. By
and large, the 49ers did what they had always
done — kept their own counsel.

It is not unfunny, nor totally without rele-
vance, that things reached the point where quarterback John Brodie didn't know who was pay-
ing him.

That came to pass in the early summer of
1966, when Brodie agreed to an offer from
the Houston Oilers of the American Football
League, with the proviso that the 49ers had the
right to match it. Shortly thereafter, the two
leagues agreed to merge.

When he heard about it, Brodie had an engaging reaction. "Somebody owes me money,"
he said.

And somebody did. Brodie would play for one
team, the 49ers; but legally he was entitled to
the amount offered by another, the Oilers.

The amount itself was enough to justify the
merger. According to the best accounts, it was
$920,000.

In folklore, Brodie would go down as "the
million dollar quarterback," and fans were ready
to remind him of this, especially when he had
a bad day. John took it in stride. "After all," he
said, "I've been called worse."

It is noteworthy that Brodie's greatest years
came after he had done the one thing no right-
handed quarterback should do: He broke his
right arm. More accurately, the Minnesota Vik-

ings did it for him in the third game of the 1963 season. It was after this game — San Francisco's third defeat of the year and tenth in a row if you count all five preseason games — that Jack Christiansen replaced Red Hickey as the 49ers' head coach. It was the only time the club had changed coaches in the middle of a season.

High tide for Hickey had been his experiment with the Shotgun formation in 1960 and 1961. The formation had lost only twice (both times to Green Bay, but everybody lost to Green Bay those years) in between its birth against Baltimore in 1960 and its death against the Bears in 1961.

The strength of the Shotgun lay in the fact that defenses had to set themselves for three possible plays (the straight run, the sweep, and the pass). Its advantages over the T-formation were varied: For one thing, the defense had to spread even when the offense didn't; for another, the run off the fake pass was always a threat. Not the least of the Shotgun's virtues was the fact that the 49ers were the only team using it. Enemy defenders, drilled from birth against the T, found themselves aligned against blockers who shouldn't be there, and searching for blockers who should.

The end of the Shotgun was immaculately planned and perfectly executed. By 1961, George Halas and Clark Shaughnessy of the Bears had divined that the Shotgun carried the seeds of its own destruction.

For Chicago's Halas, the remedy was simplicity itself. The power of the three options off the Shotgun, he reasoned, existed because there *were* three options, rather than through the effect of any one of them. Take away one of those options and the whole thing would collapse.

Halas spread his defensive ends and told them their sole job was to wait for the sweep, whether one came or not. This they did, and when the sweeps came they stopped them. The sweeps stopped coming, and the remaining elements of the Shotgun lacked the variety to sustain a winning effort. Chicago won the game 31–0. The era of the Shotgun was over. Hickey used the Shotgun more sparingly as the 49ers, off to a 4–1 start, tailed off to 7–6–1 for the season. By season's end Brodie was running the offense from the T.

Three different coaches — Hickey, Christiansen and finally Nolan — occupied the head man's position for the 49ers during the sixties. And while they were occupied, Vic Morabito and Lou Spadia were preoccupied.

With the formation of the American Football League in 1960, the Oakland Raiders had come into being. At first their competition for the Bay area's football dollar was insignificant. They played in spidery Frank Youell Field, which many high school stadiums would put to shame, and had won-lost records of 2–12 in 1961 and 1–13 in 1962.

But things changed. In truth, to cap the earlier discussion on the point, the case can be made that if the Raiders hadn't come to Oakland, the 49ers might still be playing their games at Kezar Stadium. The Raiders moved into the splendid new Oakland Coliseum, whose customer comforts Kezar could not hope to match. The Raiders began to win. A 13–1 season of 1967, followed by a 40–7 victory over Houston that propelled them into the Super Bowl, helped crystallize San Francisco's decision to change coaches once more. Exit Christiansen; enter Nolan.

But the balance appeared to have swung. The next season, the Raiders, with another division winner, packed them in at the Coliseum while the 49ers were playing to half-empty stands at Kezar. The next two Super Bowls would be won by AFL teams: the Jets in 1969 and the Chiefs in 1970.

When the final merger of the leagues came, the 49ers' aboriginal Cleveland companions

from the All-America Football Conference found themselves in a group with a similar name: the American Football Conference.

This then was the special background that made the first NFL meeting between the AFC Raiders and NFC 49ers, in the final game of the 1970 season, so critical to the future of the San Francisco team. If the 49ers had lost that game, once again Oakland would have been the only division winner in the area. This time the 49ers would have been directly to blame.

But the 49ers did win that game and with it the NFC West. They repeated as division titlists in 1971 and 1972. All seemed serene as they prepared for 1973, albeit their recent first-round draft choices hadn't been panning out and they lacked an outside running attack. One preseason rumor had Brodie going to Green Bay in exchange for MacArthur Lane. Instead, Brodie stayed on, only to announce before the season was halfway done that the year would be his last as a player.

San Francisco's annual preseason loss to Los Angeles was, in the studied opinion of coach Nolan, "the worst football exhibition I ever saw," and things failed to improve as the 1973 season began. With Brodie at quarterback, the 49ers led the Super Bowl champs, the Dolphins, at halftime in their opening game at Miami. But the heat got to Brodie and several other 49ers, and Miami won. That, as it turned out, was the way the season was going to go.

The oddsmakers, among other people, didn't believe it. As late as the next-to-last game of the season, the 49ers were favored to win by six points, and why not? They were going up against the New Orleans Saints, whom they had ruined 40–0 earlier in the season. But instead of winning by six, the 49ers lost by six. As usual, the 49ers came to the final game of the season with something at stake. This time it was last place in the division.

But under Tony and Vic Morabito and under Lou Spadia, the team had survived years far worse than 1973. In fact, its very 5–9 won-lost record in 1973 gave the club a high first round draft choice. Make that two top-round draft choices, since another had been picked up in a deal with the New England Patriots.

And on the final day of the 1973 season it was Albert who officiated as Brodie's jersey number, 12, was officially retired, like its wearer, for all time, to hang alongside Joe Perry's 34, Leo Nomellini's 73, Hugh McElhenny's 39 in what passes in San Francisco — and very properly so — for football immortality.

There are two things that Josie and Jane Morabito, the widows of the team's co-founders, will not permit club president Lou Spadia to do on his own.

"The two things I can't do," Spadia has said, "are move the team out of San Francisco or change the name '49ers.'"

Which just about says it all.

The Names
and Numbers

San Francisco 49ers Victories
1946-1973

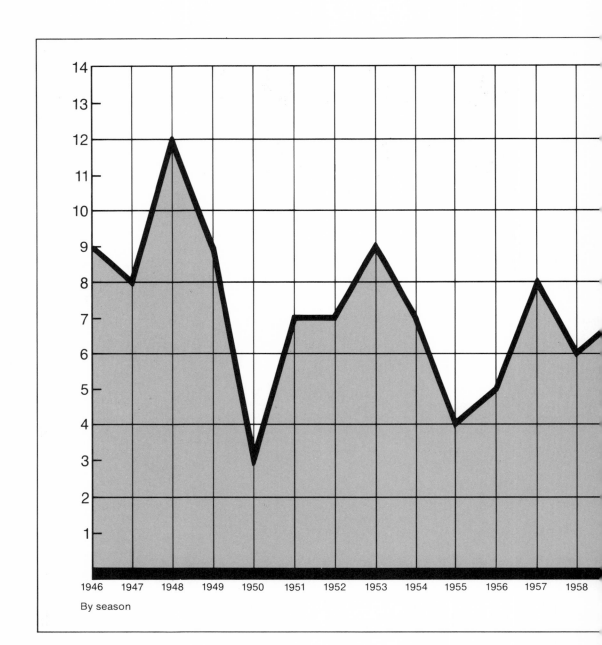

By season

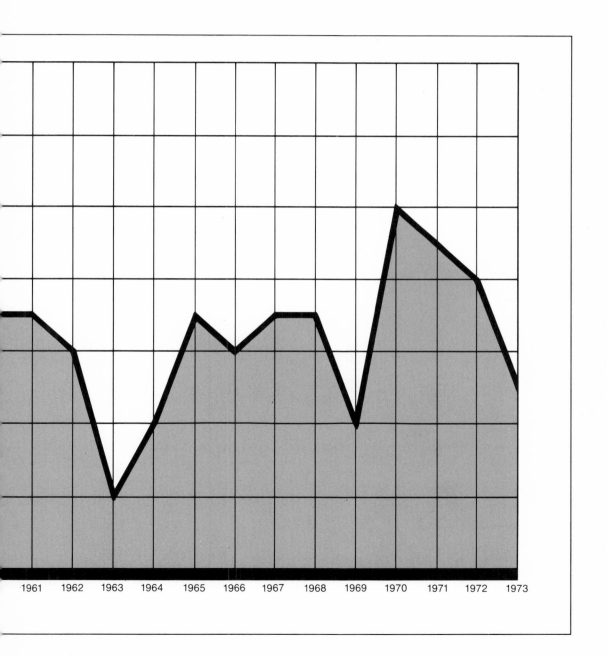

1961   1962   1963   1964   1965   1966   1967   1968   1969   1970   1971   1972   1973

49ers
All-Time
Scores

All-America Football Conference

1946
9—5—0, second place, Western Division
Coach: Lawrence (Buck) Shaw

	49ers	Opp.
New York Yankees ...(H)	7	21
Miami Seahawks ....(H)	21	14
Brooklyn Dodgers ...(H)	32	13
Chicago Rockets ....(A)	7	21
Miami Seahawks ....(A)	34	7
Los Angeles Dons ...(A)	22	14
Buffalo Bills ....(A)	14	17
Cleveland Browns ...(A)	34	20
Buffalo Bills ....(H)	27	14
Cleveland Browns ...(H)	7	14
New York Yankees ...(A)	9	10
Brooklyn Dodgers ...(A)	30	14
Chicago Rockets ....(H)	14	0
Los Angeles Dons ...(H)	48	7
	306	186

1947
8—4—2, second place, Western Division
Coach: Lawrence (Buck) Shaw

	49ers	Opp.
Brooklyn Dodgers ....(H)	23	7
Los Angeles Dons ...(H)	17	14
Baltimore Colts .....(H)	14	7
New York Yankees ...(H)	16	21
Buffalo Bills ....(A)	41	24
Baltimore Colts .....(A)	28	28
Chicago Rockets ....(A)	42	28
Cleveland Browns ...(H)	7	14
Los Angeles Dons ...(A)	26	16
New York Yankees ...(A)	16	24
Cleveland Browns ...(A)	14	37
Chicago Rockets ....(A)	41	16
Brooklyn Dodgers ....(A)	21	7
Buffalo Bills ....(H)	21	21
	311	264

1948
12—2—0, second place, Western Division
Coach: Lawrence (Buck) Shaw

	49ers	Opp.
Buffalo Bills ....(H)	35	14
Brooklyn Dodgers ...(H)	36	20
New York Yankees ...(H)	41	0
Los Angeles Dons ....(H)	36	14
Buffalo Bills ....(A)	38	28
Chicago Rockets ....(A)	31	14
Baltimore Colts .....(A)	56	14
New York Yankees ...(H)	21	7
Baltimore Colts .....(H)	21	10
Chicago Rockets ....(H)	44	21
Cleveland Browns ...(A)	7	14
Brooklyn Dodgers ....(A)	63	40
Cleveland Browns ...(H)	28	31
Los Angeles Dons ...(A)	38	21
	495	248

1949
9—3—0, second place
Coach: Lawrence (Buck) Shaw

	49ers	Opp.
Baltimore Colts .....(H)	31	17
Chicago Hornets ....(H)	42	7
Los Angeles Dons ....(H)	42	14
Bufalo Bills ....(A)	17	28
Chicago Hornets ....(A)	42	24
Cleveland Browns ...(H)	56	28
Buffalo Bills ....(H)	51	7
New York Yankees ...(A)	3	24
Cleveland Browns ...(A)	28	30
Baltimore Colts .....(A)	28	10
Los Angeles Dons ...(A)	41	24
New York Yankees ...(H)	35	14
	416	227

Playoff
New York Yankees ...(H)	17	7

AAFC Championship
Cleveland Browns ...(A)	7	21

National Football League

1950
3—9—0, sixth place, National Conference
Coach: Lawrence (Buck) Shaw

	49ers	Opp.
N. Y. Yankees ....(H)	17	21
Chi. Bears ....(H)	20	32
Los Angeles ....(H)	14	35
Detroit ....(A)	7	24
N. Y. Yankees ....(A)	24	29
Detroit ....(H)	28	27
Baltimore ....(H)	17	14
Los Angeles ....(A)	21	28
Cleveland ....(A)	14	34
Chi. Bears ....(A)	0	17
Green Bay ....(A)	21	14
Green Bay ....(H)	30	14
	213	300

1951
7—4—1, third place, National Conference
Coach: Lawrence (Buck) Shaw

	49ers	Opp.
Cleveland ....(H)	24	10
Philadelphia ....(A)	14	21
Pittsburgh ....(A)	28	24
Chi. Bears ....(H)	7	13
Los Angeles ....(H)	44	17
Los Angeles ....(A)	16	23
N. Y. Yankees ....(H)	19	14
Chi. Cardinals .....(A)	21	27
N. Y. Yankees ....(A)	10	10
Detroit ....(A)	20	10
Green Bay ....(A)	31	19
Detroit ....(H)	21	17
	255	205

1952
7—5—0, third place, National Conference
Coach: Lawrence (Buck) Shaw

	49ers	Opp.
Detroit ....(H)	17	3
Dallas Texans ......(A)	37	14
Detroit ....(A)	28	0
Chi. Bears ....(A)	40	16
Dallas Texans ......(H)	48	21
Chi. Bears ....(H)	17	20
N. Y. Giants ....(A)	14	23
Washington ....(A)	23	17
Los Angeles ....(A)	9	35
Los Angeles ....(H)	21	34
Pittsburgh ....(H)	7	24
Green Bay ....(H)	24	14
	285	221

1953
9—3—0, second place, Western Conference
Coach: Lawrence (Buck) Shaw

	49ers	Opp.
Philadelphia ....(H)	31	21
Los Angeles ....(H)	31	30
Detroit ....(A)	21	24
Chi. Bears ....(A)	35	28
Detroit ....(H)	10	14
Chi. Bears ....(H)	24	14
Los Angeles ....(A)	31	27
Cleveland ....(A)	21	23
Green Bay ....(A)	37	7
Baltimore ....(H)	38	21
Green Bay ....(H)	48	14
Baltimore ....(H)	45	14
	372	237

1954
7—4—1, third place, Western Conference
Coach: Lawrence (Buck) Shaw

	49ers	Opp.
Washington ....(H)	41	7
Los Angeles ....(A)	24	24
Green Bay ....(A)	23	17
Chi. Bears ....(A)	31	24
Detroit ....(H)	37	31
Chi. Bears ....(H)	27	31
Los Angeles ....(H)	34	42
Detroit ....(A)	7	48
Pittsburgh ....(A)	31	3
Baltimore ....(A)	13	17
Green Bay ....(H)	35	0
Baltimore ....(H)	10	7
	313	251

1955
4—8—0, fifth place, Western Conference
Coach: Norman (Red) Strader

	49ers	Opp.
Los Angeles ....(H)	14	23
Cleveland ....(H)	3	38
Chi. Bears ....(A)	20	19
Detroit ....(A)	27	24
Chi. Bears ....(H)	23	34
Detroit ....(H)	38	31
Los Angeles ....(A)	14	27
Washington ....(A)	0	7
Green Bay ....(A)	21	27
Baltimore ....(A)	14	26
Green Bay ....(H)	7	28
Baltimore ....(H)	35	24
	216	308

1956
5—6—1, third place, Western Conference
Coach: Frankie Albert

	49ers	Opp.
N. Y. Giants ....(H)	21	38
Los Angeles ....(H)	33	30
Chi. Bears ....(A)	7	31
Detroit ....(A)	17	20
Chi. Bears ....(H)	21	38
Detroit ....(H)	13	17
Los Angeles ....(H)	6	30
Green Bay ....(A)	17	16
Philadelphia ....(A)	10	10
Baltimore ....(H)	20	17
Green Bay ....(H)	38	20
Baltimore ....(H)	30	17
	233	284

1957
8—4—0, second place, Western Conference
Coach: Frankie Albert

	49ers	Opp.
Chi. Cardinals ......(H)	10	20
Los Angeles ....(A)	23	20
Chi. Bears ....(A)	21	17
Green Bay ....(H)	24	14
Chicago ....(A)	21	17
Detroit ....(H)	35	31
Los Angeles ....(H)	24	37
Detroit ....(A)	10	31
Baltimore ....(A)	21	27
N. Y. Giants ....(A)	27	17
Baltimore ....(H)	17	13
Green Bay ....(H)	27	20
	287	295

Western Conf. Playoff
Detroit ....(H)	27	31

1958
6—6—0, fourth place, Western Conference
Coach: Frankie Albert

	49ers	Opp.
Pittsburgh ....(H)	23	20
Los Angeles ....(H)	3	33
Chi. Bears ....(A)	6	28
Philadelphia ....(A)	30	24
Chi. Bears ....(H)	14	27
Detroit ....(H)	24	21
Los Angeles ....(A)	7	56
Detroit ....(A)	21	35
Green Bay ....(A)	33	12
Baltimore ....(H)	27	35
Green Bay ....(H)	48	21
Baltimore ....(H)	21	12
	257	324

1959
7—5—0, fourth place, Western Conference
Coach: Howard (Red) Hickey

	49ers	Opp.
Philadelphia ....(H)	24	14
Los Angeles ....(H)	34	0
Green Bay ....(A)	20	21
Detroit ....(A)	34	13
Chi. Bears ....(H)	20	17
Detroit ....(H)	33	7
Los Angeles ....(A)	24	16
Chi. Bears ....(A)	3	14
Baltimore ....(A)	14	45
Cleveland ....(H)	21	20
Baltimore ....(H)	14	34
Green Bay ....(H)	14	36
	255	237

1960
7–5–0, third place, Western Conference

Coach: Howard (Red) Hickey	49ers	Opp.
N. Y. Giants ....(H)	19	21
Los Angeles ....(H)	13	9
Detroit ....(A)	14	10
Chicago ....(A)	10	27
Green Bay ....(A)	14	41
Chicago ....(H)	25	7
Detroit ....(H)	0	24
Dallas ....(A)	26	14
Baltimore ....(A)	30	22
Los Angeles ....(A)	23	7
Green Bay ....(H)	0	13
Baltimore ....(H)	34	10
	208	205

1961
7–6–1, fifth place, Western Conference

Coach: Howard (Red) Hickey	49ers	Opp.
Washington ....(H)	35	3
Green Bay ....(A)	10	30
Detroit ....(A)	49	0
Los Angeles ....(H)	35	0
Minnesota ....(H)	38	24
Chicago ....(A)	0	31
Pittsburgh ....(A)	10	20
Detroit ....(H)	20	20
Los Angeles ....(A)	7	17
Chicago ....(H)	41	31
Minnesota ....(H)	38	28
Baltimore ....(H)	17	20
Green Bay ....(H)	22	21
Baltimore ....(H)	24	27
	346	272

1962
6–8–0, fifth place, Western Conference

Coach: Howard (Red) Hickey	49ers	Opp.
Chicago ....(H)	14	30
Detroit ....(A)	24	35
Minnesota ....(H)	21	7
Baltimore ....(H)	21	13
Chicago ....(H)	34	27
Green Bay ....(A)	13	31
Los Angeles ....(H)	14	28
Baltimore ....(A)	3	22
Detroit ....(H)	24	38
Los Angeles ....(A)	24	17
St. Louis ....(A)	24	17
Minnesota ....(A)	35	12
Green Bay ....(H)	21	31
Cleveland ....(H)	10	13
	282	320

1963
2–12–0, seventh place, Western Conference
Coach: Howard (Red) Hickey (3 games);

Jack Christiansen	49ers	Opp.
Minnesota ....(H)	20	24
Baltimore ....(H)	14	24
Minnesota ....(H)	14	45
Detroit ....(A)	3	26
Baltimore ....(A)	3	20
Chicago ....(H)	20	14
Los Angeles ....(A)	21	28
Detroit ....(H)	7	45
Dallas ....(H)	31	24
N. Y. Giants ....(A)	14	48
Green Bay ....(A)	10	28
Los Angeles ....(H)	17	21
Chicago ....(A)	7	27
Green Bay ....(H)	17	21
	198	391

1964
4–10–0, seventh place, Western Conference

Coach: Jack Christiansen	49ers	Opp.
Detroit ....(H)	17	26
Philadelphia ....(A)	28	24
St. Louis ....(H)	13	23
Chicago ....(H)	31	21
Green Bay ....(A)	14	24
Los Angeles ....(A)	14	42
Minnesota ....(H)	22	27
Baltimore ....(A)	7	37
Minnesota ....(A)	7	24
Green Bay ....(H)	24	14
Chicago ....(A)	21	23
Baltimore ....(H)	3	14
Los Angeles ....(H)	28	7
Detroit ....(A)	7	24
	236	330

1965
7–6–1, fourth place, Western Conference

Coach: Jack Christiansen	49ers	Opp.
Chicago ....(H)	52	24
Pittsburgh ....(H)	27	17
Baltimore ....(A)	24	27
Green Bay ....(A)	10	27
Los Angeles ....(A)	45	21
Minnesota ....(H)	41	42
Baltimore ....(H)	28	34
Dallas ....(A)	31	39
Detroit ....(A)	27	21
Los Angeles ....(H)	30	27
Minnesota ....(A)	45	24
Detroit ....(H)	17	14
Chicago ....(A)	20	61
Green Bay ....(H)	24	24
	421	402

1966
6–6–2, fourth place, Western Conference

Coach: Jack Christiansen	49ers	Opp.
Minnesota ....(H)	20	20
Baltimore ....(A)	14	36
Los Angeles ....(H)	3	34
Green Bay ....(H)	21	20
Atlanta ....(A)	44	7
Detroit ....(H)	27	24
Minnesota ....(A)	3	28
Los Angeles ....(H)	21	13
Chicago ....(A)	30	30
Philadelphia ....(H)	34	35
Detroit ....(A)	41	14
Green Bay ....(A)	7	20
Chicago ....(H)	41	14
Baltimore ....(H)	14	30
	320	325

1967
7–7–0, third place, Coastal Division

Coach: Jack Christiansen	49ers	Opp.
Minnesota ....(A)	27	21
Atlanta ....(H)	38	7
Baltimore ....(A)	7	41
Los Angeles ....(A)	27	24
Philadelphia ....(A)	28	27
New Orleans ....(H)	27	13
Detroit ....(H)	3	45
Los Angeles ....(H)	7	17
Washington ....(A)	28	31
Green Bay ....(A)	0	13
Baltimore ....(H)	9	26
Chicago ....(H)	14	28
Atlanta ....(A)	34	28
Dallas ....(H)	24	16
	273	337

1968
7–6–1, third place, Coastal Division

Coach: Dick Nolan	49ers	Opp.
Baltimore ....(A)	10	27
St. Louis ....(H)	35	17
Atlanta ....(H)	28	13
Los Angeles ....(A)	10	24
Baltimore ....(H)	14	42
N. Y. Giants ....(A)	26	10
Detroit ....(A)	14	7
Cleveland ....(H)	21	33
Chicago ....(A)	19	27
Los Angeles ....(H)	20	20
Pittsburgh ....(A)	45	28
Green Bay ....(H)	27	20
Minnesota ....(H)	20	30
Atlanta ....(A)	14	12
	303	310

1969
4–8–2, fourth place, Coastal Division

Coach: Dick Nolan	49ers	Opp.
Atlanta ....(A)	12	24
Green Bay ....(A)	7	14
Washington ....(H)	17	17
Los Angeles ....(H)	21	27
Atlanta ....(H)	7	21
Baltimore ....(A)	24	21
Detroit ....(A)	14	26
Los Angeles ....(A)	30	41
Baltimore ....(H)	20	17
New Orleans ....(A)	38	43
Dallas ....(A)	24	24
Chicago ....(H)	42	21
Minnesota ....(A)	7	10
Philadelphia ....(H)	14	13
	277	319

1970
10–3–1, first place, AFC Western Division

Coach: Dick Nolan	49ers	Opp.
Washington ....(H)	26	17
Cleveland ....(H)	34	31
Atlanta ....(A)	20	21
Los Angeles ....(A)	20	6
New Orleans ....(H)	20	20
Denver ....(H)	19	14
Green Bay ....(H)	26	10
Chicago ....(A)	37	16
Houston ....(A)	30	20
Detroit ....(A)	7	28
Los Angeles ....(H)	13	30
Atlanta ....(H)	24	20
New Orleans ....(A)	38	27
Oakland ....(A)	38	7
	352	267

NFC First Round Playoff

Minnesota ....(A)	17	14

NFC Championship

Dallas ....(H)	10	17

1971
9–5–0, first place, Western Division

Coach: Dick Nolan	49ers	Opp.
Atlanta ....(A)	17	20
New Orleans ....(A)	38	20
Philadelphia ....(A)	31	3
Los Angeles ....(A)	13	20
Chicago ....(H)	13	0
St. Louis ....(A)	26	14
New England ....(A)	27	10
Minnesota ....(A)	13	9
New Orleans ....(H)	20	26
Los Angeles ....(H)	6	17
N. Y. Jets ....(A)	24	21
Kansas City ....(A)	17	26
Atlanta ....(H)	24	3
Detroit ....(H)	31	27
	300	216

NFC First Round Playoff

Washington ....(H)	24	20

NFC Championship

Dallas ....(A)	3	14

1972
8–5–1, first place, Western Division

Coach: Dick Nolan	49ers	Opp.
San Diego ....(H)	34	3
Buffalo ....(A)	20	27
New Orleans ....(A)	37	2
Los Angeles ....(A)	7	31
N. Y. Giants ....(H)	17	23
New Orleans ....(H)	20	20
Atlanta ....(A)	49	14
Green Bay ....(A)	24	34
Baltimore ....(H)	24	21
Chicago ....(A)	33	21
Dallas ....(A)	31	10
Los Angeles ....(H)	16	26
Atlanta ....(H)	20	0
Minnesota ....(H)	20	17
	353	249

NFC First Round Playoff

Dallas ....(H)	28	30

1973
5–9–0, fourth place, NFC Western Division

Coach: Dick Nolan	49ers	Opp.
Miami ....(A)	13	21
Denver ....(A)	36	34
Los Angeles ....(H)	20	40
Atlanta ....(A)	13	9
Minnesota ....(H)	13	17
New Orleans ....(H)	40	0
Atlanta ....(H)	3	17
Detroit ....(A)	20	30
Washington ....(H)	9	33
Los Angeles ....(A)	13	31
Green Bay ....(H)	20	6
Philadelphia ....(H)	38	28
New Orleans ....(A)	10	16
Pittsburgh ....(H)	14	37
	262	319

49ers
Records

SCORING
Most Points
Lifetime — 737, Tommy Davis
Season — 114, Gordy Soltau, 1953
Game — 26, Gordy Soltau vs. Los Angeles,
Oct. 28, 1951
Most Touchdowns
Lifetime — 80, Joe Perry, 23 in the AAFC
Season — 14, Alyn Beals, 1948, AAFC
13, Joe Perry, 1953
Game — 4, Bill Kilmer vs. Minnesota,
Oct. 15, 1961
Most Points After Touchdown Made
Lifetime — 347, Tommy Davis
Season — 62, Joe Vetrano, 1948, AAFC
52, Tommy Davis, 1965
Game — 9, Joe Vetrano vs. Brooklyn,
Nov. 21, 1948, AAFC
Tommy Davis vs. Detroit,
Oct. 1, 1961
Tommy Davis vs. Chicago,
Sept. 19, 1965
Most Field Goals Made
Lifetime — 130, Tommy Davis
Season — 26, Bruce Gossett, 1973
Game — 5, Bruce Gossett vs. Denver,
Sept. 23, 1973
Longest Field Goal
54, Bruce Gossett vs. New Orleans,
Oct. 21, 1973

RUSHING
Most Attempts
Lifetime — 1,667, Joe Perry
1,475, Joe Perry in NFL games
only
Season — 258, J. D. Smith, 1962
Game — 31, J. D. Smith vs. Baltimore,
Oct. 7, 1962
J. D. Smith vs. Chicago,
Oct. 14, 1962
Most Yards Gained
Lifetime — 8,689, Joe Perry
7,344, Joe Perry in NFL games
only
Season — 1,049, Joe Perry, 1954
Game — 174, Joe Perry vs. Detroit,
Nov. 2, 1958
Most Games, 100 or More Yards
Lifetime — 22, Joe Perry
Season — 5, Joe Perry twice, 1953 and 1954
Longest Run From Scrimmage
89, Hugh McElhenny vs. Dallas Texans,
touchdown, Oct. 5, 1952

PASSING
Most Passes Attempted
Lifetime — 4,540, John Brodie
Season — 427, John Brodie, 1966
Game — 54, John Brodie vs. Chicago,
Nov. 13, 1966
Most Passes Completed
Lifetime — 2,468, John Brodie
Season — 242, John Brodie, 1965
Game — 31, Steve Spurrier vs. Minnesota,
Oct. 14, 1973
Most Yards Gained
Lifetime — 31,950, John Brodie
Season — 3,112, John Brodie, 1965
Game — 371, Y. A. Tittle vs. Baltimore,
Dec. 13, 1953
Longest Pass Completion
83, John Brodie to Dave Parks vs. Los
Angeles, touchdown, Nov. 8, 1964

Most Touchdown Passes
Lifetime — 214, John Brodie
Season — 30, Frankie Albert, 1948, AAFC
John Brodie, 1965
Game — 5, Frankie Albert vs. Cleveland,
Oct. 9, 1949, AAFC
John Brodie vs. Minnesota,
Nov. 23, 1965
Steve Spurrier vs. Chicago,
Nov. 19, 1972
Most Passes Had Intercepted
Lifetime — 224, John Brodie
Season — 28, Y. A. Tittle, 1955
Game — 6, John Brodie vs. Detroit,
Nov. 4, 1973

PASS RECEPTIONS
Most Pass Receptions
Lifetime — 407, Billy Wilson
Season — 80, Dave Parks, 1965
Game — 12, Bernie Casey vs. Chicago,
Nov. 13, 1966
Most Yards Gained
Lifetime — 5,802, Billy Wilson
Season — 1,344, Dave Parks, 1965
Game — 231, Dave Parks vs. Baltimore,
Oct. 3, 1965
Most Touchdown Passes
Lifetime — 49, Alyn Beals, 46 in the AAFC
49, Billy Wilson
Season — 14, Alyn Beals, 1948, AAFC
12, Dave Parks, 1965
12, Gene Washington, 1972
Game — 3, by 6 players

INTERCEPTIONS
Most Interceptions By
Lifetime — 41, Jimmy Johnson
Season — 10, Dave Baker, 1960
Game — 4, Dave Baker vs. Los Angeles,
Dec. 4, 1960
Most Yards Returned . .
Lifetime — 548, Jimmy Johnson
Season — 155, Kermit Alexander, 1968
Game — 94, Al Randolph vs. Chicago,
interception, Dec. 11, 1966
Longest Return
94, Al Randolph vs. Chicago, touchdown,
Dec. 11, 1966

PUNTING
Most Punts
Lifetime — 511, Tommy Davis
Season — 79, Tommy Davis, 1964
Game — 11, Pete Brown vs. Chi. Bears,
Oct. 17, 1954
Highest Average
Lifetime — 45.3, Tommy Davis
Season — 48.2, Frankie Albert, 1949, AAFC
45.7, Tommy Davis, 1959
Game — 54.5, Larry Barnes vs. Chi.
Cardinals, Sept. 29, 1957
Tommy Davis vs. Chicago,
Nov. 19, 1961
Longest Punt
86, Larry Barnes vs. Chi. Cardinals,
Sept. 26, 1957

PUNT RETURNS
Most Punt Returns
Lifetime — 124, Joe Arenas
Season — 43, Bruce Taylor, 1970
Game — 9, Ralph McGill vs. Atlanta,
Oct. 29, 1972
Most Yards Returned
Lifetime — 1,103, Bruce Taylor
Season — 516, Bruce Taylor, 1970
Game — 133, Bruce Taylor vs. Houston,
Nov. 15, 1970
Longest Punt Return
94, Hugh McElhenny vs. Chi. Bears,
touchdown, Oct. 19, 1952

KICKOFF RETURNS
Lifetime — 174, Abe Woodson
Season — 37, Abe Woodson, 1962
Game — 7, Abe Woodson vs. Detroit,
Sept. 23, 1962
Most Yards Returned
Lifetime — 4,820, Abe Woodson
Season — 1,157, Abe Woodson, 1952
Game — 210, Abe Woodson vs. Detroit,
Nov. 11, 1962
Longest Kickoff Return
105, Abe Woodson vs. Los Angeles,
touchdown, Nov. 8, 1959

49ers Team
Records

SCORING
Most Points
Season — 495, 1948, AAFC
421, 1965
Game — 63 vs. Brooklyn (40),
Nov. 21, 1948, AAFC
52 vs. Chicago (24), Sept. 19, 1965
Most Touchdowns
Season — 69, 1948, AAFC
49, 1953
Game — 9 vs. Brooklyn, Nov. 21, 1948,
AAFC
7 vs. Dallas Texans, Oct. 26, 1952

NET YARDS GAINED
Season — 5,767, 1948, AAFC
4,904, 1961
Game — 597 vs. Baltimore, Dec. 13, 1953

RUSHING
Most Rushing Attempts
Season — 603, 1948, AAFC
523, 1951
Game — 56 vs. Los Angeles Dons,
Sept. 19, 1948, AAFC
vs. Baltimore, Oct. 29, 1950
vs. Detroit, Oct. 25, 1953
vs. Green Bay, Oct. 10, 1954
Most Yards Gained
Season — 3,663, 1948, AAFC
2,498, 1954
Game — 390 vs. Baltimore, Oct. 24, 1948,
AAFC
324 vs. Minnesota, Oct. 15, 1961

PASSING
Most Attempts
Season — 500, 1966
Game — 54 vs. Chicago, Nov. 13, 1966
Most Completions
Season — 278, 1969
Game — 31 vs. Minnesota, Dec. 14, 1973
Most Yards Gained
Season — 3,487, 1965
Game — 345 vs. Baltimore, Dec. 13, 1953

49ers
All-Time
Roster

A

Abramowicz, Dan, WR, Xavier, Ohio ...1973
Albert, Frankie, QB, Stanford 1946-52
Aldridge, Ben, HB, Oklahoma State 1952
Alexander, Kermit, DB, UCLA 1963-69
Arenas, Joe, HB, Omaha 1951-57
Atkins, Bill, HB, Auburn 1958-59
Atkins, David, RB, Texas-El Paso 1973

B

Babb, Gene, FB, Austin 1957-58
Babcock, Harry, E, Georgia 1953-55
Bahnsen, Ken, FB, No. Texas State 1953
Baker, Dave, HB, Oklahoma 1959-61
Balatti, Ed, E, No college 1946-47
Baldwin, John, C, Centenary 1947
Banaszek, Cas, T, Northwestern 1968-73
Banducci, Bruno, G, Stanford 1946-54
Barnes, Larry, FB, Colorado 1957
Barrett, Jean, T, Tulsa 1973
Bassi, Dick, G, Santa Clara 1946-47
Beals, Alyn, E, Santa Clara 1946-51
Beard, Ed, LB, Tennessee 1965-72
Beasley, Terry, WR, Auburn 1972
Beisler, Randy, T, Indiana 1969-73
Belk, Bill, DE, Maryland State 1968-73
Bentz, Roman, T, Tulane 1948
Berry, Rex, HB, Brigham Young ...1951-56
Bettiga, Mike, WR, Cal. St.-Humboldt ..1973
Beverly, Ed, WR, Arizona State 1973
Blue, Forrest, C, Auburn 1968-73
Boone, J. R., HB, Tulsa 1952
Beatty, Ed, C, Mississippi 1955-56
Bosley, Bruce, G, West Virginia 1956-68
Britt, Charlie, DB, Georgia 1964
Brock, Clyde, T, Utah State 1963
Brodie, John, QB, Stanford 1957-73
Brown, Hardy, LB, Tulsa 1951-56
Brown, Pete, C, Georgia Tech 1953-54
Bruce, Gail, E, Washington 1948-51
Brumfield, Jackson, E, So. Mississippi .1954
Bruney, Fred, HB, Ohio State 1953, 1956
Bryant, Bob, T, Texas Tech 1946-49
Burke, Don, LB, So. California 1950-54
Burke, Vern, E, Oregon State 1965

C

Campbell, Carter, LB, Weber State ...1970
Campbell, Marion, T, Georgia 1954-55
Campora, Don, T, Pacific 1950, 1952
Carapella, Al, T, Miami 1951-55
Carpenter, John, T, Michigan 1949
Carr, Eddie, HB, No college 1947-49
Carr, Paul, LB, Houston 1955-58
Casanega, Ken, HB, Santa Clara .1946, 1948
Casey, Bernie, E, Bowling Green ...1961-66
Cason, Jim, HB, LSU 1948-52, 1954
Cassara, Frank, FB, St. Mary's 1954
Cathcart, Royal, HB, Cal State-Santa Barbara
...............................1950
Cathcart, Sam, HB, Cal State-Santa Barbara
......................1949-50, 1952
Cavelli, Tony, C, Stanford 1949
Cerne, Joe, C, Northwestern 1965-67
Chapple, Jack, LB, Stanford 1965
Clark, Don, G, So. California 1948-49
Clark, Monte, T, So. California 1959-61
Colchico, Dan, E, San Jose State ...1960-64
Collett, Elmer, G, S.F. State 1967-72
Collier, Floyd, T, San Jose State 1948
Collins, Ray, T, LSU 1950-52
Conlee, Gerry, C, St. Mary's 1946-47

Conner, Clyde, E, Pacific 1956-63
Connolly, Ted, G, Tulsa 1954, 1956-62
Cooper, Bill, FB, Muskingum 1961-64
Cox, James, G, Stanford 1948
Cross, Bob, T, Kilgore Jr. College ..1956-57
Crow, John David, HB, Texas A&M .1965-68
Crowe, Paul, HB, St. Mary's 1948
Crowell, Otis, T, Hardin-Simmons 1947
Cunningham, Doug, RB, Mississippi .1967-73

D

Dahms, Tom, T, San Diego State 1957
Daniels, Clem, RB, Prairie View 1968
Daugherty, Bob, HB, Tulsa 1966-67
Davis, Tommy, K, LSU 1959-69
Dean, Floyd, LB, Florida 1963-64
Donnelly, George, DB, Illinois 1965-67
Donohue, Leon, T, San Jose State ..1962-64
Dove, Eddie, DB, Colorado State ...1959-62
Dowdle, Mike, LB, Texas 1963-65
Downs, Bob, G, So. California 1951
Dow, Harley, G, San Jose State 1950
Dugan, Fred, E, Dayton 1958-59
Duncan, Maury, QB, S.F. State 1954-55
Durdan, Don, HB, Oregon State ...1946-47

E

Edwards, Earl, DT, Wichita 1969-72
Elliott, Charles, T, Oregon 1948
Elston, Art, C, South Carolina 1946-48
Enriss, Al, E, S.F. State 1952
Eshmont, Len, HB, Fordham 1946-49
Evans, Ray, G, Texas Western 1950
Evansen, Paul, G, Oregon State 1948

F

Feher, Nick, G, Georgia 1951-54
Fisk, Bill, E, So. California 1946-47
Forrest, Ed, C, Santa Clara 1946-47
Franceschi, Pete, HB, San Francisco ..1946
Freitas, Jesse, QB, Santa Clara 1946-47
Fuller, John, DB, Lamar Tech 1968-72

G

Gaiters, Bob, HB, New Mexico State 1962-63
Galiffa, Arnie, QB, Army 1954
Garlin, Don, HB, So. California 1949-50
Gavric, Momcilo, K, Belgrade 1969
Gehrke, Fred, HB, Utah 1950
Goad, Paul, FB, Abilene Christian 1956
Gonsoulin, Austin, DB, Baylor 1967
Gonzaga, John, T, No college 1956-59
Gossett, Bruce, K, Richmond 1970-73
Greenlee, Fritz, LB, Arizona 1969
Gregory, Garlin, G, Louisiana Tech ..1946-47
Grgich, Visco, G, Santa Clara 1946-52

H

Hall, Forrest, HB, San Francisco 1948
Hall, Parker, HB, Mississippi 1946
Hall, Windlan, CB, Arizona State ...1972-73
Hanley, Dick, C, Fresno State 1947
Hantla, Bob, G, Kansas 1954-55
Hardman, Cedrick, DE, No. Texas St. 1970-73
Hardy, Carroll, HB, Colorado 1955
Hardy, Ed, G, Jackson State 1973
Hardy, Kevin, DT, Notre Dame 1968
Harkey, Lem, HB, Emporia State 1955
Harper, Willie, LB, Nebraska 1973
Harris, Tony, WR, Toledo 1971
Harrison, Bob, LB, Oklahoma
......................1959-61, 1965-67
Hart, Tom, DE, Morris Brown 1968-73
Hays, Harold, LB, So. Mississippi ..1968-69

Hazeltine, Matt, LB, California 1955-68
Henke, Ed, E, So. California 1951-52, 1955-60
Herchman, Bill, T, Texas Tech 1956-59
Hettema, Dave, T, New Mexico 1967
Hindman, Stan, DE, Mississippi 1966-71
Hobbs, Homer, G, Georgia 1949-50
Hogland, Doug, G, Oregon State ...1953-55
Holladay, Bob, HB, Tulsa 1956-57
Holzer, Tom, DE, Louisville 1967
Horne, Dick, E, Oregon 1947
Hoskins, Bob, G, Wichita 1970-73
Howell, Clarence, E, Texas A&M 1948
Huff, Marty, LB, Michigan 1972
Hunt, Charlie, LB, Florida State 1973

I

Isenbarger, John, RB, Indiana 1970-73

J

Jackson, Jim, HB, Western Illinois ..1966-67
Jackson, Randy, RB, Wichita 1973
Jessup, Bill, E, So. California
........................1951-52, 1954-58
Johnson, Bill, C, Tyler Jr. College ..1948-56
Johnson, Charlie, DT, Louisville 1966-67
Johnson, Jimmy, DB, UCLA 1961-73
Johnson, John Henry, RB, Arizona State
..............................1954-56
Johnson, Leo, WR, Tennessee State .1969-70
Johnson, Rudy, HB, Nebraska 1964-65

K

Kammerer, Carl, LB, Pacific 1961-62
Kelley, Gorden, LB, Georgia 1960-61
Kenny, Charles, G, San Francisco 1947
Kilgore, Jon, P, Auburn 1969
Kilmer, Bill, QB, UCLA 1961-66
Kimbrough, Elbert, DB, Northwestern 1962-66
Knafelc, Gary, E, Colorado 1963
Kopay, Dave, RB, Washington 1964-67
Kraemer, Eldred, G, Pittsburgh 1955
Kramer, Kent, TE, Minnesota 1966
Krueger, Charlie, DT, Texas A&M ..1959-73
Krueger, Rolf, DE, Texas A&M 1972-73
Kuzman, John, T, Fordham 1946
Kwalick, Ted, TE, Penn State 1969-73

L

Lakes, Roland, T, Wichita 1961-70
Land, Fred, T, Louisiana State 1948
LaRose, Dan, DE, Missouri 1965
Laughlin, Bud, FB, Kansas 1955
Ledyard, Hal, QB, Chattanooga 1953
Lee, Dwight, RB, Michigan State 1968
Lewis, Gary, FB, Arizona State 1964-69
Lillywhite, Verl, HB, So. California ..1948-51
Lind, Mike, FB, Notre Dame 1963-64
Lisbon, Don, HB, Bowling Green 1963-64
Livingston, Howie, HB, Fullerton J.C. ..1950
Lopasky, Bill, G, West Virginia 1961
Loyd, Alex, E, Oklahoma State 1950
Luna, Bob, HB, Alabama 1955
Lyles, Lenny, DB, Louisville 1959-60

M

Mackey, Dee, TE, E, Texas State 1960
Maderos, George, HB, Chico State ..1955-56
Magac, Mike, G, Missouri 1960-64
Maloney, Norm, E, Purdue 1948-49
Manley, Joe, LB, Mississippi State 1953
Masini, Leonard, FB, Fresno State ..1947-48
Matheson, Riley, HB, Texas Western ..1948
Mathews, Ned, HB, UCLA 1946-47

Matthews, Clay, E, Georgia Tech
................................1950, 1953-55
Matuszak, Marv, LB, Tulsa 1957-58
McCann, Jim, P, Arizona State 1971-72
McCormick, Dave, T, LSU 1966
McCormick, Tom, HB, Pacific 1956
McCormick, Walt, C, So. California ..1948
McElhenny, Hugh, HB, Washington ..1952-60
McFarland, Kay, HB, Colorado State .1962-68
McGill, Ralph, CB, Tulsa 1972-73
McHan, Lamar, QB, Arkansas 1963
McNeil, Clifton, E, Grambling 1968-69
Mellekas, John, C, Arizona 1962
Mellus, John, T, Villanova 1946
Mertens, Jerry, HB, Drake 1958-65
Messer, Dale, HB, Fresno State 1961-65
Meyers, Bob, FB, Stanford 1952
Michalik, Art, G, St. Ambrose 1953-54
Mike, Bob, T, UCLA 1948-49
Miller, Clark, DE, Utah State 1962-68
Miller, Hal, T, Georgia Tech 1953
Mira, George, QB, Miami 1964-68
Mixon, Bill, HB, Georgia 1953-54
Moegle, Dick, HB, Rice 1955-59
Momsen, Bob, G, Ohio State 1952
Monachino, Jim, HB, California 1951
Moore, Eugene, RB, Occidental 1969
Morgan, Joe, T, So. Mississippi 1949
Morrall, Earl, QB, Michigan State 1956
Morris, Dennit, LB, Oklahoma 1958
Morris, George, C, Georgia Tech 1956
Morton, John, LB, TCU 1953
Morze, Frank, C, Boston College ...1957-61
Mudd, Howard, G, Hillsdale 1964-69
Myers, Chip, E, N. W. Oklahoma 1967

N

Nix, Jack, E, So. California 1950
Nomellini, Leo, DT, Minnesota 1950-63
Norbert, Hank, E, Stanford 1946-47
Norton, Jim, T, Washington 1965-66
Norton, Ray, HB, San Jose State 1960-61
Nunley, Frank, LB, Michigan 1967-73

O

O'Donahue, Pat, E, Wisconsin 1952
Olerich, Dave, E, San Francisco
................................1967-68, 1972-73
Olssen, Lance, T, Purdue 1968-69
Osborne, Clancy, LB, Arizona State .1959-60
Owens, R. C., HB, Idaho 1957-61

P

Pace, Jim, HB, Michigan 1958
Palatella, Lou, G, Pittsburgh 1955-58
Parker, Don, G, Virginia 1967
Parks, Dave, E, Texas Tech 1964-67
Parsons, Earle, HB, So. California ..1946-47
Patera, Dennis, K, Brigham Young ...1968
Pavlich, Chuck, G, No college 1946
Peoples, Woody, G, Grambling 1968-73
Perry, Joe, RB, Compton J.C. .1948-60, 1963
Phillips, Mel, DB, North Carolina A&T 1966-72
Pine, Ed, LB, Utah 1962-64
Poole, Bob, E, Clemson 1964-65
Powell, Charley, E, No college
................................1952-53, 1955-57
Powers, Jim, HB, So. California ...1950-53
Puddy, Harold, T, Oregon 1948

Q

Quilter, Chuck, T, Tyler J.C. 1949

R

Randle, Sonny, E, Virginia 1967
Randolph, Alvin, DB, Iowa 1966-70

Reed, Joe, QB, Mississippi State ...1972-73
Remington, Bill, C, Washington State .1946
Renfro, Dick, FB, Washington State ...1946
Ridlon, Jim, HB, Syracuse 1957-62
Riley, Preston, WR, Memphis State .1970-72
Roberts, C. R., FB, So. California ..1959-62
Robnett, Ed, HB, Texas Tech 1947
Rock, Walter, T, Maryland 1963-67
Rohde, Len, T, Utah State 1960-73
Roskie, Ken, FB, South Carolina 1946
Rubke, Karl, C, So. California
................1957-60, 1962-63, 1965
Rucka, Leo, C, Rice 1956

S

Sabucco, Tino, C, San Francisco 1949
Sagely, Floyd, E, Arkansas 1954-56
Salata, Paul, E, So. California 1949-50
Sandifer, Dan, HB, LSU 1950
Sardisco, Tony, G, Tulane 1956
Satterfield, Alf, T, Vanderbilt 1947
Schabarum, Pete, HB, California
................................1951, 1953-54
Schiechl, John, C, Santa Clara 1947
Schmidt, Henry, T, Trinity 1959-60
Schreiber, Larry, RB, Tennessee Tech 1971-72
Scotti, Ben, DB, Maryland 1964
Sharkey, Ed, G, Nevada 1955-56
Shaw, Charles, G, Oklahoma State 1950
Sheriff, Stan, LB, Cal. Poly 1956-57
Shoener, Hal, E, Iowa 1948-50
Sieminski, Charlie, T, Penn State ..1963-65
Silas, Sam, DE, So. Illinois 1969-70
Simpson, Mike, DB, Houston 1970-73
Sitko, Emil, HB, Notre Dame 1950
Smith, Charles, E, Abilene Christian ..1956
Smith, Ernie, DB, Compton J.C. 1955-56
Smith, George, C, California 1947
Smith, J. D., HB, North Carolina A&T 1956-64
Smith, Jerry, G, Wisconsin 1952-53
Smith, Noland, RB, Tennessee State ..1969
Smith, Steve, E, Michigan 1966-67
Sniadecki, Jim, LB, Indiana 1969-73
Soltau, Gordy, E-K, Minnesota 1950-58
Sparks, Dave, G, South Carolina 1951
Spence, Julian, HB, Sam Houston 1957
Spurrier, Steve, QB, Florida 1967-73
Standlee, Norm, FB, Stanford 1946-52
St. Clair, Bob, T, Tulsa 1953-64
Stickles, Monty, TE, Notre Dame ...1960-67
Stits, Bill, HB, UCLA 1957-58
Stolhandske, Tom, LB, Texas 1955
Strickland, Bishop, FB, South Carolina .1951
Strong, Jim, RB, Houston 1970
Strzykalski, John, HB, Marquette ..1946-52
Sullivan, Bob, HB, Holy Cross 1948
Susoeff, Nick, E, Washington State .1946-49
Sutro, John, T, San Jose State 1962
Swinford, Wayne, DB, Georgia 1965-67

T

Tanner, Hamp, T, Georgia 1951
Taylor, Bruce, CB, Boston U. 1970-73
Taylor, Roosevelt, S, Grambling 1969-71
Teresa, Tony, HB, San Jose State 1958
Thomas, Aaron, E, Oregon State 1961
Thomas, Jimmy, RB, Texas-Arlington 1969-73
Thomas, John, T, Pacific 1958-67
Thornton, Rupe, G, Santa Clara 1946-47
Tidwell, Billy, HB, Texas A&M 1954
Titchenal, Bob, E, San Jose State 1946
Tittle, Y. A., QB, LSU 1951-60
Toneff, Bob, T, Notre Dame ..1952, 1954-59
Trimble, Wayne, DB, Alabama 1967
Tubbs, Jerry, LB, Oklahoma 1958-59
Tucker, Bill, RB, Tennessee State ..1967-70

V

Van Doren, Bob, E, So. California 1953
Vanderbundt, Skip, LB, Oregon State 1969-73
Vaught, Ted, E, TCU 1953

Vetrano, Joe, HB, So. Mississippi ...1946-49
Vollenweider, Jim, FB, Miami 1962-63

W

Wagner, Lowell, HB, So. California
................................1949-53, 1955
Wallace, Bev, QB, Compton J.C. 1947-49
Walker, Val Joe, HB, SMU 1957
Washington, Gene, WR, Stanford ...1969-73
Washington, Vic, RB, Wyoming 1971-73
Waters, Bob, QB, Presbyterian 1960-64
Watson, John, T, Oklahoma 1971-73
White, Bob, HB, Stanford 1951-52
Wilcox, Dave, LB, Oregon 1964-73
Willard, Ken, FB, North Carolina ...1965-73
Williams, Howie, HB, Howard 1963
Williams, Joel, C, Texas 1948
Williams, John, HB, So. California 1954
Williams, Roy, T, Pacific 1958-64
Wilson, Billy, E, San Jose State ...1951-60
Wilson, Jerry, LB, Auburn 1960
Wilson, Jim, G, Georgia 1965-66
Windsor, Bob, E, Kentucky 1967-71
Winston, Lloyd, FB, So. California ..1962-63
Wismann, Pete, LB, St. Louis .1949-52, 1954
Witcher, Dick, E, UCLA 1966-73
Wittenborn, John, G, S. E. Missouri .1958-60
Wittum, Tom, P, No. Illinois 1973
Woitt, John, DB, Mississippi State .1968-69
Wondolowski, Bill, WR, E. Montana ..1969
Woodson, Abe, DB, Illinois 1958-64
Woudenberg, John, T, Denver 1946-49

Y

Yonamine, Wally, HB, No college 1947
Youngelman, Sid, T, Alabama 1955
Yowarsky, Walt, C, Kentucky 1958

Z

Zamlynsky, Ziggy, HB, Villanova 1946